Model-Driven Software Migration:
A Methodology

T0189598

Christian Wagner

Model-Driven Software Migration: A Methodology

Reengineering, Recovery and Modernization of Legacy Systems

Foreword by Dr.-Ing. Hans-Georg Pagendarm

 Springer Vieweg

Dr.-Ing. Christian Wagner
Potsdam, Germany

Also PhD thesis „Modellgetriebene Software-Migration" at the University of Potsdam, Chair of Service and Software Engineering

ISBN 978-3-658-05269-0 ISBN 978-3-658-05270-6 (eBook)
DOI 10.1007/978-3-658-05270-6

The Deutsche Nationalbibliothek lists this publication in the Deutsche Nationalbibliografie; detailed bibliographic data are available in the Internet at http://dnb.d-nb.de.

Library of Congress Control Number: 2014933421

Springer Vieweg
© Springer Fachmedien Wiesbaden 2014

Printed on acid-free paper

Springer Vieweg is a brand of Springer DE.
Springer DE is part of Springer Science+Business Media.
www.springer-vieweg.de

Foreword

Model-driven software development offers the method of choice when it comes to manage complex software production projects. However, these concepts face some obstacles when applied to maintenance of existing software systems. In order to ally such modern methods it is frequently assumed that re-coding cannot be circumvent.

Christian Wagner demonstrates on a real-life example how existing software may be imported into a modern software development suite via application of automatic processes. Thus with modest effort a legacy code turns into a maintainable and expandable code-base. While re-programming would create a risk of introducing new bugs, the automatic conversion of legacy code removes obstacles for further maintenance and development of the code and at the same time conserves the know-how and quality contained within a well-tested proven code. The automatic conversion turn out to be by far more efficient than re-programming. Efficiency coincides with improved reliability of the software implementation process.

The concept of model-driven-software-maintenance which is demonstrated here, is very convincing and therefore hopefully will be widely adopted in the near future. Latest when facing a task which requires the integration of a variety of codes, originating from various frameworks into one single software system, there is probably no way around the methods of model-driven-software-maintenance.

Dr.-Ing. Hans-Georg Pagendarm

Acknowledgement

Primarily I want to thank my girlfriend Dunja and my parents for their support that I have experienced in all ups and downs during this work. Incidentally, I could still learn a lot about language.

From my colleagues, I would especially like to express my thanks to Henning Bordihn. Not only for his instructions and constructive criticism, but also for his sympathetic ear, which he has always had for me. Additionally Henning strongly aroused my interest for formal descriptions. I could learn from him a lot about teaching and about the structure and organization of lectures. This knowledge will remain with me all my life.

Special thanks to Sven Jörges because he is simply a friend – and of course, for the excellent proofreading work, the regular discussions on modeling theory (I have finally managed the way from the meta-level to a concrete instance of this work), current research literature and common sporting activities, whether on rocks or anywhere on a specific coordinate.

Georg Jung has a large share in planning and structuring of this thesis. He showed me how many pages two people can bring to paper in a long day. Moreover I would like to thank Julia Rehder for here excellent English vocabulary and proofreading skills.

In addition, I would like to thank Hans-Georg Pagendarm who has encouraged me in my job at the DNW and my thesis. Without him I would never have thought about the possibility.

Dr.-Ing. Christian Wagner

Abstract

Software has become part of our everyday daily life. Since the early days of software development in the 50s an innumerable amount of software is developed. In many cases, such systems are still active today which was even not anticipated by the developers. The estimated 220 million lines of code, that are written in a language which was born in 1959, are an outstanding example.

Of course all of these software systems need to be maintained and adapted to new environments. The software evolution reflects the longest phase in the software life cycle. It begins with the delivery of the application to the customer and ends with the exchange of the old system. Modern development technologies can help to minimize the problems that inevitably arise in the context of software evolution. The aim of this research is to investigate the impact and applicability of model-driven techniques in the field of software evolution.

This includes the design of a process model, the development and application of tools and methods as well as the study of several concrete use cases. The improvement in the areas of application understanding, reengineering and migration of software are addressed. The focus is to support the synchronization between the program code and the related artifacts (usually models) which is naturally lost in classical, code-centric software maintenance. Therefore, the software development and maintenance must move towards a model-centered thinking. The synchronization is ensured by a code generation step based on the model level.

The resulting method supports this approach and consists of five phases: transformation of the source code into models, model analysis, abstraction by model transformation, splitting and migration of the existing system and code generation.

The first part – the transformation of the program code – includes the development and application of tools from the fields of compiler construction and program analysis. The aim is to convert the source code into a machine readable form. The result is a representation of a control flow graph (code-model), which is visualized graphically by means of a modeling tool. Model analyzes (second phase) improve the understanding of the application. These analyzes are based on the code-models and can be flexibly adapted to the specific project situation. This includes the creation of new ones as well as the integration of external tools. The transition to the model level occurs in the third phase: A model abstraction step is applied. Thereby information can be classified in the code-models and are abstracted into a new model. The abstraction works on the programming interfaces of the underlying libraries and is therefore called *API-based abstraction.*

The first three stages form the basis for the subsequent migration of the system (step four). The migration is the remodeling of the existing software as process model. The information obtained through the application understanding will guide this step. The developed process model is also partially associated with the functionality of the existing system. After completing this step fully executable source code is generated from the migrated models (step five).

Contents

List of Figures

List of Tables

List of Source Code Examples

List of Abbreviations

ABC	Application Building Center
ADM	Architecture Driven Modernization
AnST	Annotated Syntax Tree
API	Application Programming Interface
ASG	Abstract Semantic Graph
AST	Abstract Syntax Tree
ASTM	Abstract Syntax Tree Meta-Model
BPR	Business Process Reengineering
BMBF	Bundesministerium für Bildung und Forschung
BNF	Backus Naur Form
CEP	Complex Event Processing
CFD	Computational Fluid Dynamics
CFG	Control Flow Graph
CIM	Computation Independent Model
CMDE	Continuous Model-Driven Engineering
CMM	Capture Maturity Model
CORBA	Common Object Request Broker Architecture
CSE	Continuous Software Engineering
CSV	Comma-Separated Values
DAA	Data Access Allocator
DeAs	Datenerfassungs- und Anlagensteuerungssoftware
DLR	Deutsches Zentrum für Luft- und Raumfahrt
DNW	German-Dutch Wind Tunnels
DNW-TWG	Transonic Wind Tunnel Göttingen
DTD	Document Type Definition
EBNF	Extended Backus Naur Form
EMF	Eclipse Modeling Framework
EPT	Elsa Parse Tree
EU	European Union

GCC	GNU Compiler Collection
GMF	Graphical Modeling Framework
GNU	GNU is not UNIX
GUI	Graphical User Interface
GXL	Graph eXchange Language
HPI	Hasso Plattner Institut
HTML	Hypertext Markup Language
IDL	Interface Description Language
IML	Intermediate Language
jABC	Java Application Building Center
JNI	Java Native Interface
KDM	Knowledge Discovery Meta-Model
KTS	Kripke Transitionssystem
LIF	Lanuage Independent Format
LOC	Lines of Code
LPC	Lightweight Process Coordination
MDA	Model-Driven Architecture
MDD	Model-Driven Design
MDE	Model-Driven Engineering
MDRE	Model-Driven Reverse Engineering
MOF	Meta Object Facility
NLR	Nationaal Lucht- en Ruimtevaartlaboratorium
OCL	Object Constraint Language
OMG	Object Management Group
ORB	Object Request Broker
OTA	One Thing Approach
PDD	Process Deliverable Diagram
PIM	Platform Independent Model
PSM	Platform Specific Model
PUB	Platform Independent Description
QVT	Query View Transformation
RCL	Rigi Command Language
RFG	Resource Flow Graph
RSF	Rigi Standard Format
RTE	Round Trip Engineering
RUP	Rational Unified Process

SDM	Software Design Methodology
SIB	Service Independent Building Block
SLG	Service Logic Graph
SOMA	Service-Oriented Modeling Architecture
PLC	Programmable Logic Controller
SUS	System under Study
SVG	Scalable Vector Graphics
TA	Tuple Attribute
TU	Technische Universität
TXL	Turing eXtended Language
UML	Unified Modeling Language
VCG	Visualization of Compiler Graph
XMDD	eXtreme Model-Driven Design
XMI	XML Metadata Interchange
XML	Extensible Markup Language
XPDD	eXtended Process Deliverable Diagram
XSL	Extensible Stylesheet Language
XSLT	Extensible Stylesheet Language Transformation

1 Introduction

1.1 Motivation: Why Software-Archeology?

For many years, software systems influenced almost all areas of society and have become a fundamental component of business. Modern software systems are increasingly invading classical business scenarios and together they jointly form interconnected infrastructures. Already individual business processes can be mapped completely into those infrastructures. The main reasons for this process are the requirements for increased flexibility and cost advantages. Therefore, these infrastructures form the backbone of a company and are an indispensable basis.

Implicit is a steadily increasing dependence on the infrastructure of an enterprise that affects both functionality and further development of the processes and consequently the software. Thus software aging is a problem: A failure can have far reaching consequences: the loss of money, reputation and trust. Even if software is to be regarded as an asset, maintenance and customization are very time-consuming, labor- and cost-intensive. Swanson [Swa76] as well as Canfora and Cimitile [CC00] compare this with an *iceberg*: the real extent and possible effects are not visible, but it is too risky to ignore them. Challenges in software maintenance usually relate to the size, age, and the heterogeneity of software.

Therefore maintenance and migration of software systems are also understood as search and recovery of long-lost information, as well as linking this understanding to new knowledge. Since the beginning of software development, software archeology is known and necessary. Incidental activities, depending on the complexity, are split into maintenance (minor works) and migration of software (extensive changes to a system).

First of all the need for *archaeological excavations* within a software is because of the historically developed separation of initial development and operation/maintenance. Secondly it is due to the lack of synchronization between design artifacts and the program code. Especially in the areas of software reengineering and migration this problem is evident.

During an excavation the objects found in the ground are often the only clue to the meaning and function. Applied to software yields a similar picture. The program code is the only evaluable current source of information. Draft documents are usually outdated, useless or never existed.

Furthermore, it is comparable that the source code must be analyzed first to recover its meaning and function. However, the results of an archaeological excavation and the analysis of program code differ in their reliability. While the interpretation of salvaged *archaeological objects* rarely changes, software is subject to constant change. Archeology is not an unique application, here it becomes a regular companion.

The book addresses this issue and describes a method for model-driven development of software, to synchronize design artifacts and program code. The boundary between initial development and operation/maintenance of software becomes blurred. The repeated use of software archeology on the level of program code is no longer necessary.

To understand software, information must be extracted from the program code and placed in a meaningful context. The process of application understanding is already very complicated and complex because it can not be fully automated. Nevertheless it is important to minimize the risk of errors during modifications.

In general, the understanding of a software system is supported by various abstract views. They are represented in the form of models or diagrams. These views must also be adapted if the program code changes. Synchronization is necessary, however this increases the cost of maintenance and is therefore rarely practiced. Thus models or diagrams become obsolete and the development is restricted to the implementation level. A cycle is created which requires renewed application understanding at regular intervals.

The loose coupling between code and abstract views prevents, until now, a continuous synchronization. A possible solution to this problem is the concentration of software development on one level. The implementation level is inappropriate for several reasons: The focus is on technical languages that have no relation to the subject area, they are complex and inflexible and can only be understood by a few stakeholders in the software evolution process. Accordingly, the abstract views, called *model level* hereafter, are at the center of the software evolution. Modern development technologies can help to minimize the problems that inevitably arise in software evolution. The aim of this research is to investigate the applicability and relevance of model-driven techniques.

1.2 Scientific Contribution

This work's contribution to scientific research comprises developing a methodology for model-driven migration of software systems as well as a reference implementation of the appropriate method fragments. The designed method is validated against a medium-sized software system.

Development of a Methodology

Regarding maintenance and migration of software systems, for the first time a *model-driven approach* is developed and described as a concrete method, concentrating the evolution of software on the model level. Thus avoiding the complex synchronization between code and other artifacts. This concept is successfully tested to its practicability in industrial environments using a concrete use case.

The maintenance of software is usually a costly and complex activity, which is often regarded as a stepchild in comparison to the initial software development. The separation of the two stages in the life cycle of software is historical and can be illustrated by classical process models. Referencing various laws and empirical studies, the author first of all proves the relevance of the topic, as well as showing that delimitation of levels in software development is the cause of major problems in dealing with maintenance tasks. As a consequence, a *continuous development model* is applied and extended in this book.

As a further source of problems the author identifies a lack of system knowledge, which can be attributed to the separation of source code and development artifacts. A typical step in the maintenance phase is software reengineering – the extraction of information to improve the understanding of an application in order to make changes. In general, this information/artifacts (architecture, structure of components, etc.) have been produced during the initial development of the software. However, they become obsolete over time or become lost and must be recovered again. The reason for this classic maintenance dilemma is the usual separation of development and maintenance, and the general code-centric software maintenance. The latter in particular means that the documentation of a system and the program code drift apart slowly.

The developed model-driven approach, is applied to a continuous development model in order to avoid the complex synchronization between multiple levels. There are various continuous process models rated and one of them, the eXtreme Model-Driven Design (XMDD) is selected. Software development takes place solely at the model level and replaces the program code as the central development artifact. This can be created by a code generation process from the model level. The complex synchronization between these levels is not required anymore.

XMDD is designed for the entire life cycle, but up to now only used for the initial development of software. On this basis, a method is defined which transforms already existing code-centric developed software into a *continuous and model-driven development*. An abstract and formal description of this transformation forms the scientific basis of this book and is described in the form of a methodology. This includes an expanded notation to represent and explain the procedure.

The developed process model is divided into two phases: In the first phase, the existing system will be analyzed and prepared for a modeling tool (transformation phase). The second phase (migration phase) remodels the business logic of the existing system. It deconstructs the system and connects its functionality to a model. The last step ensures the generation of fully running source code.

Reference Implementation of the Method

For the transformation of the existing system an extended syntax tree is extracted out of the program code. For this step different tools from the fields of program analysis and compiler construction were evaluated in this book. A C++ parser named Elsa/Elkhound from Berkeley University is used. A back-end is developed by the author that translates the extended syntax tree into an Extensible Markup Language (XML)-based platform-independent format.

The intermediate format is then imported into a modeling tool. The XMDD-specialized jABC was chosen because it excels especially for the continuous development of process models. Here the extended syntax tree is transformed into a control flow graph which contains a large number of attributes. A modeling language, which is based on the grammar of the programming language C++, was developed. Due to their proximity to the program code, the control flow graphs are called *code-models*.

To improve the understanding of an application as well as to provide the second phase, the migration, various static analyzes are implemented. To support inter-and intra-procedural analyzes the imported control flow graphs are linked with each other. Further investigations include the calculation of metrics and visualization of relationships between various parts of the software system. These analyzes are developed as individual process models according to the XMDD principle. In particularly this demonstrates the flexibility of the chosen model-driven paradigm.

The last step of the transformation phase validates the created models. Therefore the process is reversed. A code-generator is developed which generates the original program on the basis of the code-models again. This limits the generated code to the necessary components, and thus considerably reduces the complexity. The entire process chain is validated for quality assurance by means of *back-to-back testing*.

The second stage, the migration, is less automated in contrast to the first stage. The core is a separation of program logic and business logic, which – until now – is only manually viable. Nevertheless, this book presents methods which were able to support the process of abstraction in different ways. For this purpose the Application Programming Interface (API)-based abstraction was developed. This method uses the information about programming interfaces to extract relevant parts of the business logic. It has been shown, that all relevant business processes regarding the structure of the graphical user interface can be found.

The method uses static program analyzes and slicing techniques to find and combine the graphical elements. The procedure itself was in turn developed according to the XMDD principle. The diversity of the grammar of the languages C/C++ as well as the large amounts of data are challenging.

The further remodeling of the business logic is a manual process and is shown in this book for selected parts of the overall system. Parallel to the remodeling, the existing system has to be separated in order to link the components of the business logic with the original functionality. The advantage of this process is that only necessary interfaces are created.

It becomes particularly clear how valuable the advantages of the developed method rather than traditional code-centric approaches are. Due to the extensive automation of the process, a developer can focus on the relevant parts of the business logic, as well as being able to test his progress immediately. Additionally, the shift of the development on the much better-to-understand model level expands the circle of stakeholders: Now application and domain experts can support the developer in remodeling.

Application of the Method

As part of the evaluation of the method as well as the developed tools an industrial-used mid-size software system (more than 100.000 Lines of Code (LOC)) is available. The degree of generalization and transferability of the approach is shown by means of further smaller examples.

1.3 Outline of the Book

This book is organized as follows:

Chapter 2 introduces the general basics of the scientific disciplines software maintenance, modeling and methodology. The accessory status
of software maintenance leads to the fact that the conceptual model
of this field of study is not very stable. It therefore requires a detailed
consideration of the terms: software maintenance, reengineering and
migration. Furthermore, the role of models and their status is examined within the software development and maintenance. Basis of this
book is the design of a methodology that can describe the process of
model-driven migration. This includes the observation of methodologies regarding the development of information systems, as well as a
concrete graphical notation that is used here to describe the developed
method formally.

Chapter 3 introduces the development of the method fragments for the
model-driven reengineering and model-driven migration phases. It
uses an extended notation to illustrate the process graphically. Moreover a discussion of continuous process models as well as the selection
and explanation of one model is included.

Chapter 4: This chapter focuses on related work and tools. The previous chapters have already mentioned such work, without however dis-
cussing them. The presentation of general approaches as well as the
consideration and selection of specific tools and data formats are included. Particularly the examined tools play a central role in the
reference implementation.

Chapter 5 contains the key application of this book. Core is an outdated
wind tunnel software system, which is analyzed using the model-driven
migration and modernization method. The development of individual
method fragments follows an introduction to the existing software system and its environment. The implementation or subsequent use of
tools is based on the results from Chapter 4. The software system is
first analyzed and transferred into a graphical representation. Therefore, a parser back-end has been developed and adapted to an existing
modeling tool. Based on this representation different analyzes are executed to improve the understanding of the application. The result
of the API-based abstraction is the starting point for the migration
of the software system. This is shown on two applications of the examined system. Furthermore, a code generator has been developed,
which is able to generate a substantial part of the application code.

Chapter 6 transfers the methodology to three further applications, and summarizes the results. The three key areas: graphical representation, abstraction and code generation are also shown in the examples.

Chapter 7 summarizes the results and the book itself. An outlook is given on open research issues and possible further developments.

2 Fundamentals

Back in the 70s and 80s of the 20th Century different approaches, concepts, standards and laws in software development were published – specifically in the areas of software maintenance and evolution. Their analysis is essential for a comprehensive definition and introduction.

The principles of this book involve the domains software life cycle, software maintenance and software modeling as well as the description of the appropriate methodology.

Software maintenance (Chapter 2.2) is a component of the *software life cycle* (Chapter 2.1) and is therefore classified in its context. This determination is necessary because the used advanced model-driven development approach differs from the traditional process models. Following, *software reengineering* (Chapter 2.4) and *software migration* (Chapter 2.5) are presented as two core areas of software maintenance. The focus of this book are aged and complex software systems, also called *legacy systems*. The associated problems and uncertainties contribute to their negative reputation[1] [III81, Seite 343][Ber05][Boe86, Seite 69] in the area of software maintenance. They are described in detail in Chapter 2.3.

The model-driven approach as well as different modeling concepts are explained in Chapter 2.6. This chapter examines different views from industrial practice [Kü06, Fav04a] and scientific research. This includes the distinction of various model definitions, model types and model relations.

The formal basis of the methodology developed in this book is a graphical notation that was devised by Brinkkemper et al. [Bri96, WBSV06, WBV07]. This has already been successfully used and extended by the author of this book[2]. A description of the methodology follows in Chapter 2.7.

In this book it is emphasized that development and operation/maintenance of software systems should be a continuous process. Techniques of model-driven development can be used to optimize the process of software

---

[1]   "This perception of maintenance is Primarily a 'pest control ...'"
[2]   compare to Chapter 2.7.2 [SHA12, She08, SHA08, CON12, ISJ+09, HSM10].

reengineering and software migration. Furthermore existing software systems could gradually be extended and regenerated in a *continuous process*.

2.1 Software Life Cycle

This chapter considers different process models in software development and examines, whether and how operation/maintenance of software are represented there as well as what relevance is attributed to them. Subsequently the reason for the aging of software is explained based on principle laws in software evolution. Hence the need for maintenance will be justified. Finally, two scientific approaches are presented which emphasize the unity of development and operation/maintenance of software.

At the beginning of the software life cycle an application is developed for the first time, *creation ex nihilo*[3]. This first phase of the life cycle (*the development*) is completed on delivery of the software to the customer. All subsequent activities (operation, error correction, expansion and migration) are assigned to the second major section, *the operation*. In literature, the terms maintenance and evolution are used interchangeably [Som06, pp. 531]. In this chapter, the last section of the software life cycle is generally identified as operation/maintenance. A closer inspection and separation follows in Chapter 2.2.

So-called process models organize the development process and life cycle of software into structured phases. Certain tasks, methods and techniques are assigned to each phase. A transition criterion for phase change is defined and thus a logical order is produced.

The clear separation of development phase and operation/maintenance phase has certainly set the focus of research literature not on the entire life cycle [Ben95]. In recent decades, the first section, the development has been extensively studied and refined. The second part, operation/maintenance of software, often appears rather as an accessory or is listed only for completeness [Ben95] [Vli08, Seite 474]. This drawback is clearly recognizable in the existing process models.

2.1.1 Process Models: Classical

In scientific literature as well as in industrial practice different process models have emerged. These range in their original form from the waterfall model [Roy70] (Figure 2.1), developed in the 70s, to state-of-the-art meth-

---

[3] Latin for "creation out of nothing"

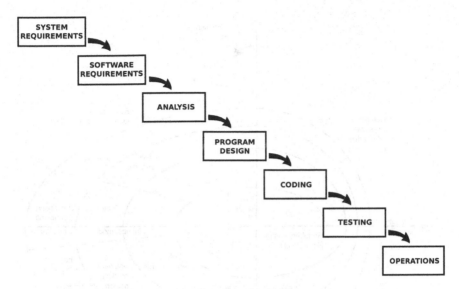

Figure 2.1: Waterfall model by Royce [Roy70]

ods like the Rational Unified Process (RUP) [Kru03]. All models have in common that they are focusing on the development of software exclusively.

The waterfall model by Royce, shown in Figure 2.1, is the first description of a relevant model of software development and the software life cycle. Despite its age of four decades it has been and still is used in a variety of projects[4]. The focus of the model is the refinement and organization of the development process in each phase. Inevitably, it is a sequential process. The transition criterion are documents that are created for each phase which leads to the term *document-driven*. Many subsequent process models are based on the phases defined in the strictly linear structured waterfall model[5].

The first phase, the development of software consists of the following phases: requirements analysis, design, implementation and testing of the software. The last section, called in most process models operation (Figure 2.1) or maintenance, is not further differentiated in contrast to software

---

[4] Until 2005, the company IBM used the waterfall model for the development of Web-sphere products [SH09]. In 2009, the market research and consulting company Forrester identified best practices in software development [Wes09]. Nevertheless still 33 % of the companies surveyed use the waterfall model for software projects.

[5] According to the process model, they are refined, summarized or iterated in several cycles.

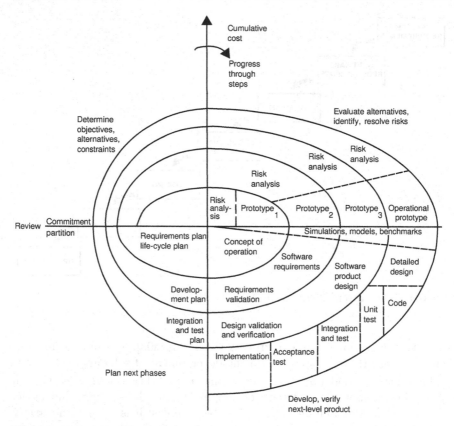

Figure 2.2: Spiral model by Boehm [Boe86]

development. Generally, there is a lack of specification in form of usable methods for adaptation, extension or migration of software.

A pragmatic solution to this problem is the *iterative* application of the process model. It is usually overlooked however, that in addition to new requirements an existing system has to be considered as well, *creatio ex aliquo*[6]. Inherently present problems are usually ignored (see Chapter 2.2).

An iterative process is a central part of the spiral model of Boehm [Boe86], Figure 2.2. It was developed in the 80s in response to problems with the linearity in the waterfall model. At the beginning of software development, different prototypes are created (Figure 2.2, 1st quadrant) to test different aspects of the software as well as to evaluate risks. Therefore, Boehm speaks

---

[6]   Latin for "creation from something"

of a risk-based methodology. Following the iterative risk assessment (1st phase) the actual software development according to the waterfall model is performed (see Figure 2.2, 2nd quadrant). To summarize, the development of software should change from an open process towards a closed loop with user feedback [Mil76, p. 266].

Boehm also discusses the applicability of his model in the operation/maintenance phase: The iterations in the model are solely used as preliminary risk assessment for the actual software development process. They do not necessarily have a direct correlation to the final product. Furthermore the model has no explicit operation/maintenance phase. Boehm said [Boe86, p. 69] that there is not a separate phase for operation/maintenance to avoid its second-class status. Software-in-use always creates new demands which are implemented in an additional maintenance spiral. The integration of existing software systems in this maintenance spiral (*creatio ex aliquo*) is not explicitly mentioned by Boehm.

2.1.2 Process Model: Continuous

In recent years[7] agile or evolutionary development methods[8] emerged in addition to the plan- or document-driven models[9] (classic). Common to all continuous approaches is the conviction that it is not possible to define all requirements at the beginning of a project. Furthermore, they focus on the integration of the user into the development process. The planning and implementation take place incrementally in small, timed steps. Adjustments or corrections are made immediately in consultation with the users.

Illustration 2.3 is a general sketch of the agile approach. At first the ideas and requirements of the customers are collected. The developers select a few requirements and implement a prototype. The prototype will be tested by the customer, which in turn creates new demands and ideas or discards old ones[10]. Thereafter the process starts again. Each iteration takes place in a short and clearly defined time frame. At the end of each iteration, a

---

[7] Initial ideas and approaches to evolutionary prototyping have already been documented in the early 80s by McCracken and Jackson [MJ82]. However, they gain importance in the last few years.

[8] The principles of these methods are defined in the agile manifesto: http://www.agilemanifesto.org.

[9] Phases, activities and goals are fixed at the beginning of the project. The progress is measured at the stage reached in the process model or at the generated documents. These models can be adapted to some degree, for example, individual phases can be iterated.

[10] This agrees with the assessment of Miller [Mil98], who states that computer users can not describe their requirements until they feel the results of their specification.

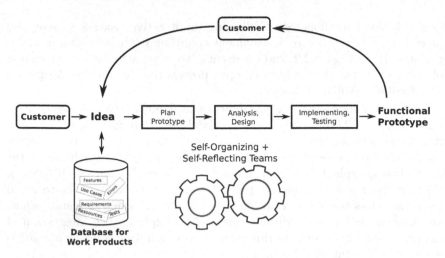

Figure 2.3: Sketch of an agile process model using the example of Scrum

running prototype (as opposed to the spiral model) must be available, which covers an increasing part of the wishes or requirements of the stakeholders.

With the help of agile process models a software life cycle model emerges, which removes the separation between initial development and operation/maintenance. Assuming that the described iteration never ends, the operation/maintenance phase is implicitly incorporated in the process model. The main difference to the plan- or document-driven models is due to the fact that the software development process does not end after the first cycle. If necessary it can be continued indefinitely. Development as well as operation/maintenance are interrelated. In the classical models, however, customer requirements can usually only be incorporated to the implementation phase and not beyond [RPTU84, p. 193].

The agile approach is to be regarded as the ideal case. The extensive effects, for example on the continuity of a development team or the evolution of the software architecture, are not discussed in this book.

At this point it must be mentioned that similarities, differences (cf. [CLC04, pp. 4]) and influences [ASRW02] between spiral model and agile methods are the subject of current controversy. Common points are the definition and status of a prototype, time periods between iterations, incorporating customer requirements and risk management into the project. From the perspective of this book, the spiral model is an intermediate step from the waterfall model to an agile software development model. Both with the aim of continuous development of software. The agile models are considered more rigorously with regards to incremental development, prototyping and customer engagement.

According to the methodology of this book, it is necessary to avoid the gap between initial development and operation/maintenance for sophisticated and useful software products. Especially it is often ignored that software products come to maturity after putting them into operation [Ber05].

Therefore the operation/maintenance phase of software should be inherently anchored in a process model[11]. *Ex aliquo* is the rule and *ex nihilo* the special case. Simultaneously the evolution of software[12] is improved by introduction of models leading to a different level of abstraction.

2.1.3 Laws in the Software Life Cycle

The need of software evolution is due to the increasing complexity in the course of the life cycle of software. Lehman and Belady [LB85] have formulated this principle in the mid-80s in several laws[13]. The first law is called *the law of continuous change*. It states that software will only be used if it is continuously adapted to the changing requirements.

> *"A large program that is used undergoes continuing change or becomes progressively less useful. The change process continues until it is judged more cost - effective to replace the system with a recreated version." [LB85, Seite 250]*

The second principle refers to the inner complexity of software. Usually, it increases by any change in the software.

> *"As a large program is continuously changed, its complexity, which reflects deteriorating structure, increases unless work is done to maintain or reduce it." [LB85, Seite 253]*

Today, these laws are still valid. They define that any software in use, is subject to evolution. It necessarily follows an increasing inner complexity. Evolution refers to the time from first operation to retirement/replacement of software (see Figure 2.5). From the perspective of the software life cycle, evolution is a part of the operation/maintenance phase.

---

[11] cf. Mills 1976 [Mil76, p. 272] and Berg 2005 [Ber05, p. 58].

[12] The concept of evolution is described in detail in Chapter 2.1.3.

[13] Lehman and Belady have formulated five Principles to the character of the software life cycle. In this book, the first two Principles are considered in detail.

Table 2.1: Empirical surveys on the percentage of maintenance in the software life cycle, partly from Müller [Mü97, p. 8]

Survey	Year	Percentage of maintenance
Mills [Mil76]	1976	75 %
de Rose and Nymann [DRN78]	1978	60 %-70 %
Zelkowitz [ZSG79, Seite 9]	1979	67 %
Cashman and Holt [CH80]	1980	50 % - 80 %
Lientz and Swanson [LS80]	1980	$\geq$50 %
Reutter [III81]	1981	70 %
McKee [McK84]	1984	66 %-75 %
Ramamoorthy [RPTU84]	1984	60 %
Grady [GC87]	1987	50 %
Moad [Moa90]	1990	60 %-90 %
Nosek [NP90]	1990	60 %
Zilahi [ZS95]	1995	$\geq$66 %
Erlikh [Erl00]	2000	85 % - 90 %
van Vliet [Vli08]	2008	75 %

Percentage of Maintenance in the Software Life Cycle

Several empirical surveys determined the amount of software maintenance in the entire life cycle (operation of software is not listed). A tabular overview of two decades can be found in Müller [Mü97, p. 8]. The percentage of software maintenance in this period was between 50 % and 80 %. Table 2.1 illustrates the summary by Müller chronologically and is extended with current surveys.

The studies in Table 2.1 point out that the lower bound of maintenance continues to rise. One survey estimates an effort of 90 % [SPL03, pp. 5].

However, these studies can only be compared with reservation. They determine the effort based on various criteria such as percentage of total budget as well as number of staff hours. Furthermore they use different definitions of maintenance, summarize maintenance and operation, are informal or are based on experience; they might also estimate future expenses. But all highlight that the percentage of maintenance is extremely high and has increased steadily in the past. Based on the principles of Lehman and Belady outlined above, it can be assumed that the proportion of maintenance steadily increases during the lifetime of software.

From Table 2.1 it can be deduced that software projects developed *ex nihilo*, only account for a small portion of all software projects. In most cases, besides new requirements of the customer, an existing software product needs to be expanded or improved. Conversely, this means that most projects do not start on a greenfield[14]. They have to deal with *legacy systems* and to incorporate them. This emphasizes the need to focus on the operation/maintenance phase.

The Maintenance Crisis

Rising costs especially have led some authors to speak of an impending maintenance or legacy crisis [SPL03, p. 6] – based on the concept of software crisis[15], which was introduced in 1968 for the first time. The authors assume that a large amount of resources are necessary for maintenance and lesser resources are available for new developments. Parnas thinks the term crisis inappropriate, since it refers to something rather short-term and unexpected. Therefore, he prefers the term *chronic disease* [Par94, p. 286].

From the perspective of this book it is not the question of whether there should be maintenance, but how much costs may be associated with it. Improvements of methods and techniques mostly have focused on software development. However, they are amortized by the growing size and the increasing complexity of software. They play a subordinate role regarding overall duration of the software life cycle (see Table 2.1). Accordingly, the interrelation of development and operation/maintenance is needed for a continuous development process for the design and maturity of long-lived software [Ber05].

2.1.4 Process Models: Research Approaches

First research approaches in this field address the above mentioned problems. In addition to the agile process models, new scientific methods holistically integrate the operation/maintenance phase into the software life cycle. Two representatives are the Continuous Software Engineering (CSE) [Web99], a former research project of the Federal Ministry of Education and Research (BMBF) at the Technical University of Berlin and the

---

14 Also called greenfield approach: Software projects that are developed from scratch must take no account to organically grown environment.

15 It was first spoken of a software crisis on a NATO conference in Garmisch-Partenkirchen (Germany) in 1968 [Mü97]. This is also considered as the birth of software engineering.

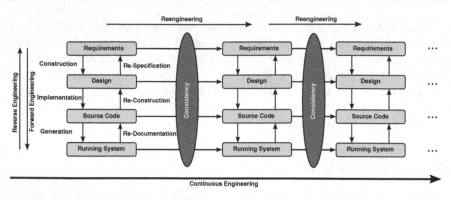

Figure 2.4: Continuous Software Engineering by Mann et al. [MBE+00]

Continuous Model-Driven Engineering (CMDE) [MS09a], developed at the Technical University of Dortmund and the University of Potsdam.

CSE addresses the continuous maintenance of software, which includes associated development artifacts[16]. It involves all phases of software development in order to avoid inconsistencies in documents, models and source code over time. Each step in the development must therefore be largely formalized. Any adjustment on one level may require changes at other levels. Therefore, effects and relationships need to be analyzed. The basic approach is shown in Figure 2.4. After each evolutionary step the consistency of all development artifacts is established, before starting with the next iteration [Web99].

The second approach (CMDE) is a continuous development approach based on the model-layer. It was originally developed for modeling and execution of process graphs. In this book it is applied to integrate existing software systems in a continuous development process (see Chapter 3.3.1). By modeling, further evolution of software is facilitated and the boundary between development and operation/maintenance is removed.

Previous approaches for continuous development and evolution of software (agile development methods, CSE, CMDE) assume that they are applied from the beginning. A subsequent switch and the insertion of a continuous process is not described yet. In literature numerous statements that emphasize the integration of existing systems into a continuous software de-

---

[16] Requirements, models, documentation, source code, etc., are various components that are part of a software development. They are commonly referred to as artifacts.

velopment process (see Chapter 2.6.6) can be found as one of the hot topics in current research.

2.2 Software Maintenance

Chapter 2.1.1 has been shown that classical process models focus on the development and not the operation/maintenance of software. As explained in the previous section, this is in contrast to the importance of the component in reality. Furthermore, the current literature for software development does not consider the final stage in detail. Vague definitions in this domain are the result.

Further information on operation/maintenance are found exclusively in special literature or published research results. Müller has named this fact in the mid-90s in his book [Mü97]. Moad [Moa90] and Parnas [Par94] argue in a similar direction. They call for a stronger commitment to the subject in teaching and at scientific conferences.

2.2.1 Operation/Maintenance Phase

The last phase in the software life cycle (Figure 2.1 and Figure 2.5) ranges from the *first operation* to the *replacement* of software. In between there are numerous bug fixes, adjustments and changes within an application. However, most life cycle models ignore the facts and hide the complexity as well as the associated problems. The most common causes are incomplete data, inconsistencies between source code and documentation, lack of records of past changes as well as lack of knowledge of the software [RPTU84].

The terms operation, maintenance and evolution must be clearly distinguished from each other prior to defining software maintenance.

The daily usage of software is called *operation*. This includes the training of users as well as providing a suitable working environment and all necessary work materials.

For the distinction between maintenance and evolution one can refer to the definition of Weiderman et al. [WBST97]. They define *maintenance* as fine-grained activity that extends over a shorter period of time and involves local changes (Figure 2.5) only. A further characteristic is the structure of the system only undergoing minor adjustments.

In contrast, the *software evolution* represents major changes, including the architecture of the system. This will be enforced when the system falls short of the user's expectations. This includes new user requirements

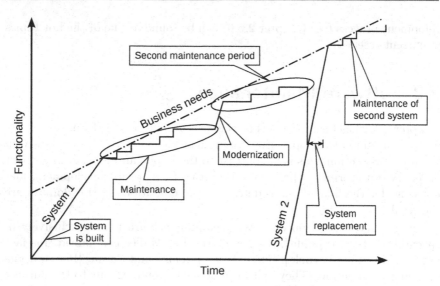

Figure 2.5: Maintenance curve from Seacord et al. [SPL03, p. 8]

or requirements that result from the company's perspective, such as new business areas. An evolutionary step (in Figure 2.5 called Modernization) meets the new demands and reduces the inner complexity. Thus it improves the quality parameters of the software. The latter can in turn lead to lower subsequent maintenance costs. The boundary between maintenance and evolution is naturally fluent. Additionally, Secord et al. [SPL03] add the replacement of a system at the end of its life cycle.

Figure 2.5 visualizes the relationships just described. The phases maintenance, evolution and replacement of a system are illustrated. The curve (solid line) describes the degree of requirements to be met by the system. The expected or required functionality is represented by a continuously increasing line (dash-dot). If the gap between these two lines is too large, a system needs to be modernized or replaced.

2.2.2 Definition of Software Maintenance

In technical vocabulary, the term maintenance is often associated with deterioration and maintenance of machines or tools. This meaning does not apply to software. Software is intangible. Nevertheless, it is subject to an aging process[17] that is driven by influences of the environment and other stakeholders. To avoid the ambiguity of this term, many authors generally described the operation/maintenance phase as software evolution [Som06].

Berg [Ber05] describes the evolution as the way to a mature software product, which is essential for the sustainable use. Lyons [Lyo81, p. 337] compares the aging of the software with a human. He notes, somewhat exaggerated, that *"unlike a child, [Software] does not grow smarter and more capable; unfortunately, it does seem to grow old and cranky."*

As already mentioned, there is no generally accepted definition of software maintenance. Various definitions emphasize different aspects. Hereafter three aspects are identified and considered in detail. In the end, a definition for this book is developed.

A German-language explanation is found in the book Duden Informatik by Claus et al. [CS06]. It refers to software maintenance as

- the exchange of algorithms,
- the addition of extra features,
- the correction of errors and
- the update of software by law.

The first two points of the definition include the fourth point. The explicit definition still makes sense, since changes in software can also be triggered by external factors[18]. Summarized the following can be stated: Maintenance is the change or extension of applied software.

Common literature for university teaching is the book *Software Engineering* by Sommerville [Som06]. Software maintenance is discussed in chapter software development and software reengineering in 22 out of 850 pages. It is defined as follows. Software maintenance is:

- referred to an installed system,
- the longest phase in the life cycle,
- the correction of errors that were overlooked in earlier phases,
- the refinement of the implementation as well as
- the improvement and adaption of the system to new requirements.

Sommerville also emphasizes that the separation of development and maintenance is not very helpful [Som06, pp. 530, 537 and 545] and that the term software maintenance usually is related to customer specific software. According to his opinion it is unfortunate that this issue occupies very little space.

---

[17] This refers to the principles by Lehman and Belady.

[18] The external factors do not refer to the requirements of the customer/user, but for example on legislative requirements or further regulations and standards, etc.

Furthermore, different standardization committees have defined the term maintenance. For example, in the IEEE Standard Glossary of Software Engineering Terminology [IEE90] maintenance is determined as follows:

> *"Software maintenance: (1) The process of modifying a software system or component after delivery to correct faults, improve performance or other attributes, or adapt to a changed environment. (2) The process of retaining a hardware system or component in, or restoring it to, a state in which it can perform its required functions.*

The standard speaks explicitly of hardware systems, however, this statement can also be applied to software systems.

The definition of software maintenance from the IEEE Standard Glossary [IEE90] is fundamental for the present book: Maintenance is a process that becomes relevant only after the delivery of software to the customer. This includes all tasks that maintain the functionality of software, including the correction of errors, the adaptation and extension of software as well as the improvement of the quality parameters and performance. The definition already contains a reference to different types of maintenance.

2.2.3 Types of Maintenance

1976 Swanson [Swa76] has distinguished three types of maintenance: *corrective*, *adaptive* and *perfective* maintenance. Additionally, he defined *preventive* maintenance, but associated it with adaptive. In the mid-80s preventive maintenance has been determined as a separate category.

Corrective maintenance, fixes bugs in the system that occur during operation. This may be due to incorrect or inadequate specifications resulting in program behavior that needs to be changed. The implementation of such adjustments is often done under time pressure and by less experienced developers. Studies of Swanson and Burton [SB89] as well as Pigoski[Pig96] show that 60 % -80 % of the employees in the maintenance team are new employees, trainees or internal students. The lack of experience inevitably results in a deterioration of the quality parameters, for example, an increasing inner complexity and erosion of a system [LB85]. As a result subsequent maintenance steps will become more complicated.

Adaptive maintenance is the adaption of software to a changed environment. These include new compilers, computer architectures, platforms or even a change of the programming language.

Perfecting maintenance means modified and new business requirements, which include new business processes or legal regulations.
Müller [Mü97, p. 7], Buss et al. [BDMG⁺94] as well as Lientz and
Swanson [LS81] indicate that 10 % of a software will be changed per
year. With the use of software, new requirements emerge to improve
the developed product.

Preventive maintenance is also called predictive maintenance. It summarizes all activities, which reduce the inner complexity of software.
Thus it simplify future maintenance tasks and making it more cost-
effective. For example, refactoring [FBB⁺99] is a known representative. Others are changing the architecture, restoration and update
documentation, eliminating redundancies or the detection of dead
code [Ken81]. Some of the activities described are already being performed by compilers. This compiler optimizations are very useful, but
deceptive, because the actual problems still remain in the source code.

Another type of maintenance is described in both the IEEE Standard
1219-1998 [IEE99], as well as in the ISO 14764 standard [ISO99]: the *emer-
gency maintenance*. It is defined as an unplanned maintenance activity,
which has to be carried out without delay in order to maintain a running
system. Usually not the fault, but its impact is mitigated. The bug itself
is fixed in the next maintenance cycle. It is generally associated with corrective maintenance. Furthermore the two standards distinguish between
planned and unplanned maintenance activities.

In literature maintenance is divided into further groups: Reutter [III81]
defines seven, Berg [Ber05] five. For this book, the above mentioned four
types are fundamental.

Müller [Mü97] and other sources present surveys about the effort allocation within the individual types of maintenance.

Table 2.2 illustrates that the cost of corrective maintenance has not
changed in the last decades. It is constant at about 20 %. Therefore the
other three categories account for 80 %. This proportion should not be
broken down any further due to the significant variations within these categories. This is mainly due to different interpretable definitions for adaptive
and perfective maintenance. Furthermore, a maintenance task can not al-

---

19 Unfortunately the publication of Nosek and Palvia does not contain all information.
However, they conclude that the proportions of different types of maintenance have
not or only slightly changed compared the ten-year-older study of Lientz and Swanson [LS80]. All information that could be found in the publication are included in the
table.

Table 2.2: Studies on the proportion of the types of maintenance, partially
taken from Müller [Mü97, Seite 9], and extended

Survey	Year	corr.	perf.	adapt.	prevent.
Lientz and Swanson [LS80]	1980	17 %	65 %	18 %	-
Reutter [III81]	1981	8 %	57 %	35 %	-
Martin [MM83]	1983	18 %	28 %	48 %	4 %
Ramamoorthy [RPTU84]	1984	20 %	55 %	25 %	-
Grady [GC87]	1987	23 %	50 %	21 %	6 %
Nosek [NP90][19]	1990	17 %	54 %	11 %	-
Zilahi [ZS95]	1995	24 %	16 %	60 %	-
van Vliet [Vli08]	2008	21 %	50 %	25 %	4 %

ways be assigned to one category[20]. It should also be emphasized that the
preventive maintenance only has a minimal role. Especially in the field
of customer specific software, it creates no immediately recognizable value.
Thus it is very difficult to sell it to the investors.

2.2.4 Tasks of Software Maintenance

Figure 2.6 compares the proportion of initial development to the entire
software life cycle. It shows clearly how small the proportion of initial
development is. Furthermore it describes the three main tasks of software
maintenance: *Understanding*, *Change* and *Test*, respectively *Validate*.

In 1979 Fjeldstad and Hamlen [FH79] established a 20-40-40 ratio in this
context. 20 % initial development costs as well as 40 % program understanding and incorporation of changes. The latter also involves testing.
Van Vliet [Vli08, p. 471] separates into isolation (change analysis), modification (the actual change) and testing (execution of regression test). He
assigns 40-30-30 % to the three areas, which is of a similar magnitude as
Fjeldstad and Hamlen. Again, these numbers are only intended as a rough
guide: According to Tilley et al. and Canfora et al. [TS95, CC00] the cost of
the program comprehension depend on the software complexity and could
be up to 90 %.

The term "Understanding" in the Figure 2.6 denotes the recognition of
structure or architecture of the system, the system properties and the in-

---

[20] Pigoski proposes to combine adaptive and perfective maintenance to the term "enhancement".

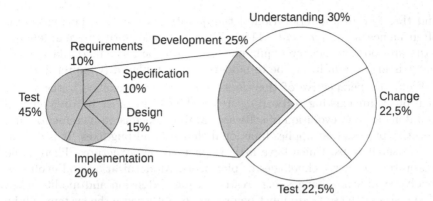

Figure 2.6: Software life cycle: the initial development effort in relation to maintenance, based on van Vliet [Vli08, pp. 15 and 471]

ternal operation. It includes determining the control and data flow information, syntactic and semantic analysis as well as presenting derived or abstracted information (Chapter 2.4). The two other terms "Implementation", the implementation of the planned changes and "Testing" to validate the changes are self-explanatory. This book will concentrate on the first two areas, the creation of information from a given program and changing the program itself.

The three main tasks (Figure 2.6) were further refined by Müller [Mü97, p. 28]. Accordingly, typical duties of a maintenance engineer are:

- the analysis of the system specification and design,
- the survey of users
- the examination of program code and documentation,
- the tracking of an error to the source,
- the design of the program change,
- the implementation of the change,
- validating and testing and
- customizing the documentation.

In fact, not all steps are necessary or possible. Further procedures (also called reengineering patterns) for individual points are described in Demeyer et al. [DDN09].

After a closer examination of the last major section in the software life cycle it has to be summarized that the maintenance of software (except for preventive maintenance) ultimately leads to an increase of inner complexity and therefore to a deterioration of the quality parameters. This change is often named as *design drift*. This will be accepted until the maintenance costs are too high or new requirements can not be met. In the last resort the existing system has to be to modernized or replaced (Chapter 2.5).

From the perspective of this book, software maintenance is the modification of an existing software system. The term must be divided into maintenance and evolution of software. Maintenance is an incremental and iterative process that applies functional changes and bug fixes. It is carried out in small steps, which have little impact on the structure. There is no adaptation to new technologies or platforms. Modernization and evolution involve significant changes, e.g. restructuring, extension and modification. Vast parts of the software must be preserved. Otherwise the system will be entirely replaced.

None of the previously mentioned definitions relates to the complexity aspect inherent in systems which are being used for quite some time and are subject to scheduled or unscheduled maintenance. These so-called legacy systems are significant in software maintenance.

2.3 Legacy Systems

Many software systems *live* significantly longer than their developers had expected. They must be adapted constantly to changing circumstances and face numerous larger and smaller modifications during their lifetime. This results in old software artifacts being symbiotically coalesced with the company (a pile of data by Canfora and Cimitile [CC00]). These systems are designated as legacy systems. They represent a particularly complex scenario of software maintenance and evolution. This is characterized by high costs, design drift, using old programming and development languages, little and less useful documentation as well as no test cases (Chapter 2.3.2).

Scalise et al. [SFZ10] assume that today not only old and monolithic systems, but also object-oriented applications (written in Java or C++) comply with legacy systems. Sneed [Sne84] underlines that systems older than five years already belong to the category of legacy systems.

2.3.1 Characteristics of Legacy Systems

The term legacy system has already been used several times in context of software maintenance. In the following the exact meaning of the term is elaborated and criteria for the evaluation of legacy systems are defined.

Many definitions of legacy systems are informal or stereotyped, for example in Seacord et al. [SPL03, p. 1]: *"legacy code is code written yesterday"* or Wu et al. [WLB+97]: *"legacy systems ... are also a road block to progress"*.

The concept is based on the translation of the English term *legacy*. Mens and Demeyer use the definition of the Oxford English Dictionary [MD08]:

> *"A sum of money, or a specified article, given to another by will; anything handed down by an ancestor to a predecessor."*

Thus it is an item of certain value, which is inherited. In terms of software systems it means that such systems have already "survived" several generations of developers, administrators and users. They represent a great value for the company and may be described as business-critical[21].

The inheritance of a system from one generation to the next naturally results in a loss of knowledge. This system-specific knowledge must be learned anew by each generation (system and application understanding). A system can age at various levels, e.g. technical basis, quality of the source code, currentness of documentation and user requirements. This may lead to parts of the system not longer being manageable.

The definition of Bennett [Ben95] is based on this knowledge. He describes legacy systems as large-scale software systems that can not be maintained any longer but are essential for the company[22]. Furthermore, Bennett et al. developed the SABA model [BRM99]. It describes a decision model to analyze software systems relating to their legacy level and demonstrates strategies for the further handling.

Seacord et al. [SPL03, p. XIII] as well as Brodie and Stonebraker [BS95] define legacy system similar to Bennett, but the perspective has changed. They note that legacy systems resist against modifications[23]. Indirectly, the active role is given to the system.

Rada [Rad00, p. 233] uses a business point of view for his definition. He associates the loss of knowledge implicitly to heredity. Furthermore legacy systems contain domain-specific knowledge about the area in which they are used. To recover this, a system must be analyzed and restructured[24].

---

[21] Software systems that are called business-critical include a huge amount of knowledge about the business processes within the company. Their breakdown causes very high costs and delays the continuation of the business operations.

[22] *"Large software systems that we don't know how to cope with but that are vital to our organization."*

[23] *"Software systems become legacy systems when they begin to resist modification and evolution."*

[24] *"Software systems in the domain of interest that can impact legacy knowledge about the domains and feed domain analysis and reengineering effort to produce domain assets or new application systems."*

A detailed and more technical definition then the ones previously mentioned is based on Bisbal et al. [BLWG99b] and descends from Singh and Huhns [SH05, pp. 67]. This definition serves as the basis for this book:

> "'[...] legacy systems would be those who run on obsolete hardware and operating systems and over nonstandard network. [...] Legacy systems often involve a substantial database component, which is poorly modeled if at all [...] Legacy systems tend to support rigid user interfaces. "'

The criteria described above can be objectively checked. In detail, they cover hardware, operating system, communication facilities, data storage and user interface of legacy systems. The case study in this book is evaluated based on this definition. Further criteria are deduced from the definition above. A good guide is also provided by Seacord et al. [SPL03, pp. 4] and Warren [War99, pp. 4,21].

2.3.2 Criteria for the Evaluation of Legacy Systems

For the evaluation of legacy systems these can be divided into axiomatic (primary) criteria and derived (secondary) criteria. In the following each criteria receives a unique number with the prefix CLS.

Axiomatic Criteria

CLS01 There is no or only outdated documentation.

CLS02 There are no or few test cases to check components and the overall system.

CLS03 The original developers or users are no longer available, orientation is time consuming and difficult.

CLS04 The system is a part of everyday business and incorporates business knowledge, a failure leads to substantial losses.

CLS05 The maintenance of hardware and software components from third parties has expired.

CLS06 The compilation of the system takes a very long time.

Derived Criteria

CLS07 The knowledge of the internal architecture of the system is no longer present.

CLS08 The overall system is only understood to a limited extent.

CLS09 There are different versions of the system, the allocation of these variants, and their maintenance is difficult.

CLS10 Small maintenance tasks require a lot of time.

CLS11 There is a backlog of change requests, since fixing errors has become a regular and permanent task.

CLS12 The source code contains duplicated areas.

The criteria are distinctive features of a legacy system. The list could also include further items, such as probability of occurrence and types of errors, frequency of changes and quality of the source code – long methods, large classes or long parameter lists, also known as *Code Smells* [FBB+99]. They are not the primary characteristics of a legacy system and hence are not considered further. A catalog with various issues and criteria can be found in Sommerville [Som06, pp. 548].

2.3.3 Strategies for Coping with Legacy Systems

From a business perspective, there are four different strategies for dealing with legacy systems [CC00]. It is possible,

- to completely replace the system,
- to freeze the current state without further changes,
- to hold on to maintenance despite cost or
- to modernize the system.

The freezing of the current system state and the adherence to maintenance are not relevant for this book. Neither do they contribute to improving the state nor do address the (main) causes of the problem.

Premise for those strategies is a profound understanding of the internals of a software. Reengineering of data and their internal processing in particular are necessary requirements for both: the new development [BLWG99b] and the modernization of software.

2.4 Software Reengineering

Seacord et al. [SPL03] define software reengineering as an engineering process with aiming to generate *evolvable system*. In general, it includes all activities following the delivery to the customer to improve the understanding of the software as well as to improve various quality parameters, for example the complexity, maintainability, extensibility and reusability. Thus, it helps to prolong the life time of a software system.

Reengineering is applied to both software maintenance and software evolution. However, scope, effort and use of various technologies differ considerably in these two areas. Evolution is based on the understanding of the whole systems. It is expensive, while maintenance usually investigates localized problems.

The generic term reengineering summarizes a variety of software techniques. They are used to understand, to improve and to validate existing software. In general reengineering is costly and complex. Compared to a greenfield approach, however, it is often a pragmatic and less risky alternative [SPL03, pp. 10] [War99, pp. IX and 12][25].

Reengineering is used to port a system to a new platform, to introduce new technologies, to extract knowledge and design[26], to break a monolith[27] and to reduce the dependence from its developers (see Chapter 2.3.2).

As described in Chapter 2.3, legacy systems are the most complex form in software evolution. In most cases targeted reengineering is indispensable for saving inherent business knowledge.

It has to be mentioned that software is not only the program code, but also all the artifacts produced during the development. They must be integrated into the reengineering process.

2.4.1 Definitions of Software Reengineering

The term reengineering includes various concepts and methods. The definition of the term itself is more specific, in comparison to software maintenance. Numerous publications use the reengineering taxonomy of Chikofsky and Cross [CC90] from 1990. The authors define reengineering as:

> *"... the examination [understanding] and alteration of a subject system to reconstitute it in a new form and the subsequent implementation of the new form."*

The definition describes three steps of the software reengineering process. In a first step, relevant information from the system must be extracted (*reverse engineering*). All existing artifacts are taken into account. Secondly, the system is changed (*transformation*) and finally this modification is real-

---

[25] Warren refers to the article, "The Evolutionary Growth of Software Reengineering and the Decade Ahead" by Ulrich. It was published in 1990 in the Journal of the American Programmer 3 (10).

[26] Knowledge concerning to the internal structure or business processes, etc.

[27] Software is called monolithic if it has no clearly structured architecture. Various aspects such as persistence, logic, exception handling and user interfaces are intertwined and not separated.

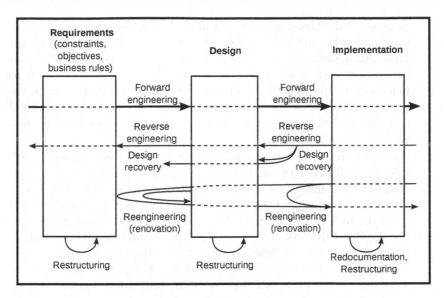

Figure 2.7: Conceptual model of software reengineering [CC90]

ized (*forward engineering*). The final step is similar to an ordinary software development step.

Figure 2.7 shows the conceptual model of software reengineering. There, Chikofsky and Cross defined further terms of the Re*-family. Each term is linked to one or more of the three levels of abstraction. They cover the main levels – requirement, design and implementation.

Forward engineering is the traditional software development process. It describes the gradual refinement from a higher to a lower level of abstraction: from requirements down to the source code.

Reverse engineering step contains the analysis of existing software systems. It examines structures, states, behavior and relationships of system elements. The objective is the extraction and the representation of information at a higher level of abstraction[28]. This process is called modeling (see Chapter 2.6). The models can be of graphical or of textual nature.

The recovery of descriptions is done by abstraction: the omission of detailed information and the aggregation of information to something

---

[28] A comprehensive and current summary of reverse engineering techniques and tools can be found in Canfora and Di Penta [CDP07].

more general. Therefore, a wide range of tools for analysis of source code and other artifacts exists. However, the interpretation of the information obtained must always be left to the developer. He must balance between levels of abstraction and level of detail: abstract as much as possible and still preserve all necessary details. In general the process of reverse engineering is semi-automatic. Reus et al. [RGD06] call this an interactive reconstruction of models to understand and explore software systems.

The source code is not necessarily the basis for reverse engineering. All existing artifacts are candidates, for example, documentation, design diagrams or comments in a version control systems. Since there is no formalized correlation between documentation and code, the latter is often the only reliable source of information [Mü97, Seite 28][War99, Seite 5][Ben95][CC00]. This is certainly the main motivation for many reverse engineering techniques that deal with program code. Also, the definition of reverse engineering in the IEEE Standard 1219 for software maintenance [IEE99][29] contains only the program code as source of information.

The result of system analysis is the basis for the transformation and forward engineering steps. Thus, reverse engineering is the foundation of the reengineering: A software system can only be changed when it is understood.

Redocumentation refers to the creation of a semantically equivalent representation on implementation level. An alternative representation of source code is, for example, a control or data flow diagram.

Design recovery creates design artifacts of a system under observation by integrating additional information (e.g. documentation and domain knowledge). Implementation-specific information is removed. It illustrates the relationships between various components of a system. For the approach presented here, design recovery is a basic activity.

Restructuring is the transformation from one form of representation to another without changing the functionality. For example, this includes the introduction of coding guidelines, improving the control flow (e.g. replace `goto` by `if-then` constructs), the removal of duplicated source code or the execution of a refactoring. Since it does not change the semantics, these adjustments are not visible to the stakeholders. Restructuring always takes place within one level of abstraction. Here it differs from the IEEE Standard 1219 for software

---

[29] 3.1.11: *"The process of extracting software system information (including documentation) from source code."*

maintenance. The standard repeatedly considers the implementation level solely[30].

In addition to the conceptual model of Chikofsky and Cross further terms in the Re*-environment have been established in recent years. Often, they focus one aspect of a software system. The following terms are introduced by various authors (e.g. Seacord et al. [SPL03, pp. 11] or Warren [War99, pp. 48]) and are relevant for this book.

Retargeting refers to the migration of a system to a new hardware platform. Usually, bottlenecks like performance or procurement of spare parts should be eliminated.

Revamp encapsulates a text-based[31] user interface in a modern graphical user interface. For this purpose, a layer between the original and the new surface is constructed to bind the text-based elements to their equivalent in the new graphical user interface. From the maintenance point of view, the advantage of this technique is at the same time its biggest drawback: Since no changes to the existing system have to be conducted, the problems still remain. However, they will be hidden behind a pretty facade (Chapter 4.7).

Rearchitecture applies changes to the original architecture of a legacy system. Usually, it is still organized centrally, which leads to problems and dependencies in software maintenance tasks. In the course of modernization often a distributed architecture is introduced. As a prerequisite, the existing system have to be split into different components. This is not always possible with legacy systems (see Chapter 2.5.3). Well-defined interfaces emerge due to the introduction of a distributed architecture. Thus replacement of individual parts of the system is possible [WNS+97].

Redesign with reuse specifically focuses the maintenance of business knowledge inherent in a system. By reusing this knowledge, it should be preserved and made accessible to new applications. This can be done by integration or wrapping (see Chapter 2.5.2) into a new system. Distributed systems are particularly well suited because data and functionality are hidden behind well-defined interfaces.

Redesign with reuse is defined similarly to rearchitecture. However, they pursue different goals. Whilst rearchitecture operates exclusively

---

[30] B.1.7: *"The translation of an unstructured program into a functionally and semantically equivalent structured program. Restructuring transforms unstructured code into structured code to make the code more understandable, and thus more maintainable."*

[31] They are also called *"Green Screen System"* based on the first IBM terminals with green letters on black background.

in an existing system, redesign with reuse tries to integrate or reuse the old knowledge base into a new system.

In the context of monolithic systems the extraction and reuse of individual parts or components are associated with high costs. Even if the components are adjusted, the original problems may persist. However, the gradual modernization of these elements is now enabled.

The model-driven migration of software systems described in this book primarily addresses rearchitecture and redesign with reuse (after Chikofsky and Cross both are associated with the term design recovery). The adjustment to a new platform (retargeting) is implicit when components are prepared for a modern system.

The previously introduced terms are based on the definition and conceptual model of Chikofsky and Cross. To complete the picture of software reengineering, additional definitions are introduced below. They do not separate different methods or levels, but focus the anticipated improvements or orient themselves towards the costs, risks as well as non-functional requirements such as quality parameters.

Reengineering: Arnold [Arn93] defines software reengineering as:

> *"any activity that: (1) improve one's understanding of software, or (2) prepares or improves the software itself, usually for increased maintainability, reusability, or evolvability. In this definition, the term "software" includes – in addition to source code – documentation, graphical pictures and analyses."*.

The process is not fully automated. Arnold describes exemplary that an automated test of the semantic equivalence of an old and a new system is not possible.

Reengineering (Tilley [TS95][32]): The definition of the Software Engineering Institute at Carnegie Mellon University is as follows:

> *"Reengineering is the systematic transformation of an existing system into a new form to realize quality improvements in operation, system capability, functionality, performance, or evolvability at a lower cost, schedule, or risk to the customer."*

The definition is very similar to Arnold: In addition costs and risks are taken into account.

Reengineering: McClure [McC92] speaks of the examination and modification of software using automated tools, *"Reengineering is the software maintenance automation"*[33].

---

[33] The detailed definition is as follows: *"Reengineering is the processs of examining an existing system (program) and/or modifying it with the aid of automated tools to:*

Reengineering (German-language encyclopedia): The Duden Informatik [CS06] defines reengineering as a *"modification of existing systems with the goal of quality improvement"*. This includes all activities that occur after the introduction of a software system. Reasons for reengineering can be a new environment, reuse of software components or improving maintainability.

The Kleine Informatiklexikon [ZS95] limits reengineering to determining manual control flow and data flow information, as well as the architecture with the help of automated methods for syntactic and semantic analysis.

Both definitions do not capture the existing conceptual models, for example by Chikofsky and Cross.

Reengineering (IEEE 1219-1998 [IEE99]): The IEEE standard for software maintenance automatically assumes that reengineering is the redevelopment of a software system.[34]

The latter definition addresses one important point from the other definitions. The discrepancy centers around the question of whether a system's functionality can be extended in reengineering or if the system has to be semantically equivalent to its predecessor. Some authors [Som06, Pre86] exclude a functional extension because they assume that the risk is not assessable. Berg [Ber05] refers enhancements only on maintenance, but not on software reengineering.

Other authors argue that with extensive work on a system, such as the change of platform, new functionality is automatically integrated into the system [Mos09, IEE99, CC90]. This book agrees with this opinion: A functional extension should not and can not be excluded from the reengineering of a software system.

The book is based on the definition and the conceptual model of Chikofsky and Cross [CC90]. Additionally, it is expanded to include the above mentioned terms: redesign with reuse, rearchitecture and retargeting.

2.4.2 Levels of Software Reengineering

In their taxonomy (Figure 2.7) Chikofsky and Cross already divide software-reengineering into different levels and use them to define a conceptual model.

---

[1] Improve its future maintainability, [2] Upgrade its technology, [3] Extend its life expectancy, [4] Capture its components in a repository where CASE tools can be support it, [and 5] Increase maintenance productivity."

[34] B.1.6: *"A system-changing activity that results in creating a new system that either retains or does not retain the individuality of the initial system."*

A hierarchical view of the individual levels and their relationships in software reengineering is published by Byrne [Byr92]. For the author, the concept of abstraction is the central idea. The degree of abstraction depends on the circumstances and objectives of the reengineering project.

Each level determines specific characteristics and forms of representation. The result is a hierarchy of levels: The most accurate and detailed information can be found on the bottom, the implementation level. The density of information decreases towards the top.

Information from higher levels are only implicit in the underlying levels. They are replaced by concrete level-specific representatives, for example, requirements are mapped in architecture and design decisions. In general, this corresponds to a 1:n-relationship. One requirement affects n-different places in the layer below.

Changes within a level only affect the underlying, but not the level above. Furthermore, it can be deduced that the only reliable level is the lowest (according to Figure 2.7). All others do not necessarily represent the current state. Fragmentary or outdated information about a layer must be reconstructed in a reverse engineering step.

Changes to a system must be implemented in the correct level, e.g. architectural changes should be carried out in the design level. The effects are then propagated downwards.

The classification and naming of the levels is not universally defined. Chikofsky and Cross (Figure 2.7) are based on the phases of the software development process (requirements, design, implementation). Instead, Bergland [Ber78] divided into source, module and system level. The Horseshoe Model (Figure 2.8) adds the functional representation as an additional layer, but – in comparison to Chikofsky and Cross – omits the requirements level.

The Horseshoe Model in Figure 2.8 is developed in the CORUM II (Common Object-based re-engineering Unified Model) [KWC98] project at the Software Engineering Institute at Carnegie Mellon University[35]. The aim was to categorize the variety of different tools and approaches in the area of architecture recovery and to create a common data model for the tools that act at different levels of the software reengineering process.

It is based on the three areas of software reengineering. The reconstruction of an architecture requires the consideration of different levels. In reverse engineering (Reconstruction) lost information is reconstructed. They are adequately replaced in forward engineering (Refinement). The Transformation of the old to the new system can take place at any level.

---

[35] The CORUM II model is the successor of the CORUM model, which was solely focused on reengineering of source code [WOL+98].

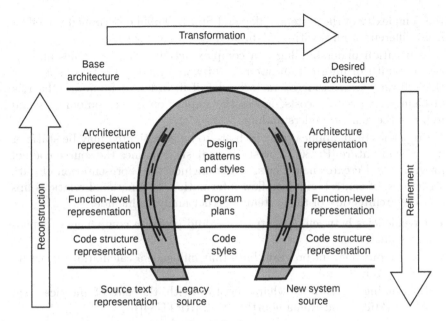

Figure 2.8: Horseshoe Model [KWC98]

2.4.3 System and Application Understanding

A central point of the previously discussed fundamentals is the understanding of the system as well as the application (e.g. Figure 2.6). Usually, the maintenance developer does not have the same knowledge as the developers of the original system. He needs to make *"the system"* his own for a successful reengineering process[36].

Large software systems generally consist of a landscape of different software products that are developed or bought and grown over many years. System understanding examines the connection and the interaction between different products. The result is an overview of the functions and the role of the subsystems: system understanding.

If a single program is the focus, we speak of application understanding. The aim is to understand the internals of the software sufficiently, that modifications can be made safely. Bennett [Ben95] defined program understanding as a major activity in software reengineering. Depending on

---

[36] See Chapter 2.4.1: Only when a software system is understood, it can be changed.

the complexity of the system Tilley and Smith [TS95] determined the effort
from different studies with 50 % to 90 % (see Figure 2.6).

Application understanding is a complex activity that combines and filters a wealth of information about a software system. Certain aspects of
the software are considered in more detail in order to minimize the risk
of changes, to reduce costs, assess the impact on other components and
improve the general understanding.

Properties of an application which are to be investigated may be static or
dynamic in nature [Pre86]. The static analysis examines the source code of
programs and creates new views. These include the representation of data
structures, of control and data flow information, of functional relationships
and the architecture of the system. Further analyzes include:

- dependencies between data structures and program components (dependency analysis),
- filtering out relevant program lines that influence a calculation (program
  slicing [Wei84]) and
- determining measurable characteristics with the aid of metrics (e.g.
  Müller [Mü97] and Ramamoorthy et al. [RPTU84]).

The dynamic analysis of a program is done during execution, while its
behavior is recorded. This information is filtered and visualized in a model.
The developers are often interested in the consumption of resource, the use
of data, the relationship between functions, or the use of concurrent areas
in parallel processing.

Top-Down and Bottom-Up Approaches

Basically, there are two different approaches for the investigation of software. The study of the architecture starts with a look from the *top* (top-
down). The first results are then refined from top to bottom with the help
of various hypotheses. The opposite direction (bottom-up) starts with the
source code and extract information, structures and other artifacts which
are necessary to form an abstract representation at the next higher level
(e.g. architecture).

Combinations of the two methods are possible and recommended. The
preferred approach of Weiderman et al. [WBST97] uses the top-down approach for system understanding. Often, a general overview of the architecture of the system is sufficient to recognize relationships. For a detailed
analysis of a program the bottom-up approach is essential.

The application understanding requires tools for the visualization of the
extracted information. In this context graphs are a valuable and impor-

tant form of representation (see Chapter 4.4). An overview on software visualization, as well as techniques and tools can be found by Zeller [Zel04].

The method developed in this book addresses the understanding of the internals of a program. Here the source code from individual applications is analyzed and abstracted using filters. Chapter 5.6 shows that this approach is also applicable for system understanding.

2.4.4 Excursus: Business Process Reengineering

Objective in reengineering of software systems are the documentation, preservation and improvement of business processes. Because of the relationship of concepts, software reengineering should be defined here against Business Process Reengineering (BPR) known from economics.

Johanson et al. [JMPWI93] define BPR as a fundamental and radical redesign of business processes of an enterprise in order to achieve dramatic improvements in efficiency and performance (cost, quality, service, etc.).

A business process usually consists of several connected steps and involves large parts of a company. Its goal is the production or provision of an asset, a service or a product.

In general, the reengineering of business processes also triggers a reengineering of the relevant software systems. These must be adapted to the new or modified requirements. Thus the BPR has obviously a broader basis than software reengineering. The respective goals are similar, but the focus is different.

In the future these two areas will coalesce as today's software systems penetrate into all areas of a company and integrate them.

2.5 Software Migration

The following chapter merges the previous concepts. In this book, the migration of software is assigned exclusively to the field of software evolution. Frequently, the software migration is associated with legacy systems and the complex and complicated restoration projects associated with it. As explained in Chapter 2.3, the demand do maintain the system and its inherent business logic, especially from an economic point of view, is very high for old systems. Because of the central importance of the systems they can not be shut down or redeveloped. Some of the aforementioned features and identified problems are high maintenance costs, a lack of documentation and a bulk of requirements that can not be incorporated into the current system (detailed in Chapter 2.3.2).

2.5.1 Definition of Software Migration

In this book, software migration is defined as splitting and transferring software to a new platform or technology (transformation) – with the goal to meet new requirements and to improve future maintainability. The existing functionality is to be preserved in order to prevent the loss of business knowledge. This view is based on Bisbal et al. [BLWG99b]. The authors restrict migration to information systems and define it as follows:

> *"Legacy Information System Migration (...) allows legacy systems to be moved to new environments that allow information systems to be easily maintained and adapted to new business requirements, while retaining functionality and data of the original legacy systems without having to completely redevelop them."*

Functionality (the maintenance of domain knowledge and business logic), *data storage* and *usage* of a system determine the key aspects of software migration. Particularly kind-of-use decides whether an existing system, even if only for a certain period, can be switched off entirely or partially. A comprehensive understanding of system and application is basis for a migration of software.

2.5.2 Migration Methods

Various methods for the handling of existing systems, often legacy systems, are described by Müller [Mü97], Demeyer et al. [DDN09], Seacord et al. [SPL03] and Bisbal et al. [BLWG99b]. In summary, these fall into three categories: new development, wrapping and migration.

New development is denoted in literature as *Big Bang* or *Cold Turkey* approach [BS95, pp. 8]. Parallel to the existing system, a second, completely new one, is developed. (cf. Figure 2.5, System 2). The new development approach is associated with huge costs and the risk that parts of the company may not be operational during the transition phase, the new system does not meet the requirements or that it is already outdated upon completion[37]. The *Second System Effect* could emerge: The over-development and over-specification of the new system. This problem was first described by Brooks [Bro95].

---

[37] Further risks are described by Brodie and Stonebraker [BS95, pp. 9]. These include delays in development, dependencies to other systems, etc.

Wrapping enables transformation of parts of the original system. Advantage is that software components can be reused, which have been known and tested for years. In this context Seacord et al. [SPL03] defined this as black-box modernization. Merely knowledge of the external interfaces is required.

Unfortunately, this method has solely a short term solution character. Since the basic problems are not necessarily solved. Further steps, such as the replacement of the wrapped components, are strictly necessary. A prerequisite for wrapping is the decomposability of the existing system (see Chapter 2.5.3)[38]. Ideally, the new system can access data and functionality of the legacy application and vice versa. Typical problems occur with the persistence of data, synchronization, as well as exception and error handling. Wrapping is often used during the transition from procedural to object-oriented programming languages [Mü97, p. 112]. Weiderman et al. [WNS+97] state that wrapping is in combination with modern middleware systems more effective than trying to completely investigate a system. They differentiate between the wrapping levels job, transaction, program, module and procedure level. Seacord et al. [SPL03, pp. 226] separate additionally between component-based and object-wrapping.

Migration of software systems strikes the balance between the two above mentioned methods. It moves the existing system in a flexible environment while maintaining its functionality. Liebhart [Lie10] denotes the fundamental revision of a system as modernization.

This sustainability-oriented way is more complex than wrapping, but less risky than a new development (see definition p. 40). A schema for the migration of object-oriented systems is provided by Demeyer et al. [DDN09, pp. 182]. In addition, the authors explain incremental steps to migrate software systems. It is defined by Seacord et al. [SPL03] as white-box modernization[39].

Migration of software systems is primarily aimed at long-term issues, such as improved future maintenance, comprehensive understanding of the system, reduced maintenance costs, as well as more flexibility for further requirements [Lie10]. Liebhart [Lie10] and Demeyer et al. [DDN09] consider the inclusion of the users as a key success factor in the migration process.

---

[38] The wrapped components must be largely side-effect free. The communication and dependencies to other components should be kept as low as possible.

[39] Black- and white-box modernization differ in the depth of understanding, Liebhart [Lie10]. In black-box modernization only the inputs and outputs are analyzed, whereas white-box identifies the components of a system and their dependencies.

In reality, a strict separation of the methods is not possible. A specific activity can be categorized into several methods, for example, migration can also include wrapping or development of individual parts. Therefore, each part of the system must be considered separately.

2.5.3 Migration Strategies

Based on the migration methods for dealing with legacy systems, different scenarios for the transition from an old to a new system are possible. The strategy must consider the functionality and data management of the existing system. In terms of functionality, Simon [Sim92] describes three different ways of a transition:

The *Cut-and-Run* method turns the old system off and activates the new system. This is done in one step and is therefore associated with very high risk. There is no experience regarding the new system. Untested components are used and users have little confidence. This strategy is in line with the new development and is listed here for completeness only.

The *Phased Interoperability* approach renews incrementally individual parts of the legacy system and transfers them to the new system. Both systems form a unit. A significant reduction in risk is a clear advantage of the latter strategy. Demeyer et al. [DDN09, pp. 181] generally recommend to migrate systems incrementally. They depict useful patterns for the application in migration projects. The functional separation of system parts and components is essential for this complex task and not always possible with monolithic systems. Brodie and Stonebraker [BS95, pp. 15] distinguish three different types of architectures:

Decomposable architectures can be separated in individual applications, databases and interfaces. Each component of the system has a well-defined interface and is independent of the others. Usually, they depend on the database only.

Undecomposable architectures represent the worst case. These systems can only be regarded as a black box. It is impossible to separate individual system functions.

Semi-decomposable or hybrid architectures are a mixture of the two above. Parts of a system, e.g. the graphical user interface, can be separated. Others, however, such as the database, are closely connected to the logic and can not be decomposed. This increases the complexity in the analysis and in the migration of a system.

The *parallel operations strategy* runs old and new system simultaneously, all operations are performed in parallel on both systems. Once the new system covers the functions of the old system, the latter is switched off. In contrast to the cut-and-run approach the confidence with the new system increases during development. Thus, at any time a quick change between old and new is possible.

Data Migration

To avoid inconsistencies, considerations for data migration are necessary especially for the last two methods. Usually, the database schema evolves over time. As is customary, during migration the scheme is adapted to the new circumstances and old habits are removed. The timing, in relation to the migration of the functionality, may vary. The data can be migrated before, in parallel or after[40].

A closer examination of the adaptation of database schemata and data migration is not part of this book (cf. Bisbal et al. [BLWG99a, BLWG99b], Brodie and Stonebraker [BS95] as well as Wu et al. [WLB+97]).

Conclusion

In this book the extension of a reengineering method towards the migration of information systems is described. The premises reside in the migration of a system to a new platform, the removal and replacement of functionality, ensuring a consistent usability of the system as well as the preservation of a maximum proportion of the existing source code and thus the business logic. The method contains wrapping and new development (Chapter 2.5.2) of individual parts for the migration. Expected positive effects are the increased flexibility, a better understanding of the internals and simplified future maintenance steps.

As with the phased interoperability strategy, the legacy and the new system form a composite. This approach reduces the risk, but increases the complexity in return. The latter is counteracted due to the use of models (Chapter 2.6) and modeling tools.

2.6 The Concept of Modeling

The use of models and model transformations acquires a central role in a model-driven software migration approach. In the following chapter the characteristics of a model are introduced at first in general, and then in the

---

[40] Details for data migration can be found in Seacord et al. [SPL03, pp. 232] and Bisbal et al. [BLWG99a].

context of computer science. This includes a differentiation of the concepts of model-based and model-driven, the properties of modeling languages as well as different types of model relationships and model transformations. The focus is not only the current state of research, but also the use of modeling in the industrial context.

Models have been applied in various disciplines of engineering, mathematics and philosophy [Lud03, Bro04] for many decades, partially for centuries. Their significance has been increasing constantly since the 90s in the comparatively young computer science, especially in software development.

In 1973, the mathematician and philosopher Stachowiak associated three main features to models in his General Modeling Theory [Sta73]:

Mapping Feature: *Models are always models of something, namely illustrations, representations of natural or artificial originals that can itself be models.*

Reduction Feature *Models do not capture all of the attributes represented by the original, but only those which are relevant for the particular model characteristics and/or model users.*

Pragmatic Feature *Models are not clearly associated with their originals per se. They fulfill their function a) as a replacement for certain – recognizing and/or acting, using – model subjects, b) within certain time intervals and c) under restriction to certain mental or actual operations.*

Stachowiak determines that a model is the abstraction (Reduction) of a real or artificial object (Mapping). The model has been created for someone (human or artificial model user) and for a specific purpose. It *works* only in this particular context. The model can be used to make specific predictions or conclusions about the subject (Pragmatic Feature).

Thus, models help to simplify and understand complex issues and problems. They separate certain aspects from the object under study – *Separation of Concerns* –, reduce complexity and focus on a certain amount of information. Models provide a common basis for communication and are particularly helpful in dealing with heterogeneous systems.

The model features defined by Stachowiak are the basis for the model definition in the context of computer science. Within this discipline, the knowledge of the modeling of software systems is strongly influenced by the industry. Especially the Object Management Group (OMG) [OMG12d] plays a significant role with its framework of standards. In the following, the emergence of two key standards is briefly explained. They are necessary for the distinction between the two terms model-based and model-driven. A formal consideration of the subject of modeling, model definitions, modeling languages as well as model transformations can be found below.

2.6.1 Software Development at an Abstract Level

In the early stages of software development models were used as sketches, manuals, documentation or description of ideas [Sei03]. They were applied in very specific areas. These include, for example, the Petri Nets [Pet62]. They were developed in 1962 and describe distributed systems.

The introduction of the Unified Modeling Language (UML) has increased the influence of models in software development. The UML consists of a family of languages and was developed by the OMG, an industry consortium. Version 1.0 has been released in 1997 as a standard. Now it is a de facto standard in software development and in teaching at universities.

The UML is mainly oriented to object-oriented systems and a collection of graphic modeling languages. It enables the description of a software system from different points of view [41]. The current version 2.3 [OMG12c] contains over a dozen different notations. The components itself are not developed from scratch. Principally, they are based on many existing modeling notations, for example, Petri nets, or the 4+1 view model of Kruchten [Kru95].

Initially, the UML was exclusively used for the description and specification of software systems. This sketch and documentation character has the natural disadvantage that a specification is typically created once and not further adapted to changing circumstances. Thus, it will be discarded later, because the synchronization with the source code is lost. In this book, this kind of model usage is referred to as *model-based*. Seidewitz [Sei03] calls it code-centric development.

Built on the model-based development, the necessity arose to focus software development more on models and by doing so turning them into the pivotal artifact [Sei03, MCF03, BBJ07, DVW07][42].

Software development, which is based on this principle is referred to as *model-driven*. In this context, Kühne [Kü06] speaks of bound (in the model-driven design) and unbound (in the model-based design) models. In con-

---

[41] These aspects relate to the static and dynamic aspects of a software system and to the different phases in the software development process. The available modeling languages can be specifically used in certain phases, for example, for the description of system requirements, software architecture and other design decisions.

[42] Bézivin and Seidewitz describe models as primary artifact of development. In a similar direction go van Deursen et al., they define models as an integral part of model-driven software development. Mellor et al. [MCF03] want to create real things by model transformation.

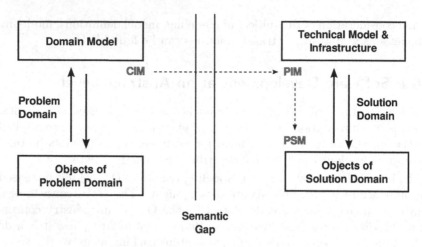

Figure 2.9: The concepts of MDA: CIM, PIM, PSM in problem domain
and solution space

trast, Brown [Bro04] states that a clear definition of the term model-driven
is not recognizable. He notes that the description – as a semi-automatic
code generation from abstract models – is becoming more widespread.

The Model-Driven Architecture (MDA)

In 2001, the industry and the OMG have taken this trend into account with
the preparation of the MDA [MM03, OMG12b]. Moreover, the OMG has
changed their motto of *"Everything is an object"*, to *"Everything is a model"*.

The result is a complex set of standards that are grouped together under
the MDA[43]. To control the complexity of software development, the MDA
distinguishes between descriptions of the domain and solution space [Sch06].

Figure 2.9 presents the three main concepts of the MDA [MM03]. The
problem domain (left side) represents physical objects that exist in a particular domain. These are abstracted and summarized to concepts of the
domain (CIM) [Sch06]. The Computation Independent Model (CIM) is also
called the language of the subject domain. It is independent of the problem
to be solved.

For a specific problem, first a model in the solution space (right side)
is created in accordance with the domain concepts described in the CIM.

---

[43] The UML is now also a part of the MDA.

The Platform Independent Model (PIM) describes a possible solution of the problem and is independent of technology.

The technical implementation is described in the Platform Specific Model (PSM). According to the MDA, the PSM is created from the PIM with the help of several transformation steps (Chapter 2.6.5). The importance of the semantic gap between the technical domain and the solution space will be discussed later in more detail.

Critical Aspects of the Model-Driven Architecture (MDA)

In sum, the MDA description and the associated standards have a circumference of several thousand pages, spread across a plethora of documents. Inconsistencies in and between the documents arose [Fav04a], because of the extent, the quantity and of the various versions. For this reason and because of the lack of theoretical foundation (for example, the semantics of the model relationships), the OMG has experienced a lot of criticism from the research community [Fav04a, AK02, AK03, Sei03, GPHS06].

In this context it should be noted that the roots of the UML and MDA are in industrial and not in academic research. Both standards represent a pragmatic perspective of the use of conceptual models in development.

As a consequence, academic research has attended to model-driven development more intense retrospectively [BBJ07]. It has already influenced the creation of version 2 of the UML [AK01]. Furthermore, a new branch of research has emerged: The new discipline is named Model-Driven Engineering (MDE). The goal is to establish a formal basis for the concepts of software modeling [Fav04b].

MDE is described as an open approach, which contains no specific concepts and methods. The concepts are summarized in a so-called Mega-Model[44]. It includes the description of systems, models and meta-models as well as their relationships [Fav04a, Fav05, Bé05]. Favre [Fav04a] describes MDE as a global approach for software development. Now existing results and artifacts can be integrated. Fundamental is the discovery of elementary concepts in order to reduce the complexity of software development. The MDA is a possible incarnation of the MDE [Fav04a].

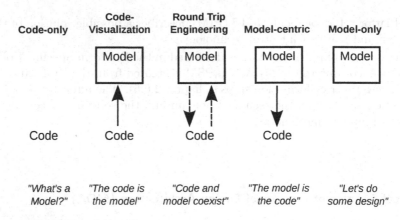

Figure 2.10: Modeling Spectrum

Models and their Usage

Brown [Bro04, pp. 316] defines five types of model usage in software development. In Figure 2.10[45], the spectrum ranges from the informal use, to the sole use of models.

Code-only is used by the majority of software developers, Brown [Bro04]. The model is hidden as an abstraction in the source code, in shared libraries and object hierarchies (characterized by packages, modules and interfaces). The modeling of software is done informally, for example at a white board or as a thought in the mind of the developer.

Code-Visualization helps to understand the structure and behavior of software. Some aspects of the program code are represented in a modeling language. These descriptive models are also referred to as code or implementation models.

Round Trip Engineering (RTE) synchronizes the program code with the corresponding model and vice versa. Changes to either side, e.g. design changes, are automatically transferred to the other. RTE presupposes that at least function bodies can be generated from models.

---

[44] The Mega-Model is based on the model definition of Seidewitz [Sei03], the model of relations of Bézivin [BBJ07] as well as the Meta-Model and ontology relationship by Atkinson and Kühne [AK03].

[45] According to Brown this figure is based on John Daniels. Unfortunately, the author does not provide further information regarding the source. In my own research the primary literature could not be found either.

Model-centric targets the generation of fully executable source code. The model is the primary artifact of software development. Mainly, the generation uses external libraries, services and standard third-party applications and integrates existing legacy systems and data.

Model-only: Models are used to describe the application domain and/or the solution space. The models serve as a basis for discussion, communication within or outside a community, and create a common linguistic basis. The implementation is thereby separated from the model. As an example, the author cites the outsourcing of the implementation and maintenance of systems.

The latter two types are assigned to the model-driven development. Here, models assume the central role in software development. In contrast, the first two categories can be related to model-based development. However, they differ in the degree of formalization. Depending on the type of application and focus, RTE can be applied to a model-based as well as to a model-driven development.

In the present book, code visualization is used to investigate and understand existing source code. Based on the results the source code is converted into a model-centric development.

2.6.2 Model Definition

In the following, different model definitions are considered in the context of software modeling. The OMG defines the term model in the UML-Standard as follows:

> *"A model is an abstraction of a physical system, with a certain purpose."*

From a pragmatic point of view the limitation on physical systems is understandable, however incomplete. Stachowiak and further authors extend this restriction to *mental* or *unreal* systems[46].

Bézivin and Gerbé put the pragmatic feature of a model (Stachowiak) in the center of their definition [BG01].

> *"A model is a simplification of a system built with an intended goal in mind. The model should be able to answer questions in place of the actual system."*

They formulate, as well as the OMG, that a model is a simplification/abstraction of a system for a particular purpose. But it is not further re-

---

[46] This is in line with other disciplines such as mathematics or physics.

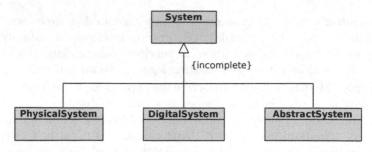

Figure 2.11: Refinement of the system concept by Favre [Fav04a]

stricted. The aim of a model is to allow certain questions and conclusions, without having to consider the actual, possibly real system.

Seidewitz [Sei03] deploys models as the primary artifacts of software development and defines the term as follows:

> *"A model is a set of statements about some system under study. Here, statement means some expression about the SUS that can be considered true or false (...)."*

A model consists of a set of statements that allow conclusions (true or false) about the system. A model is formally correct, if the statements about the system evaluate to true. The reduction feature by Stachowiak is indirectly part of this definition. It assumes that the set of statements about a system is a summary of a small set of features of the system. Additionally, Seidewitz states that the System under Study (SUS) does not necessarily have to exist for real.

To summarize, the definitions result in three focus areas, which have to be taken into account in the modeling of systems: the system, the model and the relationship between them.

Kühne [Kü06] formalize this point and defines that a model is an abstraction of a real or language-based system that allows predictions or deductions. He describes the relationship between a model and a system with the following syntax:

$$S \lhd M, \tag{2.1}$$

where $\lhd$ represents a one-to-many relationship.

Furthermore, Favre [Fav04a] states that the term system is insufficiently defined by Stachowiak (he described it as *something of* or as *original*) and substantiates it. For the modeling of software he proposed that a system can

be either physical, digital, or abstract (see Figure 2.11). Physical systems
are observable elements or phenomena of the real world, digital are located
in the memory of a computer and processed by a processor, and abstract
systems are ideas and concepts in the minds of people. Additionally, systems
can be divided for further refinement.

Models, depending on their relationship to the system (subject), are classified differently. Most authors distinguish two classes of models [Sei03,
Kü06, Fav04a].

A model which represents an existing SUS[47] is also referred to as a *descriptive model*. These models are frequently encountered in the reverse
engineering and can be used for analyzing and documenting a system.

If the model is used as a template for the creation of a system (forward
engineering), for example as a specification, then it is called a *prescriptive* or
specification model. The interpretation of the model describes a possible set
of systems. Especially in model-driven software development, specification
models represent the primary use-case. They are often data- or control
flow-oriented [Sei03].

Models that feature both characteristics are declared as *transient* models [Lud03, HM08]. On the one hand, they represent a SUS and on the
other hand they use this model to specify new systems. Especially this
characteristic makes transient models interesting for software migration.

2.6.3 Modeling Languages

The definition of a modeling language is necessary for the appropriate use of
models. Such a language has a certain degree of abstraction and represents
domain-specific concepts. It consists of elements and their relationship to
each other (syntax), the semantics and a representation (notation), see also
[KK02, AK01, MCF03].

Syntax: The syntax description of a model is often referred to as abstract
syntax. It describes the components and elements of the language
as well as rules. The rules are usually defined by a grammar. They
describe how the elements relate to each other. Using these rules, a
model can be checked for validity against the modeling language.

Notation: The notation is the concrete expression of the abstract syntax
(also known as *concrete syntax*). In general, the elements of a modeling language can be expressed in textual or graphical notations. Van

---

[47] Ludewig [Lud03] restricts the existence of the SUS. By using the weather forecast or
estimate costs in software projects as example, he explained that it (the SUS) does
not necessarily have to exist for real.

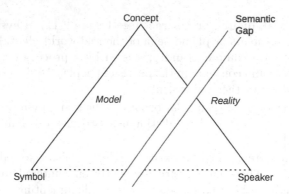

Figure 2.12: The semiotic triangle

Deursen et al. [DVW07] suggest to use textual notations for logic and graphical notations for structure representations. Schmidt [Sch06] believes that the learning curve is lower with graphical presentation. Experience with the creation of notations and their advantages and disadvantages are discussed by Kelly and Pohjonen [KP09]. The UML mostly consists of graphical notations.

Semantics: The semantics describes the meaning of model elements. It is mandatory to assign a meaning to each symbol. Usually the semantics is expressed in natural language [AK02]. It does not matter whether a model exists in textual or graphical notation. Without this relation, the use of models, as a representative for certain aspects of a system, is not possible.

The theory of the meaning of characters is a branch of semiotics. In 1923, Ogden and Richard [OR23] have described a semiotic triangle. This triangle (Figure 2.12) shows the relationship between a speaker, a thought or a reference (designated object or artifact) and the representative symbol[48].

In Figure 2.12 the symbol is located in the lower left corner of the semiotic triangle. It contains the notation in the context of a modeling language. The concept of the mental and conceptual representation of the symbol is located at the top of the triangle. It describes the abstract syntax, the boundary conditions (rules) and the semantics

---

[48] In linguistics originally the relationship between a concept (idea), a word (symbol) and an object (speaker) is used. Since the term object applies differently in computer science, the terminus speaker, introduced by Ogden and Richards, is used in this book.

of the modeling language (cf. Stahl et al. [SVEH07, pp. 28]). The abstract syntax defines the elements of the concept and their relationship. This includes the specification of rules for the well-formedness of the language. The semantics defines the meaning of language elements. They can be formally specified or given intuitively.

Ogden and Richards described the concept as a thought or reference. In this book, the term concept is used because it blends in better in the area of modeling (see Figure 2.9). Notation, abstract syntax and semantics together characterize the model.

The speaker in the lower right corner is the meaningful element – *concrete nouns* or *abstract noun* of the real world.

The mapping from symbol to speaker or vice versa is concept-dependent and can never happen directly (dashed line). The concept must be involved. Consequently the mapping is always dependent on the syntax and semantics of the concept (indirect relationship). The homonym *row* is a good example. Depending on the context, to argue or a row of seats, the symbol is connected with another speaker.

Usually the concepts are formulated in natural language or given implicitly (for example as a thought). In this case a semantic gap (see Figure 2.12) occurs between the concept and the meaningful element. The semantic gap is defined as the meaning-based difference between the model and the speaker.

The gap in Figure 2.12 and Figure 2.9 between the problem domain and the solution space is also described by Mellor et al. [MCF03] and Schmidt [Sch06]. It especially occurs when a speaker, not familiar with the domain, tries to interpret a model of the domain. But this is not the only significant gap. Additional gaps may occur within the solution space, e.g. the transformation of a model in programming language constructs. Selic [Sel03, p. 22] indicates that modeling languages are often not formally defined. In this case, semantic gaps appear between the PIM and the PSM as well as between the PSM and the program code. Selic would like to improve the transformation to the program code with a series of small and incremental transformation steps.

To avoid ambiguities and to allow automatic processing, the semantics of a model should be defined as formal as a programming language according to Seidewitz [Sei03]. For Favre [Fav04a] formal languages such as B [Lan96], VDM [Jon90] or Z [ISO02] are unsuitable. They cause additional costs and their usefulness is not clearly demonstrated for the development of information systems.

The Characteristics of Meta-Models

To check if a modeling language has been applied correctly, a description
of the language itself is required. This language description can also be expressed with the help of a model [AK03]. The *meta-model* defines the syntax
and semantics of the modeling language [SVEH07, p. 29]. This includes the
abstract syntax as well as rules about the interrelation of the elements of
the abstract syntax. Meta-models are specification models. They describe
a class of systems (in this case the system is the modeling language). For
instance, in the UML, the individual components of the modeling languages
are specified as UML class diagrams. The rules are expressed in the Object
Constraint Language (OCL) at meta-model level [Obj10]. The associated
semantics is described in natural language.

The well-formedness of models can be verified with the help of meta-
models. Furthermore, they play a central role as a data exchange format
and for development tools in the OMG standards[49].

The relationship between model and system, between models and the
definition of meta-models are subject of current research. Meta-models are
models in the proper sense. Their specific role within a model hierarchy is
expressed by the prefix *meta*[50].

Kühne [Kü06] and Favre [Fav05] formalize the development and the relationship of models and describe a formal basis. Both authors come to the
conclusion that the repeated application of a non-transitive, acyclic operation is a prerequisite for the meta-model status. This operation creates a
type-schema of all elements [Bé05, Sch06].

Favre [Fav05] uses a mathematical approach based on set theory and
defines various relationships between systems (the representationOf or μ-
relationship is non-transitive) and models (the elementOf or ϵ-relationship
is non-transitive and the includeIn or ς-relationship is transitive). A specific
pattern of these relationships ($\mu\epsilon\mu$-pattern) leads to a meta step (the con-
formsTo relationship, abbreviated with χ, see Figure 2.13). This elevates a
model in the meta-model status.

In contrast, Kühne [Kü06] studies the relationship between models only
([Kü06, p. 369]). He assumes that the system is already represented as

---

[49] For this purpose the OMG has specified the XML Metadata Interchange (XMI) for-
     mat [Obj07]. With the help of this format all UML models can be stored in XMI.
[50] Weather a model can be referred to as a meta-model depends on several factors.
     These include the context of the speaker and the type of relationship between the
     models. A model can be a meta-model from the system's point of view, but not
     from the perspective of the model. Furthermore, a model-to-model relationship does
     not automatically lead to a *meta*-state (cf. Kühne [Kü06], Favre [Fav05], Gašević et
     al. [GDD06, pp. 127]).

model. He divides the model-to-model relationship in `tokenModelOf` (transitive) and `typeModelOf` relationship (non-transitive). Kühne further distinguishes between ontological and linguistic instantiation and typifies both model relationships. The application of a `typeModelOf` relationship done twice raises a model in the meta-model status. If both types of instantiation can be used is not clarified yet.

It is generally noted that the meta-model view is always relative to the position of the observer.

Meta-models play a significant role in the present book. Usually they are implicit or defined by an implementation and not specified in a modeling language (Chapter 3.3.2).

2.6.4 Model Relationship

The previous section considered different relationships between a system, the model and the meta-model. The type and the semantics of the relationship are among the most controversial point in model-driven development.

In the MDA only the `instanceOf` relations exists, i.e. between model and system as well as between model and meta-model. These are borrowed from the object-oriented development. In the research literature this type of relationship is widely discussed and criticized [AK02].

Other authors consider this relationship from two different directions: Seidewitz [Sei03, p. 2] differs between descriptive and prescriptive models, depending on which of the two sides is the starting point. If a system is described by a model, Seidewitz named this relation as *representation*. Conversely, the system is created by an *interpretation* of the model.

In the MDE-concept Favre [Fav05] and Bézivin [BBJ07] introduce the `representationOf` (μ-relationship) and `conformsTo` relationships (χ-relation) (see Figure 2.13). The former represents the relationship between model and system, and the latter between model and meta-model.

The term Round Trip Engineering (RTE)[51] is often referred to in this context. Source code and models are to be synchronized automatically[52]. Changes to the model have a direct impact on the source code and vice versa. After a modification of the model the reinterpretation of the model and the resulting adjustment of the source code seams to be possible. The way back, the representation of the code as a model, is limited. This is due

---

[51] Compare to Figure 2.10 and definition on p. 48.
[52] According to Seidewitz this affects both the interpretation and representation of the relationship between model and system.

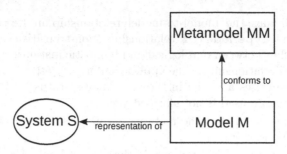

Figure 2.13: Base relations in MDE [BBJ07]

to the abstraction step, which must be applied each time the source code is changed. According to Selic [Sel03] this can be done manually only.

Until now, the properties of an abstraction have been described informally. Based on formula 2.1 Kühne formalized the abstraction and defined a function α:

$$M = \alpha(S). \tag{2.2}$$

An α exists when for each M a model to a system S exists. The abstraction function α consists of the composition of a projection (filter) π, a classification of elements and relationships β and τ the translation into another representation (for example, a different modeling language):

$$\alpha = \tau \circ \beta \circ \pi \tag{2.3}$$

The filter π is a structure-preserving, mathematical representation that summarizes elements and reduces their information. The abstraction function β is a classification function. Elements are grouped on the basis of their common attributes and relationships to common types. This step results in a loss of information. Consequently the model never holds the same information content as the system itself (reduction feature). Thus, the conditional application of RTE is justified. Conversely, a model can be enriched with information to convert it partially or completely into source code or any other form of representation.

In [SWM10] related approaches to RTE and the RTE capabilities of several existing tools are compared. Together with Steffen et al. differences in the context of continuous model-driven development are identified: Central argument of this paper is that in model-driven approaches the program code should be fully generated and the development of the software concentrates on model level [SJWM09]. In this context RTE is unnecessary. The advocated model-driven approach is explained in detail in Chapter 3.3.1.

Another relationship between models is the generalization. It is also discussed in detail by Kühne [Kü06] and mentioned here for completeness only.

The book is based on the formalization of Kühne and the naming scheme of Bézivin und Favre.

2.6.5 Model Transformation

The appropriate use of models in model-driven software development is the automated transformation to other models or artifacts (source code, structured documents, etc.) [Fav04a]. Transformation functions provide the ability to document and reuse expert knowledge [MCF03, WUG03]. Mellor et al. [MCF03] define model-driven development as a transformation:

> *"Model-driven development is simply the notion that we can construct a model of a system that we can then transform into the real thing."*

Schmidt emphasizes the advantage of the resulting artifact, with respect to the model, as being consistent. He refers to this as *correct-by-construction*. In general, three different types of transformation can be distinguished:

Model-to-model, transforms a model from one modeling language to another. By the transformation information can be added (refined) or lost (abstraction).

Model-to-code: This transformation is often referred to as a model-to-text or code generation. It generates a model from a textual description, for example, program code or other structured representations such as Extensible Markup Language (XML). The program code does not necessarily have to be executable.

Code-to-model: The transformation is primarily used in software reverse engineering. Information contained in the source code will be represented at model level.

Many authors [DVW07, MCF03, Fav04b, Lud03, Kü06, GLZ06] rightly argue that source code is also a model[53]. Thus, the three different types of transformations can be reduced to one. However, this separation is main-

---

[53] The source code is a model of the calculation performed on one or more processors [Lud03].

tained here to emphasize the reverse and forward engineering steps that relate to the program code.

Description of Model Transformations

A prerequisite for model transformation is that the abstract syntax and the semantics of the source and the target model are well known and understood. Therefore, meta-models play a central role in model transformations. Sendall and Kozacynski [SK03] as well as Weis et al. [WUG03] distinguish three different classes of model transformations:

Classical programming languages: In various modeling tools and languages, it is possible to manipulate the models by means of a programming interface[54]. The transformation is described in a classical programming language.

Intermediate representation: Many tools enable the export of models as a structured document. For this, the XMI format specified by the OMG is commonly used. This XML-based format can be manipulated using the Extensible Stylesheet Language Transformation (XSLT) language.

Transformation language is a language that describes and applies transformations. They are far more abstract than the first two methods and do not require detailed knowledge about interfaces or structured elements as well as their representation at the model level.

Transformation languages abstract from many aspects, which are implemented either in a classical programming language, or in the domain of XSLT taken over by the XSLT processor. This includes operations such as searching for items or patterns, as well as the creation, deletion and modification of model components [WUG03]. Sendall and Kozacynski [SK03] state that abstractions are the core aspects of a transformation language. They should be intuitive and cover a large proportion of all occurring cases.

Model transformations are distinguishable in textual and graphical notations. For example, the OMG defined the textual language Query View Transformation (QVT) [Obj11c] to describe transformations between modeling languages. Sendall and Kozacynski [SK03], Weis et al. [WUG03] and Moody [Moo09] prefer graphical notations. The present book uses different graphical transformations to explore models that were obtained from a reverse engineering step. Further languages are presented in Chapter 4.5.

---

[54] also known as Application Programming Interface (API)

2.6.6 Models and Software Evolution

Favre [Fav04a] criticized that research in the area of software modeling focuses on an idealized world full of models. However, for fifty years the software development has been code-centered and at best models are used for description purposes. According to the topic of this book, he states that models should play a central role in both the development and the maintenance, respectively the evolution.

There are mostly theoretical considerations for the use of models in software migration and evolution. The focus is the transient nature of models. Transient models enable – along with model transformations – the scheme of reconstruction, transformation and refinement shown in Figure 2.8.

Selic [Sel03] described advantages of models in software evolution. He emphasized that models are

- implementation and technology independent,
- closer to the problem domain and
- they enable the generation of program code from models.

In contrast to pure programming languages, models can be provided to a much wider audience. Selic predicts that in the future, users create or adapt their software by themselves based on models[55].

Van Deursen et al. [DVW07] presume that the cost for development and maintenance will be reduced by the use of models. In the future maintenance tasks are to be implemented through a series of model transformations. From the perspective of the authors model migration and evolution enable a continuous process. In addition, they describe other potential research topics in this area. One of them is the reconstruction of models from source code, in particular from legacy systems.

In this context, many authors [Sch06, GLZ06, DVW07, Sel03] suggest that models should interact with existing systems. This includes the use of existing libraries and the integration of legacy code and middleware systems.

Rugaber and Stirwalt [RS04], Scalise et al. [SFZ10] and Favre [Fav04a] use the term *model-driven reverse engineering (MDRE)*. They describe explicitly the use of models in reverse engineering to address maintenance problems. Models are used to represent aspects of software on an abstract level. These models form the basis for a new system, which is partially or fully generated. Rugaber and Stirwalt, for example, define a textual language to describe the domain, the model and the transformation between

---

[55] In Chapter 3.3.1, an approach, which offers a user-centered development of software, is presented.

the two. Favre [Fav04a] defines MDE as a composition of model-driven forward and reverse engineering.

Additionally, the OMG has recognized the importance of model-driven reverse engineering and created a new working group with the title Architecture Driven Modernization (ADM) [OMG12a]. Its goal is, based on the MDA technology, to support the industry in the maintenance and evolution of software.

Due to the short history of this area, the subject is highly topical and little explored. Currently, it is characterized by the pragmatic view of the industry and the OMG. The research attempted to explore the complexity of the field and to provide a formal basis for precise definitions. Especially the importance of models, modeling languages, their relationship and the development of a formal basis are subject of the current discourse.

Models can pave the way to a continuous software evolution. The research community has agreed that the modeling of software will improve the maintainability. But so far there are no concrete examples or applications on an industrial scale.

2.7 Software Design Methodologies

The software development process consists of a variety of different methods and artifacts. Especially larger projects with different development teams and philosophies must be synchronized and harmonized. *Method Engineering* [Bri96] is concerned with the diversity and the interaction of methods and artifacts along the software development process.

Method Engineering has its origins in the development of information systems and the underlying software development methodologies [BJO85, Bri96]. Brinkkemper defines Method Engineering as a composition of *methods, techniques, tools*, along a *methodology definition*.

A method is a concrete instance of a software development process. One technique that can be automated by a tool represents a fragment of this development process [BSH99]. Such method fragments [HBO94, SH96] can be concepts, criteria, notations, or artifacts (cf. [Rol97]).

The term methodology is an abstract concept and refers to the study of methods [KA04]. In contrast a method is a concrete instance of a methodology. One method consists of a collection of method fragments as well as related templates and rules for their composition. Based on these fragments, a development process is derived that is tailored to a specific project situation. Often the terms methodology and method are used interchangeably [Rol97, p. 3].

In this book a methodology for model-driven migration and evolution of software systems is defined for the first time. It is formalized using the concepts and notations from the research area of methodologies. The method itself and each method fragment are introduced in Chapter 3.

2.7.1 Situational Method and Research Overview

The adaptation of a software development process to a specific project situation is also called a *Situational Method*. Brinkkemper [Bri96] defined Method Engineering as a

> *"discipline to design, construct and adapt methods, techniques*
> *and tools for the development of information systems"*

In the following a brief history and current research topics in the field of Software Design Methodology (SDM) are presented. The overview of the research topics will consciously not be part of Chapter 4 (Related Work). In this book methodology is used as a tool only and is not part of the research.

SDM has its origins in the 70s. It includes process models, presented in this chapter, as well as specific forms, for example data flow oriented design or functional decomposition (cf. Bergland [Ber78]). SDM is generally used for structuring and organizing the development of information systems. The well-known models in the software development process or software life cycle consist of phases and describe an abstract view of the process. Method Engineering refined these models with specific methods and adapts them to specific project situations. In many publications the RUP is discussed and used as a research object [Die02, KA04]. With the increasing complexity of software systems, software development methodology and their building blocks (concepts and methods fragments) become important.

Lyytinen [Lyy87] as well as Kumar and Welke [KW92] early took the view that the existing software development process for information systems is too general. It needs to be adapted to the specific project situation. This idea was picked up by van Weerd et al. [WBSV06] and further refined. The authors examined the incremental development of software development processes. Their aim was to analyze and construct method fragments. They assumed that an evolutionary change in the development process is associated with less risk and less resistance or problems with the developers, e.g. in comparison to holistic approaches, such as the Capture Maturity Model (CMM) [Hum88].

Today there is a large number of languages and notations for method fragments. They describe certain aspects of software in detail. Among these
languages, the UML has become the de facto industry standard [Sei03]
(see Chapter 2.6.1). Furthermore, there is a variety of other problem-
oriented concepts, such as description languages for software architectures
(e.g. AADL [FGH06]) or autonomous systems (cf. ASSL [Vas08]). However,
none of these languages describe the development process in general.

In SDM research there are different trends for detection/identifica-
tion/recognition and construction as well as dealing with model fragments.
Due to the large number of existing fragments and their project-specific use
an extensive area of research is created.

Harmsen et al. [HBO94] and Rossi et al. [RTR+00] developed approaches
to evaluate method fragments. The information obtained will be annotated
to the method and to the fragments in order to take them into account in
future projects. This coincides with the propagated incremental evolution
of the software development processes by van Weerd et al.

Based on different kinds of knowledge Karlsson and Ågerfalk [KA04] developed configurable packages and templates to adapt the development process to the environment. Ralyté et al. [RDR03] use different strategies for
the configuration of fragments. The authors applied a generic process model
in order to enable a spontaneous adaptation of the development process. A
real world example of a Situational Method comes from Dietzsch [Die02].
He describes and improves the business processes of an insurance company.
The composition of methods in specific contexts is discussed in detail by
Rolland and Prakash [RP96].

SDMs provide a neutral basis to represent and to harmonize different
approaches. The technique is non-invasive and therefore easy to integrate
into an existing development process. Further applications can be found for
example in management and in consulting of software projects [Hid97].

2.7.2 Process Delivery Diagrams

The methodology developed in this book, the model-driven software migration and evolution consists of various techniques and methods that are
located in different areas of software engineering. Here the aim is not an
incremental improvement of the software development process, but the documentation of the migration method, the technique, the applied tools and
the artifacts on a neutral basis. It is described how the fragments interact
and which parts of the process require manual intervention. Furthermore,

the influence of changes in the methods fragments, changes in techniques or tools, are conveyed.

To illustrate the developed methodology as well as the associated method fragments a formalism of Saeki [Sae03] is applied. It includes the description of the relationship between processes (activities, tasks) and products (concepts, documents, models, diagrams). Therefore, Saeki uses conventional UML class and UML activity diagrams. Van Weerd and Brinkkemper et al. [WBSV06, WBV07] have extended this approach and named it Process Deliverable Diagram (PDD). With adjustments, PDDs are very suitable

- to mark the individual artifacts that are required in the process as well as the creation, usage or reusage of them,
- to document the resulting order and
- to elucidate the influence of the artifact on the migration process.

eXtended Process Deliverable Diagram (XPDD)

PDDs have been successfully applied in larger projects in the context of European research [She08, SHA12] [HJM+10, CON12]. Therefore the PDD notation was extended by Jung and the author of the book [JWMB10, SHA08] to illustrate the influence of individual process steps on method fragments. Originally, the notation of van Weerd et al. allowed directed edges between process (activity) and product aspects (concept) only[56]. The focus of van Weerd et al. was the description of the results of a Situational Method. Therefore, only directed edges between process and product were necessary. This restriction was removed and backward edges (of concepts back to activities) were introduced. The latter were originally defined in the notation of Saeki. Now, there is a separation of product aspects in inputs and results (outputs) of an activity. The convention to illustrate inputs on the left and results on the right side significantly improving the readability (compare Figure 2.14)

Another change in contrast to van Weerd et al. is that not every activity must be associated with a concept.

To keep an overview over larger method descriptions, activities and concepts can create a hierarchy. This is in contrast to van Weerd et al. which provided only a refinement of concepts. Activities or concepts and their associated sub-activities or sub-concepts can be identified by an unambiguous name. Furthermore, if a concept or an activity is used in another PDD, it must have the same name. Within a method, this name must be unique.

---

[56] This means that processes produce products, but the products can not be used as input again.

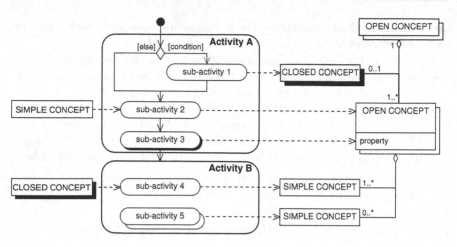

Figure 2.14: Representation of an eXtended Process Deliverable Diagram
(based on [WBV07])

Figure 2.14 shows a template of the adapted notation. The authors called
it XPDD.

Structure of XPDDs

XPDDs are based on the UML notation. The migration process (activity)
is described as an UML activity diagram. On the left and on the right the
products are represented as UML class diagrams. Figure 2.14 illustrates the
division into the triple

$$(Input, Activity, Result).   \tag{2.4}$$

In general, the UML diagrams retain the intended semantics. All changes
or extensions of the diagrams are described below.

- Usually the process description in the form of an UML activity diagram
  is in the middle of an XPDD. It describes the sequence (for example,
  analysis of source code, retrieval of information by reverse engineering,
  modeling, abstraction, transformation and code generation) that is necessary for the migration of a software system.
- Product aspects are represented by UML class diagrams. They are connected with an activity by a directed, dashed edge. The additional edge
  type characterizes the relationship between activities and concepts (for
  example, Figure 2.14 between sub-activity 2 and simple concept). For rela-

tionships within concepts the existing UML relations (association, aggregation, composition, inheritance) as well as multiplicities are available.

Concepts represent conditions or results of activities. Conditions are all relevant inputs, which are necessary for the migration process. Mainly, they comprise source code, models, filters and tools. Results in the context of migration are descriptions of source code, abstractions as well as analysis results.

Notwithstanding the UML standard, there are additional syntactic and semantic extensions in the XPDDs. To enable a hierarchical structure of the diagrams, all nodes are divided into simple and complex nodes[57].

Simple activities denote an atomic process. Similarly, simple concepts denote a data type and are not further refined. This contrasts with the complex nodes. They are marked with an extra shadow beneath the node (see Figure 2.14) and are differentiated into open (transparent shadow with a black frame) or closed nodes (black shadow). Open nodes contain sub-activities or sub-concepts. They represent a relevant fragment of the process. They are described in the same or in another XPDD. In contrast, closed activities are not process relevant and hence not considered further.

In sum, the three resulting combinations are shown in Figure 2.14:

1. **simple** activity/concept, see sub-activity 1,
2. **open complex** activity/concept, see sub-activity 5 and
3. **closed complex** activity/concept, refer to the closed concept in the upper part of Figure 2.14 or sub-activity 3.

The resulting XPDD notation allows a compact and intuitive representation of activities and their impact on the software migration process. Through the extension, such as hierarchy of activities and concepts, models can be incrementally refined. They can be modified and expanded incrementally by sub-activities or sub-concepts. This creates a comprehensible overview of the overall process. This is advantageous when, as applied in the present study, many different technologies and methods fragments are involved. The notation is easy to use and does not interfere with the process.

2.8 Summary

The subject of the present study was classified within the context of the software life cycle. Based on the historical development the separation of

---

[57] This is in contrast to van Weerd et al. [WBV07], here only concepts can be further refined.

development and operation/maintenance of software has been worked out and resulting problems were discussed. A first attempt to overcome the described problems is shown in the form of the continuous model-driven development. In this book an existing software system is converted into a continuous evolution process.

In general, working on a system is in the scope of software maintenance. Here, various types were presented and classified in the context of the book. An own definition of software maintenance is developed.

Usually legacy systems play a central role in the maintenance domain. For examination of these systems, criteria for their recognition are developed. Later they will be used to classify existing systems.

Typical work in the evolution of software is reengineering, the retrieval of information, the migration and the transfer of systems to a modern environment without fundamental changes (system understanding). These aspects are central components of the developed method which prepares existing systems for model-driven migration.

Furthermore, modeling theory was considered. The aim is to move the evolution of the software from the code to the model-layer.

Since in the present study an entirely new method is developed, it must also be formally described. At the end of this chapter an introduction into methodology research was given. Software development methodologies have been introduced and a specific notation was explained.

3 Model-Driven Software Migration

Based on the Fundamentals (Chapter 2), the general problem in the evolution of software systems is discussed in Chapter 3.1. Thereafter a novel solution is developed (Chapter 3.2) and refined in detail (Chapter 3.3 and following). Furthermore, the relevance and necessity of the subject are proved by actual contributions in scientific literature.

3.1 Problem Description

In general, software reengineering is used to recover information that are located exclusively in the code or in related artifacts. Together they present an overall view of a system and they are the basis for further development. Hunt and Thomas [HT02] called this process software archeology. In Chapter 2.4 it has already been explained that this activity is very costly, in terms of time and man power. Nevertheless, this step is inevitable especially in the context of legacy systems (see Chapter 2.3). It reduces the risk of errors in further development as well as future costs and expenses.

An extensive software reengineering is, corresponding to cost and complexity reasons, no regular or normal activity in the field of software maintenance. It is mainly applied to larger changes in software evolution (see Chapter 2.4). Usually, there is a lack of time and resources to conduct a reverse engineering in advance, in order to prepare an overview of a system and update all existing artifacts. In general, the developers rely on the existing and not always up-to-date information.

The complexity in software reengineering is primarily caused by a very high proportion of work that can not be automated. Mainly, this includes the *system understanding* and *application understanding* (Chapter 2.2.4 and Chapter 2.4.3). Sneed [Sne84] and Berg [Ber05] explain that software renovation is a labor-intensive manual task with basic tool support. Sommerville [Som06] assumes that major changes within a software can not be automated and therefore require manual effort.

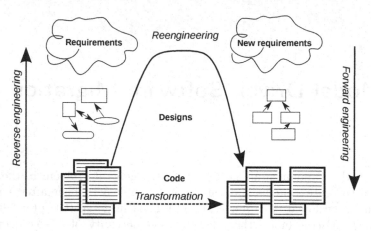

Figure 3.1: Process of Software Reengineering

Classical software reengineering[1] transforms software systems at the level of the program code. In general, existing source code is examined in order to abstract specific information and to provide these in the form of models. These models contribute to the understanding of the system and form the basis for extensions or changes at the implementation level. This includes adjustments to a new platform or programming language as well as changes in the architecture (see Chapter 2.2.3). Demeyer et al. [DDN09, p. 9] illustrate the process in Figure 3.1. It starts at the source code of the original system and ends with the adjusted system.

In Figure 3.1 the modification of software at the implementation level is shown by the broken line. The solid line in the middle describes different categories and levels of artifacts that are obtained during the analysis of the system. Usually they are discarded after the adaptation of software which, at the end, is a major disadvantage.

Unfortunately, this deficit does not emerge immediately. The effects can only be noticed during future maintenance. The artifacts obtained (models and system overview) form the basis for the initial system understanding and further development. However, the following activities[2] are focused exclusively on changes at the implementation level. Since the artifacts above are not adjusted they are no longer considered and become *obsolete*. As a

---

[1] The classic software reengineering is in the following delineated from the model-driven reengineering (Chapter 3.2).

[2] These include the usual maintenance tasks such as error correction, exchange of algorithms and smaller adjustments.

result, the synchronicity of the artifacts and the implementation is lost again.

Following the laws of Lehman and Belady (Chapter 2.1.3) the inner complexity of the software will increase again and another classic reengineering is necessary. Due to outdated artifacts this must necessarily start at the source code. The developers can not, or only to a very limited extent, build on the experiences and results from the previous reengineering process. Cost and effort are comparable or even grow. In particular, the labor-intensive and complex process of reverse engineering is performed again.

Due to the cost and complexity of software reengineering, the recovered information must be preserved beneficially for the future development of the software itself as well as for other projects in their environment. Therefore usage and recycling of information obtained must be a central goal.

To summarize, the described problems are based on the loose coupling of models and program code. In order to maintain synchronization, two or more levels must be considered. The automation of this task is difficult or impossible to implement.

This book provides a continuous, model-driven development process, which focuses on high level artifacts. Accordingly, these are the basis for the future evolution of software.

The model-driven development (Chapter 2.6.1) outlines a possible solution to the problem of many loosely coupled levels. It places the model level in the center of the development and thus avoids the manual, repetitive and error-prone updating of multiple levels. Originally, this methodology was created for the development of green-field systems. So far, the application of model-driven methodologies in reengineering and evolution is limited to a small number of examples in academic research (see Chapter 2.6.6).

3.2 The Model as Central Artifact

In the following, the application of model-driven methodologies in software evolution is considered in general. In particular, the model level, the stakeholders involved in the evolution, the emergence of a continuous development process and the definition of the term *model-driven evolution* are to be discussed.

While in classical reengineering the artifacts (mostly design-level models) provide a basis for application understanding[3], their importance and role in *model-driven reengineering* change radically. All modifications or enhance-

---

[3]   See also the model-based development in Chapter 2.6.1.

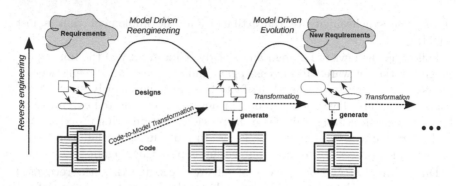

Figure 3.2: Model-driven software reengineering and migration

ments to a software are now applied exclusively at a more abstract level above the program code: *the design or model level*. Therefore it represents the basis and central artifact of model-driven software evolution.

Figure 3.2 extends the graphic of Demeyer et al. and explains the developed methodology. On the left, the transformation from the code-centric to model-driven development is depicted. This step is necessary only once. It corresponds to a reverse-engineering in the classical sense (see Chapter 2.4). Based on the existing code, models with a focus on abstraction and remodeling of functionality are created. These form the basis for the model-driven evolution of software, illustrated on the right side. The transformation (broken line in Figure 3.1) is now shifted from the lowest level to the model level. Furthermore, it is illustrated that the program code of an application is generated from the descriptions in the model level in each evolution step.

In this context Brown [Bro04] predicted a disappearance of the traditional forward and reverse engineering by introducing model-driven techniques. Favre [Fav04a] and the methodology in this book integrate the two phases in model-driven software evolution. Thus, forward engineering is the generation of program code and reverse engineering the unique transfer of program code to the model level as well as any further analysis of models (obtaining information, see Figure 3.2).

By concentrating all changes and enhancements to one central artifact the existing distinction between initial and further development should no longer be necessary. Conversely, a continuous process of model evolution is enabled. The generation of source code, the topicality and the synchronicity of models and program code are guaranteed. The new focus significantly contributes to the development of a continuous evolution of software.

Definition of Model-Driven Software Evolution

In this book model-driven software evolution is defined as follows:

> *"The model-driven software evolution defines models as the central artifacts of the development. In the first step the models are obtained by a unique reverse-engineering from the existing program code. All other maintenance and evolution steps are applied to the model level. After each step of evolution the source code of a software is fully generated from the model level."*

In 2003, Sendall and Kozaczynski [SK03] documented the shift in software development from pure programming languages to the model level. They describe the structure and the behavior of an application from a certain point of view. The creation of program code is enabled through various transformations (see Chapter 2.6.5). They are applied to the model level (in Figure 3.2 labeled with "generated").

Mellor et al. [MCF03] and Selic [Sel03] have described that executable systems can be created with the help of model-driven approaches from abstract descriptions. Selic further explains that models take over the role of third-generation programming languages (3GL-languages). In the historical context it is comparable with the transition from assembler towards programming languages (see Chapter 3.3).

The shift of software development to the model level introduces another level of abstraction. For Atkinson and Kühne [AK03] model-driven development is characterized by the trend towards abstraction[4].

By describing software on an abstract level, the possibility to involve further stakeholders in the development process does arise. Thereby the semantic gap (Chapter 2.6.3) is further decreased, while the application understanding is improved.

The developed approach focuses on the analysis of existing systems, the extraction of information, the creation of models at the design level and their coupling with the existing functionality. The created models describe the internal processes of software.

---

[4]   David Wheeler formulated this relationship as follows: *"All problems in computer science can be solved by another level of indirection... Except for the problem of too many layers of indirection."*

3.3 Continuous Software Development

As introduced in Chapter 2.6.6, the developed methodology automatically
leads to a continuous development cycle at the model level. One can not
distinguish between initial development and evolution. In Chapter 2.1.2 it is
described that software development and maintenance form two sides of the
same coin. The realization of a continuous development cycle will overcome
the historically developed division of *creatio ex nihilo* and *creatio ex aliquo*.
In the following different continuous development approaches are examined
for their suitability for the presented model-driven methodology.

In Chapter 2.1 three representatives for continuous process models are
specified, agile development, CSE as well as CMDE. In detail, the agile
methods are considered in Chapter 2.1.2.

Each of these three process models focuses on one or more levels in software development. While agile methods are still very much code-centered,
CMDE focuses exclusively on the model level. In contrast, the CSE (Chapter 2.1.4) is designed more general. It is a holistic approach that takes
all levels of software development into account. It is associated with all
artifacts, which results in a high complexity.

The CSE introduces a synchronization phase between two development
steps. Therein all artifacts involved in the development process (see Figure 2.4) have to be updated. This is very time consuming. Additionally an
extensive formalization and automation of the process is necessary to estimate or calculate dependencies and cross effects. The complexity strongly
depends on the number and degree of formalization of the artifacts involved
(including the program code). In general, one can assume that the synchronization of the artifacts begins at the implementation level, since this
always contains the "latest" information (Chapter 2.2).

The CSE concept is similar to the Round Trip Engineering (RTE) presented in Chapter 2.6.4. The main differences between the two is the synchronization time and the involved levels of software artifacts. While RTE
attempts to automatically synchronize the design and the implementation
level after each change, CSE establishes semi-automatic consistency of all
artifacts after an evolutionary step only. In Steffen et al. [SWM10] it has
been discussed that RTE may lead to partially undecidable problems. Thus
not all aspects can be synchronized[5].

---

[5]   In this article static and dynamic aspects of the RTE are distinguished and their
      feasibility within the UML notation is investigated. The result was that many tools are
      able to synchronize the structural properties of classes. However, there are difficulties
      regarding relationships and multiplicities of classes as well as dynamic aspects.

Selic [Sel03, p. 21] also doubts that the automated updating of models according to changes in the program code will be feasible. He argues that the ability of abstraction of a human is not comparable with the capacity for abstraction that results from the summary of program code by a computer program. Hearnden et al. [HBLR04, p. 97] argue similarly: They refer to a boundary between the real and the abstract, which can only be passed by a human, similar to writing down an idea that exists as a thought.

With the introduction of consistency phases in CSE the synchronization after each modification is obsolete. Depending on the number of artifacts involved however, this leads to a huge and largely manual effort[6].

In contrast the third approach, the CMDE does not incorporate all artifacts and levels of software development. It concentrates on the model level (Figure 3.2) only. All operations involving the development and evolution of software focus on this level. The lowest layer, the source code, is basically generated from this description and should not be changed. The complex balance of all artifacts, described above, is avoided.

For the first time, the CMDE methodology is used and applied in the field of software evolution. Focus is the semi-automatic integration of an existing software system into a continuous model-driven methodology.

3.3.1 Continuous Model-Driven Engineering

CMDE highlights the description and execution of business processes. In times of fast-moving markets, software systems are subject to frequent changes. CMDE addresses this from a business perspective. On the one hand the stakeholders get more control over policies and processes to decreases costs. On the other hand they can hand over the development and maintenance of process modules to third parties to shorten the time to market [MS09a, p. 106]. Today the success of a company increasingly depends on how quickly it can adapt to changes in the market.

To control the processes within a company, it is essential to shift them down to the business and application experts – away from electronic data processing [MS09a]. Application- as well as business-experts have to be able to continuously monitor business processes and to change them independently of the data processing. Furthermore they are part of the software life cycle [KJMS09] and are integrated into the development process [MS09b]. A first predecessor of CMDE, the Lightweight Process Coordination (LPC)

---

[6] Coding standards, such as Misra-C [Mis11] from the automotive industry, can reduce the complexity by limiting the capabilities of programming languages. Thereby, they simplify the synchronization.

method was already established at the end of the 90s in the context of telecommunication applications [MS04].

The adaptation of business processes has a particular impact on the underlying systems (Chapter 2.4.4). According to the authors of CMDE [MS09a] the necessary agility can not be reached with traditional software development methods. Therefore, the authors propose a holistic modeling, which works on one central artifact exclusively. This artifact can be verified, tested and executed.

CMDE combines several current paradigms of software development. These include [MS09a, p. 106]:

Model-Driven Development: Models become the central artifact in development. They represent an abstraction of the overall system and serve as a template for the generation of program code (see Chapter 2.6.1).

Process Modeling forms the basis of the formal description of business processes. Process models are represented using visual notations. They are used for communication with business experts and are the interface between data processing and business. The process models used in CMDE not only document the system, but can also be executed. Thus they avoid the gap between the model and the behavior (program code).

eXtreme Programming focuses on the direct involvement of all stakeholders in the development process. It supports the joint development and continuous improvement of business processes [MS09b]. Similar to eXtreme Programming at the implementation level, various prototypes of models arise during the development. At any time they can be reviewed, tested and simulated. Now, stakeholders are able to check the progress and have a direct influence on the overall development.

Aspect Orientation: A model can describe different aspects of a software. At the end these are woven together to an executable program. Aspects also support the reuse of components.

Service Orientation: With CMDE executable and verifiable process models are developed. Together with the application experts, they are refined until atomic functionalities emerge. Often, the necessary services are available at the lowest level. The services can cover a wide range of functions: from purchased components to distributed technologies such as middleware systems[7] or web services[8] to self-written code. Service orientation helps to prevent monolithic systems and enables the reuse of functionality.

CMDE manages the expansion of software-development towards the problem domain through inclusion of further stakeholders[9] in the development process. As described in Chapter 2.6.1 (Figure 2.9), generally there is a semantic gap between IT experts and actual users. By involving the users the gap will decrease. But it will never completely disappear[10].

Involvement of Stakeholders

The opening of the process leads to an extension of the user group and transfers the *What?* to the application experts. They can keep track of process changes (market-driven evolution), can detect errors early and thus give direct feedback [MS09b]. The data processing remains responsible for the *How?*. This results in a strict separation with clearly defined responsibilities [MS09b].

Especially efforts have to be made to integrate existing systems into a model-driven development, the extension of the user group and the explicit modeling of business processes can be a powerful incentive and advantage. Mellor and Selic [MCF03, Sel03] state that users now have the opportunity to design their software themselves. The development of software is enhanced with a closed loop feedback by the users. CMDE is a logical step towards a continuous software life cycle.

Other authors in the area of model-driven development suggest similar concepts such as the CMDE, usually without describing it in comparable level of detail. Selic [Sel03] explains that software development by end users seemed to be the future. This goal is getting closer by the further development of software techniques. Selic identified advantages especially in the implementation-independent description of software by models. Due to the additional abstraction these are closer to the problem domain and thus closer to the end user. The semantic gap is smaller. The author proceeds on the assumption that it is easier to specify models. Therefore a development by end users is made possible. Software can be generated

---

[7] Middleware systems are communication systems that interact between different platforms. They are a component of distributed architectures and build a bridge between different applications and platforms.

[8] Web services represent a special type of middleware systems. Currently, they are state of the art. A special feature is that the communication is conducted via Internet protocols.

[9] Mainly domain experts are involved.

[10] The reasons for the existence of a semantic gap are discussed in detail in Chapter 2.6.3.

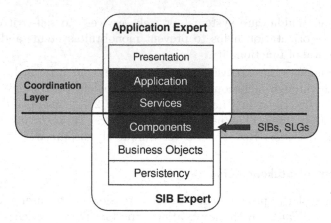

Figure 3.3: jABC – Coordination Layer (Steffen et al. [SMN+07])

from models if an adequate formalism is provided. For Selic this is the core of model-driven development.

Additionally Mellor et al. [MCF03, Seite 15] anticipate the gap between IT professionals and end users to decrease due to the high level of abstraction. The creativity will shift from the code to the model level. Models are closer to the language of the domain.

In contrast to the observations of the authors above, the CMDE methodology is much more specified in detail. The target of the authors Margaria and Steffen [MS09a] was not only the development of the theoretical framework, but also the practical implementation. They developed a method consisting of different method fragments (Chapter 3.3.2) and a corresponding development tool (compare Chapter 4.4). The following chapter explains the method and briefly presents the application in industry and research.

3.3.2 eXtreme Model-Driven Design (XMDD)

The XMDD method represents a concrete implementation of the CMDE methodology. It is a graphical, library-based approach to orchestration and modeling of system behavior [MS04]. XMDD inserts an additional layer of coordination into the common three-tier architecture. The layer is located between the program logic and the user interface (Figure 3.3).

Due to this additional level, now two different types of program logic can be better separated. The *component* or *service-specific* program logic works locally within a component. It has no interaction with other components. Usually it is characterized by implementation-specific details and rarely subject to change[11].

In contrast, the *coordination (program) logic* connects different parts of the software system. It describes the dynamic behavior of the application on a coarse-grained level. This level is subject to much more frequent adjustments (see Chapter 3.3.1).

XMDD uses a graphical, model-driven method for the specification of the coordination layer. It contains different execution units (Service Independent Building Blocks (SIBs)), which are connected to a process model (Service Logic Graph (SLG)). The granularity of the models and the nodes is highly dependent on the particular application context. Usually, no data or calculation-intensive components are modeled [MS04]. The focus is the control flow of an application. This is also referred to as the business process in the computer science meaning[12].

By abstract description of the system behavior, advantages in terms of adaptivity of these processes and the involvement of other stakeholders (see Chapter 3.3.1) emerge. The model simplifies the adaptation of the business process. The behavior is neither technically described in a programming language nor distributed over different components. It is illustrated as a central graphical representation. This hides data structures and the architecture of the underlying components [MS04]. Moreover, the execution units within the model are connected with the implemented functionality. Therefore it can be simulated or compiled into executable applications [Jör11, KJMS09].

According to Margaria and Steffen [MS04], the components are treated as black or gray boxes. This means that the interfaces are known and understood. However, the internal structure plays a minor role. In the context of software migration, this methodology is also called wrapping. In Chapter 2.5.2 this is presented in detail.

Depending on the context, these models are called Service Logic Graph (SLG) [KJMS09], coordination model [MS04], orchestration graph [MS09b] or process model. Here, the term process model is used.

XMDD is a combination of method fragments from the model-driven development, process modeling and techniques from the field of eXtreme Programming. In the following, the meta-model of XMDD, the components of the model as well as the stakeholders involved in the development are

---

[11] This includes the correct sequence of instructions and error handling.

[12] The term business process originates from the economy where it describes a process that involves several parts of a company and produces a commodity or provides a service (Chapter 2.4.4). Here the term is used for local processes within an application.

presented. A more detailed localization in the context of the present book can be found in Chapter 3.4.

Formal Basis: The XMDD Meta-Model

The process model is described by a mathematical structure, a transition system [MS09b]. It consists of nodes, edges and a designated start state. Each node is identified by an unique name and contains an action (semantics). A transition connects two nodes and has a name. The name represents the result of the execution of the corresponding action.

Originally a Kripke Transitionssystem (KTS) [MOSS99] (meta-model) provides the basis of the process model in XMDD. It consists of a quadruple $(V, AP, Act, \rightarrow)$, where [JMS08]:

- V is a set of nodes,
- AP is a set of atomic propositions that describes the basic properties of the nodes (The interpretation function $I : V \rightarrow 2^{AP}$ defines which properties apply to which node.),
- Act is a set of actions, and
- $\rightarrow \subseteq V \times Act \times V$ defines transition between two nodes.

This mathematical structure has been designed for modeling and verification of business processes. These can be simplified for the description of models in the context of model-driven migration. Here a quadruple of $(S, Label, \rightarrow, S_0)$ is used:

- S represents the set of all nodes,
- S_0 is a designated start state from the set of all states $S_0 \in S$,
- $Label$ is a set of edge labels and
- $\rightarrow \subseteq S \times Label \times S$ defines transition between two nodes[13].

Components of a Model

The nodes S of the transition system are building blocks, which can be connected to a graph (process model). A node is either atomic, and thus a proxy for a particular functionality, or it spans a hierarchy. Such a node hides another graph, hereinafter referred to as sub-graph [KJMS09].

In XMDD a process model is refined to the level of basic services with the help of the stakeholders [MS09b]. This results in complex hierarchical models that describe the functionality from the user perspective. According

---

[13] According to Mellor et al. [MCF03, Seite 15], not all models are formally described, but those which are benefit from automation and code generation.

to Moody [Moo09], the hierarchical representation of models is a property of visual notations to efficiently organize and visualize complex situations. Additionally, the hierarchy supports the reuse of individual sub-graphs [MS04].

The execution semantics behind the nodes (actions), ranges from a few lines of code to complex and implementation-dependent parts or components (see Figure 3.3). Calls to larger systems, libraries, third party software components or delegations of services are possible.

A node in the process model is referred to as SIB. A SIB is represented by a simple Java class (see Chapter 4.4) and has two characteristics. Firstly, a SIB contains all the information about its presentation. It knows its parameters, its outgoing edges, its graphical representation and contains documentation for the user as well (see Chapter 4.4).

Second, a SIB implements different types of behavior (actions) (see Chapter 4.4). For the execution semantics, the full Java language support is available. With the help of further programming paradigms other languages can also be incorporated into the behavior of a SIB. This includes the execution of native languages using Java Native Interface (JNI) or the remote execution of services via middleware systems. The outgoing edges of a SIB symbolize the possible results of the execution [MS04].

Together a set of SIBs represent a business process. They are called process model or SLG.

Stakeholders in XMDD

The creation and successive refinement of the process models is done in close collaboration with various stakeholders [MS09b]. Ideally, this can even be done by the users themselves. Advantages arise through the close cooperation, such as short development cycles coupled with immediate feedback (Chapter 3.3.1). During the development of the models the stakeholders can animate, validate and test the models. The authors of XMDD describe the process as a continuous and collaborative development process that operates on a single centralized artifact, also called One Thing Approach (OTA) [MS09b].

In XMDD adjustments to the system takes place exclusively at the model level. In the present methodology, the adaptation of models corresponds to the maintenance and evolution of software (compare to Favre [Fav04a]).

XMDD uses a role concept derived from CMDE. Different stakeholders are integrated and their individual strengths in continuous software development [MS04, MS08] reduce the gap between traditional users and IT professionals [MS09a].

Programming Experts or IT professionals are responsible for the software infrastructure, the runtime environment of the individual services, implement individual SIBs or use third party software for the connection of the required functionality.

Domain Experts classify the SIBs according to different technical criteria such as origin, version or language. They create a domain model and decide which blocks are required for the purpose of the application. Additionally domain experts can specify empty shells, which can already be used for modeling, but still have no implementation. It is the task of programming experts to implement the missing functionality.

Application Experts also called business experts model the business process, which describes the behavior of the application. Knowledge of a programming language is not necessary. The coordination of the individual modules is done graphically. During the modeling of the application the expert can perform, verify and test the models.

Users configure and use the turnkey application.

Karagiannis and Kühne [KK02, Seite 4f.] defined a similar concept of roles for a modeling platform. The authors distinguish six different roles, which are reflected in the above mentioned definitions[14].

The required building blocks are provided by the programming experts or can be pre-defined by the domain experts. Advantage of this procedure is that the developer only has to develop a small and limited part of the application. He does not have to handle the overall complexity of the system. Furthermore the implementation can be done in parallel to process modeling. Whether it is a single line of code, a complex business application or a remote service.

Applications of XMDD

XMDD was and is successfully used in various industrial and research projects. The industrial sector includes the development and testing of telecommunications services [SM99, SMC+96], the remote management and administration of computer systems [BM06], the development of large scale web applications [KM06], the modeling of supply chains [HMM+08] as well as modeling, verification and execution of test cases [MS04].

In the area of research XMDD is applied in bioinformatics [MKS08, LMS08], in the modeling of game strategies [JKPM07], in the control of robots [BJM09], in the specification of temporal properties [JMS06] and

---

[14] The roles are called: method, language, process, tool and infrastructure engineer as well as method user.

the semantic description of web services [KMSN09]. This book uses a further XMDD based project, which investigates the model-driven specification of code generators [Jör11]. The aim is to generate executable program code from the created process models.

From Code-Centric to XMDD

So far, the XMDD approach is only used for the development of new software systems as well as the documentation of business processes within an organization. Currently there are no case studies on the transformation of existing software systems in this model-driven method. An existing software system already contains a defined process model as well as the associated building blocks. Since they are usually not well documented, both can be derived from the existing source code only.

Therefore the aim must be to identify process models and to extract the necessary building blocks to describe existing software at the model level. This forms the basis to completely regenerate the corresponding source code. A similar, albeit less powerful approach is described by Reus et al. [RGD06]. They extract the business logic based on naming conventions from the program code, map it onto the model level and use it for the generation of stub-code (classes and empty methods).

Here the XMDD method is applied in the model-driven evolution of an existing software system. Key issues are the reengineering and migration of the system[15]. The system must be analyzed and remodeled. Remodeling is defined in this book as

> the mapping of the business processes of an existing code-centric developed software at model level with the aim to support software evolution as well as to regenerate the program code from the description.

Additionally it is shown in the following that various parts of the system can be exchanged. In doing so it is even possible to use different programming languages. Originally, the method developed here should improve the analysis of software as well as the application understanding by use of abstraction and the associated reduction of complexity. However, it has become apparent that this approach, in combination with the XMDD method, is equally useful for the migration of software.

Hereafter, the necessary steps and the various techniques for model-driven software evolution are presented.

---

[15] Software reengineering and migration are summarized in the following under the term evolution.

3.4 Model-Driven Evolution

In this book *model-driven software evolution* is defined as

> *the evolution of software using model-driven concepts, in which models replace the source code as the key artifact.*

The understanding of classical software reengineering changes. The role of the traditional software reverse engineering, the extraction of information from the program code, is kept, but now the goal is to transfer the system towards a model-driven evolution. This step is to be performed only once. Certain facts have to be gathered from source code and manually connected at the model level (see Chapter 3.5). The classical forward engineering step is replaced by a formalized and automated generation of partially or fully executable code (see Figure 3.2).

The transformation step, in traditional software-reengineering the adaptation of the system at the implementation level, is now represented by a chain of model transformations. Bézivin [Bé05], Brown [Bro04] and van Deursen et al. [DVW07] equate classical maintenance with model maintenance. Except that in this case the input and the output of a transformation are models.

Based on the process model described in XMDD, a new approach that allows the integration of existing and long-lasting systems into the model-driven evolution is developed. This contributes significantly to the constant evolution and continuous life-cycle model as demanded in Chapter 2.1.2.

Model-Driven Evolution illustrated

In this chapter a method for converting an existing system into the model-driven evolution is presented in detail. The method itself is described using the XPDDs supplemented by Jung and Wagner [JWMB10] (Chapter 2.7.2).

The XPDD in Figure 3.4 provides a schematic overview of the stages in the evolution of model-driven software. The entire process is divided into two phases (Figure 3.2). The first phase is the model-driven reengineering (Chapter 3.5). It starts with the source code of the existing systems. During processing, code-models[16] are created and analyzed by various analysis tools. In research the term model-driven reverse engineering [RS04, SFZ10] (see Chapter 2.6.6) has been established for the creation of models.

---

[16] Brown [Bro04] refers to the visual representation of program code as code-model or implementation model. Additionally he describes that some authors use the term diagram to outline that the term model should exclusively be used for abstract descriptions.

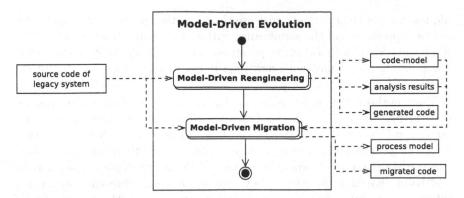

Figure 3.4: XPDD – Phases of the Model-Driven Software Evolution

The structure of the code-models is based on Canfora and Cimitile [CC00, p. 107]. They describe that a code-model consists of a control flow graph, which is decorated with additional information at the nodes. Furthermore, it includes a reference to the corresponding line in the program code.

Thus, code-models are a visual representation of program code and represent its static structure. Therefore analyzes are limited to static aspects (see Chapter 3.5.3). Thereafter based on the code-models, the code can be regenerated for validation and testing purposes.

In the second phase, the model-driven migration step is performed. It gradually remodels an application within the model level. It integrates the existing functionality and creates new or modified program code.

The role of the Maintenance Developer

The XMDD role model presented in Chapter 3.3.2 was exclusively designed for model-driven development of software. For the model-driven evolution one role must be added. The *maintenance developer* converts the source code into code-models, performs various analyzes and remodels the business logic. Primarily the first two steps serve the application understanding and support the subsequent migration of the software. Together with the business expert the maintenance developer can extract and remodel business processes. Only when the software is completely described, executable program code can be generated.

Usually the model-driven evolution addresses legacy systems. This, as already explained in Chapter 2.3, has a variety of reasons. First of all, for this kind of software systems there is a huge need for methods and tech-

niques in order to preserve or to reuse them in other projects. Secondly, the
political pressure and the significance within a company is extremely high.
A reengineering in this context promises benefits in terms of maintenance
costs, effort, compliance with new requirements and preserving the future
of the company.

Many authors in research point out the significance of the integration of
existing systems into the model-driven development, see Chapter 2.6.6. In
2007, van Deursen et al. [DVW07] outline different research topics in this
area. They think reengineering of legacy systems and their integration into
the model-driven development to be one of the future topics. Karagiannis
and Kühn [KK02, p. 8] integrate existing applications through web service
interfaces into business processes. Furthermore they use these processes to
derive a description of the interfaces for further implementations.

Currently there are only a few detailed and meaningful examples in research literature, that process existing industrial applications for model-
driven development and enable a continuous evolution. In Chapter 4 some
of the existing examples and projects are introduced. This includes the
projects MoDisco and Renaissance, which were funded by the European
Union.

3.5 Model-Driven Reengineering

Model-driven reengineering is a generic term used for the first part of model-
driven evolution. It prepares existing systems for the integration into the
XMDD method. Bézivin et al. [BBJ07, p. 2] refer to this as the abstraction
from text to models. The existing source code is transfered and analyzed
on model-layer thereby. This requires the availability of the program code
for the existing system.

Figure 3.5 represents the model-driven reengineering process in detail. It
is divided, as in classical reengineering, in three phases. Reverse engineering (Chapter 3.5.1) is the first step. The existing source code is analyzed
and transformed into a language-independent description. This description
contains information that is both implicitly and explicitly available (see
Chapter 4.2).

Subsequently, this information is imported by a modeling tool, and presented graphically. Due to their proximity to the program code the resulting models are called code-models (cf. Chapter 3.4). The platform- and
language-independent description of the program code decouples the extraction of information from the information processing within a modeling

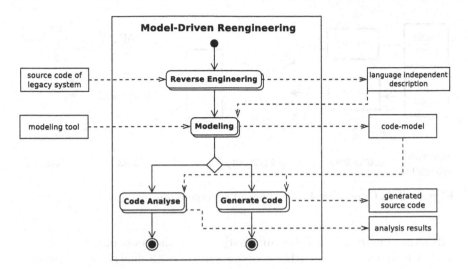

Figure 3.5: XPDD – Model-Driven Reengineering

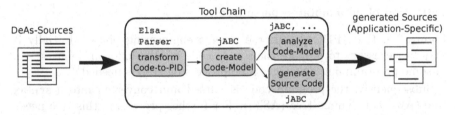

Figure 3.6: Tool chain in model-driven reengineering

tool. After the descriptions have been imported, it is possible to analyze, test, or to generate the source code from the code-models again. The tool chain is illustrated in Figure 3.6. In the presented model-driven approach, the first phase, the code-to-model transformation is to be applied exactly once (see Figure 3.2).

3.5.1 Reverse-Engineering

In the reverse engineering phase, various tools are used to extract information from the source code. The first step transforms the program code into a language- and platform-independent representation.

Arnold [Arn93, p. 11, Figure 5] and Favre et al. [FED⁺01] already described requirements for the extraction, analysis and representation. The

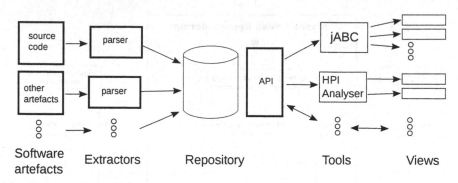

Figure 3.7: Generalized tool chain in reverse engineering

extractor (Figure 3.7) isolates information from the code and stores it in a shared memory. Various other tools can use this to analyze and visualize information in the source code.

Extraction of an annotated parse tree

Figure 3.8, the XPDD details the reverse engineering phase. Initially it may be necessary to prepare the source code for the following phases, e.g. in some programming languages a preprocessing step is needed[17].

Subsequently, the program code is parsed and converted into a syntax tree (Abstract Syntax Tree (AST)). For further processing this tree needs to be decorated with additional information. These include references to variables and method declarations.

The sequence of steps and data structures produced in this process correspond to the structure and functionality of a compiler front-end (cf. Aho et al. [ASAU99, pp. 6])[18].

As described in Aho et al., the abstract syntax tree (AST) is built during the syntactic analysis of a compiler. The AST contains information about the structure and content of each line in the source code.

The semantic analysis of the program code is followed by the syntactical analysis. This phase verifies the correctness of the static semantics. The

---

[17] This step is optional and not necessary in every case. For the sake of clarity a corresponding case is not illustrated in Figure 3.8.

[18] In general, layered architectures are divided in front- and back-end. Here front-end refers to the part of the program or component in charge of processing the input data. In programs with graphical user interface, this is generally referred to as the front-end. The back-end of a compiler by contrast is responsible for synthesis, i.e. generating the target code.

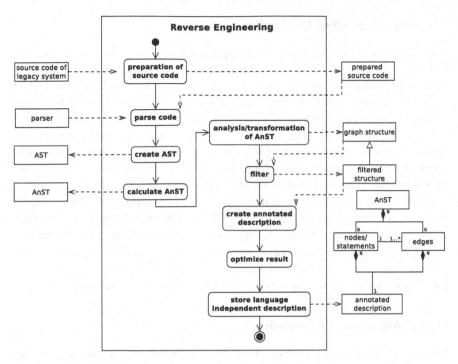

Figure 3.8: XPDD – Reverse engineering phase

analysis examines the validity and compatibility of variables, data types and operations. In general, the parser annotates additional information to the individual nodes of the AST. In the following the attributed or decorated AST is called Annotated Syntax Tree (AnST). It comprises data flow and type information about variable definitions, parameters and return values of operations including a unique name (fully qualified name). Especially the latter is required to analyze variables or function blocks to connect them to a common hierarchy (call graph).

Above all the AnST represents semantic information explicitly. It forms the basis for the platform independent description of the source code. Weiderman et al. [WBST97, p. 15] indicate that static analysis can merely be used in monolithic, not in distributed systems.

Platform-independent Description

Initially for each file or class of the existing program code a separate, annotated and platform-independent description is created. It contains a separate description for each method[19] derived from the AnST subtree. Each node of this subtree is associated with a statement (typically one line in the code) and annotated with additional information from the AnST.

By using the AnST, which – as described above – is enriched with additional aspects, the amount of information is greatly enlarged. By a subsequent filter this amount of information can be reduced depending on the necessary elements and properties (cf. Figure 3.8).

Prior to generating the output it can be further optimized. For example, strings such file paths can be consolidated. Chapter 4.2 presents further types of partially extensible language- and platform-independent formats.

In Chapter 4.1, various tools are investigated for their suitability to generate the data structures or information defined above. In the ideal case, a parser already contains the necessary information to calculate an AnST.

Formal Aspects of Code-Models

During the preparation of code-models abstraction or classification of elements does not occur. Thus the abstraction function within the meaning of Kühne [Kü06] (see Chapter 2.6.4) is the identity: $\beta = id$. The textual description is prescriptive. The transformation translates language constructs into an enriched, textual notation, which is derived from the grammar of the underlying language. Therefore the description is on the same level as the program code. Chikofsky and Cross [CC90] refer to this type of representation as restructuring or redocumentation (see Figure 2.7).

3.5.2 Modeling

The modeling phase (Figure 3.9) uses the annotated and platform independent description to graphically represent the source code as a model. The representation is based on a control flow graph. For this purpose, a modeling tool is required which can import and convert the language-independent description into an internal representation. In this case the extracted description has a transient character (see Ludewig in Chapter 2.6.2). On the

---

[19] In this book, the terms method, function, or routine are used synonymously. The author deliberately avoids a distinction of the terms regarding programming concepts or languages.

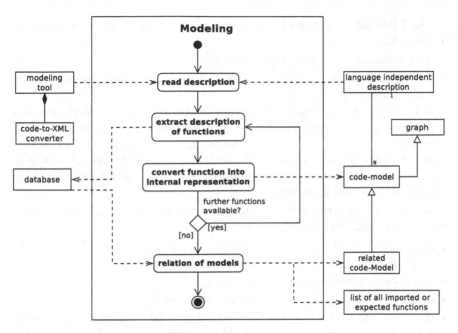

Figure 3.9: XPDD – Modeling phase

one hand the model represents the program code, and on the other, the model serves as a basis for further analysis and abstractions.

In general, the annotated description contains several control flow graphs. Each of them represent a method or a function. They are extracted from the description and a graphical representation is created. All available information, about the programming language construct and its internal relationships, are transfered to the representation of the modeling tool.

In the next step, the code-models are interconnected to a hierarchy. For this, each node in the model is examined. If a method call is found it is linked to the associated function or method. Here a filter can be applied. Often certain areas of a program, or certain functions should explicitly excluded. Usually these include functions from standard libraries. It significantly reduces the size of the resulting model and therefore its complexity.

A special case is a program statement with more than one method call. Therefore an intermediate graph is generated, which includes the method calls in the correct order. Each node is associated with the corresponding code-model again.

The following advantages result from combining the individual graphs to a hierarchy:

- A program can now be completely traversed[20] and
- the analysis of the program code or the models can now be both intra- and inter-procedural.

A condition for the transformation of source code into code-models is a corresponding representation of the syntax elements in a graphical notation. For this purpose a suitable representation must be created for each syntax element. The different types of elements are defined by the grammar of the language. Furthermore they determine both the control flow (outgoing edges) and the associated attributes[21].

Based on the described type of modeling various requirements for a modeling tool emerge. It should provide

- an interface for loading a self-defined input format and to be able to convert it into the internal representation,
- a support for the hierarchical modeling,
- arbitrary graphical representation of notations[22],
- the possibility to store arbitrary attributes to the nodes and meta-information on the model itself, including management information, such as file name or function name (see Chapter 5.5.2),
- information necessary for the generation of program code,
- the possibility of code generation as well as
- the link between nodes in the model and the corresponding behavior to animate/execute models during the migration of software.

A detailed overview of the current state of modeling tools as well as language- and platform-independent descriptions can be found in Chapter 4.

3.5.3 Model-Driven Analysis

After the preparation of the code-models, the models can be analyzed using a variety of static analysis. The aim is to improve the maintenance

---

[20] This is similar to the link structure of web pages and is therefore referred to as *browsing*.

[21] Each element has different outgoing edges and parameters. An `if` node contains the outgoing edges `then` and `else` and a description of the Boolean expression as attribute.

[22] As explained in Chapter 2.6.3 and Chapter 2.6.5, a combination of graphical notations with hierarchy is suitable for the representation of complex relationships and structures.

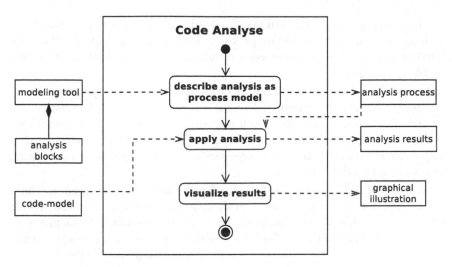

Figure 3.10: XPDD – Process of analysis

engineer's understanding. Nielson et al. [NNH99] distinguish four different types in static program analysis:

- control and data flow analysis,
- constraint-based analysis,
- abstract interpretation and
- the type and effect systems.

The model-driven migration focuses on the first type. The control and data flow analysis is assigned to the model-driven analysis of code-models. It includes the determination of metrics, the computation of dependencies between functions and the detection of dead code.

Each analysis process is described as a model again. It represents a model transformation and is applied to the generated code-models. The abstract method is described as XPDD in Figure 3.10. The procedure itself is identical to the filtering and abstraction of code-models presented in Chapter 3.6.1. Since both pursue different objectives, they are considered separately in this book. The analysis process solely extracts information. Contrary to this is the abstraction of code-models, which uses filters to generate a different representation: process model (Chapter 3.6.1).

The model transformation collects and aggregates information according to specific criteria. The benefits of a graphical description of a transformation are the simple representation, the integration of existing analysis tools

in the transformation, the arbitrary output and visualization of results as
well as the reuse of existing components. Either existing software[23] can be
used or the maintenance engineer can adapt the transformation according
to his requirements.

In addition to the application understanding, the analysis process demonstrates the model-driven approach and its scope. At the modeling level code-
models can be used, in combination with different types of transformations.
These cover the generation of test cases or the verification of systems. The
approach is limited here to the previously described domains of program
analysis and model-driven evolution.

The individual analysis and their implementation are presented in Chapter 5.5.3 in detail. They are based on the experiences collected in the process
of migration. Specific reengineering patterns are described by Demeyer et
al. [DDN09]. Especially the *Look for Contracts* pattern improves the application understanding and promotes a deep knowledge of the system.

3.5.4 Code Generation

The last phase in model-driven reengineering examines the validation of
the generated code-models. Therefore a code generator is necessary which
translates the model description back into program code. Additionally, this
generator is a central component of the forward engineering phase in model-
driven migration (see Chapter 3.6.4).

Rugaber and Stirewalt [RS04, p. 46] discuss various approaches for measuring the suitability of reverse engineering methods. The authors suggest
to measure *thoroughness* and *lucidity*. Thoroughness measures the degree of
coverage of the system to be examined by a model. Lucidity determines the
degree to which the reverse engineering method focuses on certain aspects
of a system and its representation in the program code.

To measure the defined criteria, the authors recommend to reverse the
reverse engineering step: Based on the model description, program code
is generated again. Thus a different version of the original system is created. Afterwards both programs will be compared. The reverse engineering
method is considered adequate if both systems are close together. Therefore,
the authors consider different categories.

Stub-generation: For all classes and methods as well as data structures so-
called stubs are generated. The generated system is compilable, but
has no application logic and therefore does not produce any results.

---

[23] For example, the collection of Graphviz [Gra12] tools as well as the corresponding
dot [KN02] application.

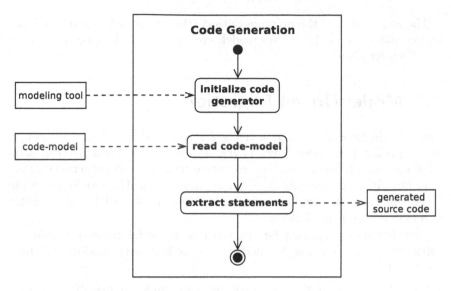

Figure 3.11: XPDD – Code generation

Line-by-line generation is describe by Rugaber and Stirewalt as the antithesis to the stub-generation. Here, the original program is reproduced line by line.

Comparing the program output: The generated program is supposed to be able to duplicate the output of the original. Both not necessarily having the same code base. Performance or use of resources, such as speed or memory consumption, are not considered in this comparison.

The last two processes, line-by-line generation and comparison of program output, are applied to model-driven migration. The line-by-line generation is used to check the resulting code-models in the model-driven reengineering step. The creation of the code generator has an integral part in this as well; along with collecting experiences regarding the existing program code, the programming language and its translation. It soon becomes apparent whether the complete program code is available and has been converted into a code-model.

Based on the preparation of the code generator and the validation of the code-models, the maintenance engineer gains experience. He is therefore also able to estimate the amount of manual handwork needed. Chapter 5.5.4 illustrates some examples. In general, the process itself is illustrated in Figure 3.11.

The comparison of the program output (third approach) forms the basis for the validation of the process models created during the migration phase (see Chapter 3.6.4).

3.6 Model-Driven Migration

Based on the information and artifacts obtained in the model-driven reengineering phase, the model-driven migration modernizes the underlying software system. Modernization is a collective term for various activities that have already been explained in detail in Chapter 2.5. Here we focus on the incremental exchange and extension of functionalities as well as the transfer of a system to a new platform.

The developed approach for the continuous model-driven migration of software systems requires the validity of some boundary conditions. These include that

- the source code of existing software is available, compilable and executable,
- all dependent libraries and compilers are available,
- the code base is frozen for the migration period and,
- an appropriate analysis tool that generates code from existing codemodels is available or is being developed.

Seacord et al. [SPL03] match this procedure to the white-box modernization. This is due to both, the program code and knowledge about the internal structure of an application (cf. Chapter 2.4.3), being required. According to Weiderman et al. [WNS+97] software systems have to be in a technically perfect condition for a white-box modernization. This can be derived from the above-mentioned conditions.

The Process of Model-Driven Migration

The XPDD in Figure 3.12 describes an overview of the main aspects of the second phase. In the first step, a process model is abstracted from the codemodels. Aim is to find parts of the inherent business processes and to isolate them from the general program logic. Individual elements of the business logic can quite reliably be found on the structure of the user interface or with the help of the parameters for program startup.

Usually the preparation and completion of the process models needs manual rework. In this phase, the objective of the maintenance engineer is to remodel the execution paths of the application. He can rely on the code-

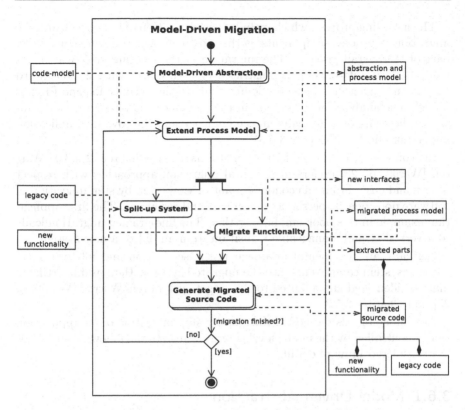

Figure 3.12: XPDD – Overview of the Model-Driven Migration

models to work out the essential aspects. Subsequently the process models
are connected to the behavior/execution. Existing legacy functionality can
be reused or replaced with entirely new functionality. In parallel the existing
system has to be separated (cf. Chapter 3.6.2).

Once the process model is completed, the original source code can initially
be recreated. This first test is necessary to proof the code generator with
the constructed abstraction and to confirm the effectiveness of the approach.
The code generator generates the appropriate code for individual process
models. The result is a mix of legacy source code for unprocessed parts and
already migrated system parts. These may include new or reused program
code that accesses old functionality.

An executable prototype can be created at any time by means of code generation. Simon [Sim92] refers to this approach as "Phased-Interoperability"
(see Chapter 2.5.3). Both, old and new systems form a unit.

The modeling process, which includes the separation of the system and the migration of process components, is the most complex and time-consuming part of the overall process. The migration of the existing system is incremental and iterative. This is illustrated in Figure 3.12 with the backward edge from the activity Generate Source Code to the activity Expand Process Model. The analyzes of the system in the reengineering phase are now valuable. They support the maintenance engineer and improve his application understanding (see Chapter 3.5.3).

In contrast to "Cut-and-Run" methods (see Chapter 2.5.3), Warren [War99, p. 23] prefers incremental migration approaches with respect to risk and cost. From an economic point of view, step by step migration of software does benefit personnel placement and resources. The first application example in this book emphasizes this. The fine-grained migration leads to a very slow and manageable transition from an old to a new system.

Basically an incremental approach is the separation and integration of existing system components into the migrated system. Here usable artifacts must be identified and adapted to the target system (cf. Warren [War99, p. 25] and Chapter 2.5.3).

Advantage of this method is the step-by-step migration of an application that is controlled by the model level (Figure 2.10). In the following sub-steps are considered in more detail.

3.6.1 Model-Driven Abstraction

The information density of the previously used code-models is well suitable for the computer-aided analysis of the source code. However, they did not fit to the concept of a model, because of the missing reduction feature. This was defined by Stachowiak and introduced in Chapter 2.6.

Program code has the disadvantage that general logic, such as details about error handling or the persistence of data, is mixed up with business logic[24]. Usually, components of business logic result from aggregating various steps of the program logic.

Therefore, prior to the remodeling of the business processes, the information in the code-models must be reduced and summarized. As already explained in the analysis phase, the abstraction step is again a model transformation and also described as a model. Of interest are aspects that can be assigned to the business logic or parts thereof.

---

[24] Business logic is defined as an abstract, implementation independent description of the problem to be solved. In contrast, the program logic comprises all execution steps corresponding to an algorithm.

It is assumed that the source code is the only source of information. All other artifacts that were created during the development of the legacy system are irrelevant. This requirement is based on the findings made on legacy systems in Chapter 2.3 and Chapter 2.4.1.

Two different types of information are initially available for the abstraction of program code: On the one hand the folder structure of the individual source files and their names, and on the other hand, the internal and external programming interfaces that are used within the software.

Abstraction of a graphical user interface

In the following the extraction of business logic is fully explained and illustrated in Figure 3.13. It is based on the programming interface of a graphical user interface.

Generally graphical elements, such as menu options and buttons, represent the starting point of possible user actions. A graphical user interface provides a defined set of actions for each user. These actions represent the set of business processes that belong to an application. By implication, this results in every element, which can trigger such a process, being the starting point of a business process within the system. Merlo et al. [MGK+93a] also use the structure of the graphical interface to transform text-based systems to systems with graphical user interfaces. They are investigating the code to detect actions that cause a change in behavior.

Due to the creation, a graphical element is represented by a method call, this can easily be found in the code-model. The parameters of the call can be analyzed, which results in advantages for the maintenance engineer:

1. He does not have to work out the structure of the graphical interface by hand.
2. He can find the functionality implemented "underneath" the graphical element.
3. Once the abstraction is created, it is available for all other programs using the same library for the graphical interface.

In general, the elements within a graphical user interface refer to functions (semantics of the elements) that are implemented in the program code. Since these are already present as code-models, they can initially be attached to the starting points of the business process. This supports the maintenance engineer in the further modeling and the migration of the system. He has direct access to the methods stored as code-model. Furthermore, he can iterate the software due to the hierarchy of the code-models. Of course, this approach can also be applied to other aspects, such as persistence.

API-based Abstraction

This type of abstractions is referred to as *API-based abstraction*. Therefore the programming interface of the graphical user interface is analyzed. All the elements that can trigger user actions are collected. These form the basis of the abstraction. The code-models are analyzed, the information is classified and results in an abstract model.

Chapter 2.6.4 introduces a formalized definition of relationships between models by Kühne [Kü06]. It concatenates a projection, a classification and a translation function. The analysis phase (Chapter 3.5.3) did not include a classification step ($\beta = id$). In contrast, for the migration it does play a central role. It is described by the API-based abstraction.

Kühne [Kü06, p. 6] denotes the classification function as Λ, so $\beta = \Lambda$, where Λ is a homomorphism. It classifies different objects and their relationships and aggregates them into a type. The elements of the graphical interface are divided into two categories (action triggering and no trigger). According to Kühne an entire abstraction consists of the projection π, the classification Λ and the translation into another representation τ. The projection reduces the code-models to all nodes, which create elements of the graphical user interface. The classification summarizes these and aggregates them to a new model (translation into another representation τ).

Fuhr et al. [FHW10] analyze the graphical user interface to detect the main functionalities of a software system. In contrast to the method presented here, they do not create a general model. They only use the graphical interface for probing and identification of commonly used functions. The authors do not derive models for the modeling of business processes.

Compared to the bottom-up method used in this approach, Debaud and Rugaber analyze [DR95] the application domain first. Following this, they attempt to find suitable functionalities within the program code (top-down).

Phases of Model-Driven Abstraction

Figure 3.13 illustrates the relationship of the individual steps that are necessary for the model-driven abstraction. For the description of the classification function (according to Kühne) a transformation language must be defined first. It supports the analysis and abstraction of a code-model. The language reflects the relevant aspects of the programming interface. It also contains the fundamental properties of a transformation as mentioned in Chapter 2.6.5. Individual components emerge from this language, which are assembled to filters. According to XMDD these filters are graphically represented and stored as a model.

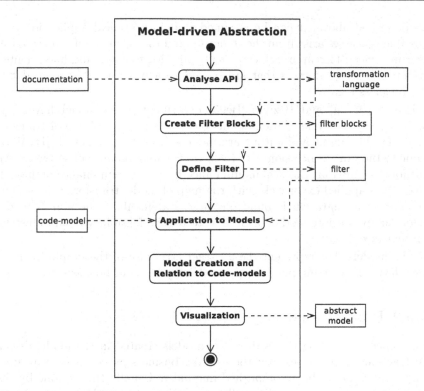

Figure 3.13: XPDD – Model-driven abstraction

In Chapter 2.6.5 different types of transformation have been presented. The transformation languages described here can be assigned to these. Sendall and Kozacynski [SK03] as well as Weis et al. [WUG03] describe various basic properties of such a language. They include adding, removing, finding elements as well as different search patterns.

Model-driven Abstraction and Maintenance

In a nutshell, the code-models serve as a starting point for the calculation of model properties. These properties range from the calculation of metrics or the documentation of the dependency graphs (cf. Chapter 3.5.3) to more complex methods like the API-based abstraction. The former plays a minor role only. Its feasibility and potential are shown in Chapter 5.5.3.

The main objective is the implementation of the last point: Business processes are semi-automatically identified and represented in a process model.

As described above, it can be assumed that in graphical applications, all possible processes arise from the structure and the elements of the graphical user interface. This approach can also be applied to command-line-oriented systems: The parameters that are passed to a program at startup define the business logic.

Brown [Bro04] and Bézivin [Bé05] describe that in model-driven approaches the life cycle of the system consists of a series of model transformations. The input and output are models. Van Deursen et al. [DVW07] came to the same conclusion with focus on the maintenance of software. All authors assume that classical maintenance becomes maintenance on model-layer. It is applied exclusively with the help of model transformations. The model-driven migration is build on these statements. The aim is to develop an appropriate method as well as to test its feasibility in an industrial context (see Chapter 5).

The models that represent the abstract structure of the graphical interface, form the starting point for manual remodeling of business processes.

3.6.2 Process Modeling

The process modeling is based on the models created in the model-driven abstraction. Aim is to extract the existing business processes step by step. This task can only be accomplished manually. Usually this is done by the maintenance engineer. Additionally, it requires a great deal of knowledge about the application .

The purpose is to recognize the existing functionality in the code-models as well as to encapsulate and refine it on coarse-grained level, until it can be connected to the existing functionality. Algorithms or filters play a supporting role only. The process of remodeling can be done incrementally and thus saves resources in the project.

The modeling process is supported by the extraction of business logic . The models created represent the set of all possible business processes. Further, the starting points of the processes have already been associated with the code-models, which describe the implementation. The maintenance engineer can therefore focus on the remodeling.

In parallel, the existing system must be split up in order to integrate the different functions into the process model. Depending on the functionality to be used the existing system must be equipped with interfaces (wrapping) or new functionality must be integrated (new implementation, Chapter 3.6.3).

An advantage is that the interfaces are defined on the basis of the process model. Therefore only a minimal set of interfaces to the existing program code is required. They link the process models to the appropriate and necessary functionality. Chapter 5.6.6 summarizes various features and rules that are central to the definition of interfaces.

The process modeling phase should start with a coarse-grained process model. Depending on the requirements of the legacy system certain aspects (e.g. user interface or persistence) should be refined. The result of the gradual approach is a controlled migration of the legacy system. The system itself is, based on the process modeling, separated automatically into various components. Furthermore, the data flow and the dependencies inside a system are revealed by the process model.

Karagiannis and Kühn [KK02] use a similar approach for remodeling. At first they define services based on the knowledge about the system. Afterwards they try to find the corresponding functionality in the program code to interconnect them. Their aim is to extract the existing functionality of an application, to reflect it on the model level, to preserve the program logic and to add the execution (semantic) to the model. In this context DeBaud and Rugaber [DR95] refer to executable domain and application models.

Due to the linking with the existing functionality, fully executable program code can be generated from the created process models at any time.

Furthermore certain recurring practices can be modeled and applied to other programs. The maintenance engineer can model new filter rules that are applied to other process or code-models. For example, subtrees (partial functions or structures) can be replaced or certain patterns can be detected.

The primary goal of the process modeling is not only the analysis and the replacement or the graphical interface. Aim is to extract, model and migrate the business processes within an application. Migration also includes the addition of new functionalities. Chapter 4.7 presents different approaches of the modernization of user interfaces. However, these approaches focus on the transformation of text-based to graphical user interface systems.

Of course it is possible to extract static and dynamic information of the graphical user interface to subsequently re-create it. Especially in the area of Complex Event Processing (CEP) there are many research opportunities in combination with the static structure and dynamic behavior. This book will focus on process models.

3.6.3 Migration and Separation of the System

To integrate existing code into the model-driven migration, it is necessary to provide it with an interface. The basis of modern systems are layered architectures with defined interfaces. For Liebhart [Lie10] one of the main problems in migration is the allocation of program components to these layers. One requirement is that the components should be changed as little as possible but should still allow to be pasted smoothly into the new architecture. Therefore he recommends the use of service concepts for the modernization of systems. He describes a concrete process model in [Lie10].

Canfora and Cimitile [CC00] focus specifically on mainframe systems. They develop a separation between the graphical user interface, program logic and data storage. With the help of program slicing the authors filter the source code according to specific input and output operations and use the result for partitioning.

Weiderman et al. [WNS+97] describe different levels. A system can be divided at job-, transaction-, program-, module-, or procedure-level.

According to Weiderman et al., the model-driven migration will concentrate on the module and procedure level. It is not intended to created an interface for each existing method. They are created in combination with the refinement of process models. The functionality of the existing system is provided for selected components only. Otherwise it would be an uncontrolled growth of interfaces.

Most likely both, the programming language and the platform, will change in the migration process. Therefore mechanisms for the remote invocation of functions are to be preferred. Many different techniques exist, ranging from remote procedure calls over middleware systems, to service architectures. These techniques differ mainly in developing-comfort and the type and dependencies of technologies involved. The basics have already been introduced in Chapter 2.6.6. Middleware techniques are well suited to make existing applications and libraries for modern systems accessible.

Furthermore, different programming languages and compilers allow direct calls between different languages (binary compatible), e.g. the languages C, C++ and Fortran and the Solaris compiler or the GNU Compiler Collection (GCC) as well as C, C++ and Java via the Java Native Interface (JNI) [Gor98].

Usually this point is the critical part of the migration process. The existing system must always be incrementally integrated within the new system. As mentioned in the fundamentals, this is not always successful without extra effort and rework. In Chapter 2.5.3 three typical cases have been explained by Brodie and Stonebraker.

All integration methods mentioned here are summarized under the term wrapping (see Chapter 2.5.2). This approach supports focusing on one aspect of the system, e.g. reuse persistence functionality. Thus, the migration can examine the behavior of the application first, and later the data.

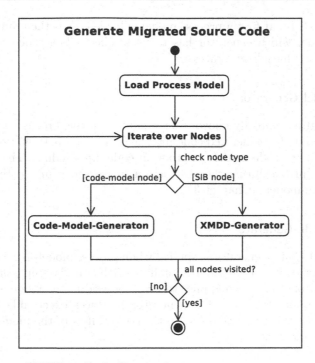

Figure 3.14: XPDD – Code Generation

For the migration of existing functionality, the maintenance engineer has to decide between reuse of existing program code or the development of new components and modules. Van Deursen et al. [DVW07] propose the use of frameworks for new components. Frameworks are libraries of components that together provide a very complex functionality. Their behavior can be configured from the outside.

In general, hybrid approaches are used which combine various wrapping techniques with the development of individual system components.

3.6.4 Code Generation

The code generation step is supposed to be able to generate executable program code at any time from the existing process models. Since the code generator has no knowledge about the migration state of the individual process model a distinction between three different types of generators has to be made.

In Figure 3.14, at first a process model is loaded. It is then differentiated at each node, which generator has to be applied. The process continues until all nodes have been processed.

Code-Model-Generator:

This generator is already known from the model-driven reengineering. It is used to validate the generated code-models (Chapter 3.5.4), and recombines the nodes in the code-models to program code, line-by-line. The generator has been adjusted during the abstraction phase according to the requirements of the models (Chapter 3.6.1).

XMDD-Code-Generator:

The XMDD-Code-Generator is applied when process models have been completely redesigned and migrated. Usually modeling tools supply one or more code generators. This also applies to the tool used in the model-driven migration (see Chapter 4.4). The generator produces executable Java code from a process model. It connects to the control flow of the model with the execution semantics.

Hybrid-Code-Generator:

Hybrid models are models that consist of a mixture of old and already migrated functionality. The code generator has to distinguish two different scenarios. The maintenance engineer could extend code-models, i.e. he inserts new statements into the code-models. This case is highly unlikely since of the advantage of model-driven development would be lost. It would be easier and causes less effort, to change the program code with a suitable development tool. But the Code-Model-Generator (Chapter 3.5.4) would cover this case.

In the second scenario, the maintenance engineer reuses an already existing functionality. For this purpose he would implement a SIB in terms of the XMDD method. It is used to access the required functionality. As already explained, it is possible to access different platforms or other programming techniques within a SIB. This implementation satisfies the requirements and the existing internal XMDD-Code-Generator can be used.

The Hybrid-Code-Generator uses the two above mentioned code generators. It analyzes a model and decides which one is applied.

3.7 Conclusion

The aim of this book is the use of a continuous development methodology in the field of software evolution. On the basis of the problem, several deficiencies of the classic software reengineering and the associated software evolution were demonstrated. An existing continuous development methodology is chosen and their method fragments are described. This also includes the formal specification of the applied transition system.

Subsequently, a solution to the problem statement by using the continuous methodology is outlined. This solution is divided into two major phases, the model-driven reengineering and model-driven migration of software. Both are separated in work packages and formalized using the XPDD notation.

The result is a clear structure and overview of the different aspects of the method. Topics such as program analysis, abstraction, modeling and modeling process play an important role. The application of the XPDD notation highlights which components of the method are to be processed fully automatically or manually. In addition, the requirements as well as the use of tools in the process are visible. Furthermore, based on the steps to be processed the effort is clearly recognizable.

The developed method operates exclusively at the model level. Thus it differs fundamentally from the existing approaches in software evolution. Basis of the software evolution process are models that are created semi-automatically from the existing program code. The processing and transformation of the models takes place in a graphical modeling tool. In the remodeling the focus is on the integration of existing functionality. This is the prerequisite for the generation of fully executable source code.

4 Related Work

As far as it is known, the methodology described in this book is the first concrete application of model-driven concepts in the field of reengineering and migration of industry-relevant software systems. The methodology requires the implementation of different method fragments.

In the following related work as well as projects from industry and research are examined for their suitability in terms of model-driven reengineering and migration. Central to this is the question, whether it is possible to reuse existing approaches. Tools and concepts are introduced, compared and evaluated. These include a number of projects that deal with model-driven technologies and software reengineering.

Different areas of computer science are related to the topic. Each of them have a very long and extensive research history. An entire overview in the areas of software reengineering and program analysis is beyond the scope of this book. Therefore, the author introduces the relevant aspects only.

Furthermore, it may occur that an aspect can be classified in several areas of computer science, for example in software reengineering and migration. In this case, the aspect is assigned to migration.

4.1 Analysis of Source Code

Analysis of the program code and further artifacts has a long history in research. A variety of analysis tools are available for numerous programming languages. Therefore, it is sensible and appropriate to examine this area of research in order to reuse one of existing tools or techniques. This chapter also describes the necessary requirements for the application in model-driven software reengineering.

A basic principle in program analysis is the extraction of specific information from the Abstract Syntax Tree (AST). As already mentioned in Chapter 3.5.1, parser front-ends are particularly suitable. Usually they provide an interface to manipulate the tree itself and the output format (back-end). Tools and output formats have been investigated for their applicability. In

detail the results are described below. Additionally, a summary can be
found in [WMP06].

The aim is the creation of code-models illustrated in Figure 3.8 and Figure 3.9. Code-models represent a control flow graph (CFG), where each
node represents a statement (declaration, loops, branches) in the program
code and is enriched with additional information. The edges represent the
possible control flow. One model is generated for each method or function
in program code (see Chapter 3.5.2). Usually an entire program emerges
from the combination of various code-models.

Requirements on the Program Analysis

Initially the requirements have to be defined for comparing and selecting
analysis tools. An obvious but necessary requirement is that the program
code is available as text or in another form of representation (e.g. debug
information). Especially in the area of third-party code these requirements
can not always be met.

The code-to-graph converter is supposed to analyze program code or similar artifacts to provide the following information:

- identifiable lines in the program code,
- symbolic and unique names for variables and methods,
- definitions of variables and functions, and
- the control flow graph.

For the latter it must be taken into account that analysis tools can offer
optimization for source code. Compilers are a well known candidate for this.
Therefore all optimizations must be disabled. Otherwise this could lead to
falsified analysis results.

Furthermore, the investigated tools are supposed to comply with the standards of the target language to meet a broader base of program code.

System Tools

A very simple and effective form to analyze a program (object files) is the
usage of the existing system tools. Many operating systems, especially in
the UNIX/Linux environment, offer a wide selection. In combination with
scripting languages this can lead to very complex and versatile tools. The
parameters and the output of programs like: nm, dem, ldd and ar were
examined. ldd and ar provide information about program libraries. nm
analyzes object files and symbols inside a library. It displays the appearance

as well as the declaration of variables and functions. dem translates symbolic names in function declarations.

Disadvantage of these programs is the missing access to the control flow of a program. Furthermore, the information in the object files can not be transferred to a line within the source code.

Debug-Data and -Formats

The results of the investigation of system programs is a lack of information in the object files. Debugging formats are supposed to close this gap. Two well-known formats are the *Dwarf* and the *Stubs* format [MKM97]. Both are supported by the GNU and SUN Solaris compilers. Generally the source code must be compiled with a certain compiler option.

The program dumpstabs, belonging to the Stubs format, can extract information like symbol-tables from object- and executable files. The Dwarf format is much more flexible and further developed than the Stubs format. Since December 2005, the version 3.0 [Wor05] of the Dwarf format is available. This includes a data access library as well as a program called dumpdwarf for command line access. The latter can extract information about compiler (e.g. version, language), source code lines, local and global symbol tables, etc.

The available information is still not sufficient. The data is based on the assembly language. This means, any programming language-specific information is removed, e.g. all loops and branches will be replaced by Goto- and Label-statements. At this level, too much information about the control flow is missing to create an appropriate code-model.

Compiler

The properties of code-models, described in Chapter 3.9, suggest the use of compilers or compiler front-ends. They already hold the necessary information internally. However, they use different output and data formats to collect and aggregate information. Here, the GCC compiler as well as the SUN C++ compiler were evaluated for their applicability.

The Sun compiler is a closed-source program. It has several options and offers a built-in source browser. The option -xsd creates a database including information about function calls, declarations and variables. Queries on the database can be prepared and executed with the help of the programs sbenter and sbquery (see SUN workshop manual [Sun01, pp. 93]).

The database does not contain information about the structure of the source code. Further, the output of the compiler is severely limited in contrast to the GNU is not UNIX (GNU) compiler. This includes, for example, the output of intermediate information during the translation of a program. The source code of the compiler is not available and therefore can not be adapted to the requirements of the project.

In contrast, the GNU Compiler Collection [Gou05, WH04] is an opensource product. The versions 2.95.3, 3.4.4, and 4.0.2 were tested in this context. To summarize, the GCC-C++ compiler is much more flexible in comparison to the SUN compiler. There is a variety of options and data formats which are able to output information during and after the translation of code. These are grouped into different categories. Important parameters for the creation of the code-models can be found in the categories: parsing, code analysis and compilation steps.

The GCC compiler passes different stages for the translation of a program (lexical analysis, syntactic analysis, semantic analysis and optimization). Each phase is further subdivided into several smaller units. The GCC-C++ can write the current state of each unit into a file. In principle there are two different output formats. They depend on the internal data. The *tree* data structure and the Register Transfer Language (RTL) can both be translated into the Visualization of Compiler Graph (VCG) format and be visualized by using the VCGtools. This format is poorly documented and very difficult to analyze. Additionally it is possible to export a control flow graph. However, the Control Flow Graph (CFG) has been optimized. Therefore it is not comparable with the original program code.

The GCC compiler output is often based on the internal format of the compiler. The disadvantage is that all language-depended elements have been removed already. Depending on the phase of the translation the output is optimized and therefore useless. Initial optimizations are applied at the beginning of the translation (parsing).

The wealth of information offered by the GCC compiler is in itself very revealing. However, individual strands of information can not be related. A primary key, for example, row and column in source code is missing. Thus, additional front-ends for the programming language C++ are examined below. In most cases they are based on the GCC as well.

In addition, it was analyzed whether the GCC-C++ can be adapted. The necessary information could be collected and printed into a self-defined format. The internal structure of the compiler was the most complex challenge. The compiler does not process phase after phase during a translation. Instead it jumps between lexical, syntactic and semantic analysis. Possibly

a program could not be stored in its entirety in the memory during translation. In the past, memory was limited and expensive. Further hurdles
were the extensive use of macros and their inadequate documentation. This
approach was rejected after a short try.

GCC_XML

GCC_XML is an extension of the GCC-C++ compiler. It generates an
XML description of the analyzed program code[1]. The description includes
all classes and methods, their parameters and symbols, name spaces and
line numbers for assignment to the program code.

A specially adapted version of the GCC-C++ compiler is included in
the project. The output of the XML description is created in parallel to
the creation of the object file – during an ordinary translation process.
All further GCC options can be used. The XML file contains information
about functions only. Function bodies are not examined. Therefore, it is
not possible to derive a control flow graph.

Sage++

Sage++ is a program transformation tool[2] [BBG+94]. It is used to extend
the C++ programming language with new language elements. One example
is pC++ for parallel programming [BBG+93]. Sage++ allows to access
the AST, the symbol table, the type table and comments in the program
code. The main function of Sage++ is *unparsing*. The developer is able to
restructure the AST according to his requirements. Thereafter the AST is
transformed back into C++ code. The manipulation of AST is implemented
as a transformation (see Chapter 2.6.5). During the analysis of Sage++
problems emerged with standard library. This due to the lack of further
development since 1997.

OpenC++-Parser

OpenC++ is another project that expands the scope of C++ language[3] [Chi95]. Developers can define domain-specific extensions without
the need to adapt a parser or the type system. For this purpose a so-called
meta-level program is created. The program is an input of the OpenC++
compiler which is then able to translate the extended C++ code. During

---

[1]   http://www.gccxml.org/HTML/Index.html
[2]   http://www.extreme.indiana.edu/sage/
[3]   http://www.csg.is.titech.ac.jp/ chiba/openc++.html

translation the compiler creates a data structure called PTree. An extensive API exists to access this tree. The tree itself contains several structural information (classes, functions, variables, types) and semantic information. A symbol table is missing. Again, this project is no longer maintained since 2001. The developers have switched to Java (Open Java[4]).

XOGastan

XOGastan implements an extension of the GCC compiler[5] [APMV03]. However, this is not like GCC_XML directly integrated into the GCC compiler, instead it uses one of the numerous output formats of the compiler. XOGastan creates an XML description of the abstract syntax tree. The compiler option -fdump-translation-unit is used to create a description for each file.

The internal structure of XOGastan is called NAST (New Abstract Syntax Tree). It is quite similar to the data structure within GCC compiler. The program gcc2gxl processes the output of the compiler and generates a Graph eXchange Language (GXL) [HWS00] description. GXL was developed for general representation of graphs. Advantage is that already several tools can edit, visualize or analyze the content of this format[6]. Furthermore XOGastan offers an API to access and manipulate the data structure.

XOGastan meets all the requirements stated above, except it covers the C language only. All C++ language elements are ignored. However the case study in this book is written in C++. Thus XOGastan is not suitable to create code-models in this use case. Nevertheless the project demonstrates the flexibility of self-developed back-ends including an API for accessing the generated data structure.

CPPX

The program CPPX[7] [DMH01] was developed at the University of Waterloo in Canada. It transforms the internal data structures of the GCC compiler into the Datrix format. The Datrix Fact Model [Hol02] consists of an extended Entity/Relationship graph. It includes syntactic and semantic information of the program code. Based on this representation CPPX is able to create the GXL, Tuple Attribute (TA) or VCG format. These are used for further program analyzes, visualization or slicing techniques.

---

4 http://www.csg.is.titech.ac.jp/openjava/
5 http://xogastan. sourceforge.net/index.html
6 http://www.gupro.de/GXL/tools/tools.html
7 http://swag. uwaterloo.ca/ cppx/

Again, the age of the project is a drawback for the application in the context of this book. Since CPPX is integrated into the GCC, the extension depends on the compiler version. The last release of the project includes GCC version 3.0.

EDG C++-Front-end

Furthermore, there are several commercial compiler front-ends and program analysis products. One of them is the Edison Design Group (EDG)[8]. EDG exclusively develops compiler front-ends and is often mentioned in scientific publications. Their products support different languages such as C, C++, Fortran and Java. The developers are active members in standardization committees of the respective language.

The EDG front-end translates the source code into an intermediate language which can be processed afterwards. The developers describe the possibility of source-to-source transformation to enrich the language C++ with new elements. Mainly the front-end is used in compilers from different manufacturers to create platform-specific code. Therefore, it offers a complex and fine-grained interface that covers the extensive aspects of the C and C++ languages. This is correspondingly complex and powerful. Furthermore, the front-end includes a preprocessor.

Elsa C++-Front-end

Elsa is a front-end for the languages C and C++. It was developed at the University of Berkeley. It is based on a GLR parser generator called Elkhound[9] [MN04] (again developed at Berkeley). Both Elkhound and Elsa are written in C++.

Elsa merely offers a front-end and a well-structured and documented API. Thus the back-end, further processing and output, has to be implemented. The projects OINK[10] and Cqual++ [CHN06] already apply Elsa in program analysis as well as the deduction of types.

Elsa is based on the C++ standard. Additionally, errors in GCC compiler as well as Microsoft Visual Studio compiler can be bypassed[11]. The input of Elsa are preprocessed C/C++ files. Hence, comments are removed,

---

[8] http://www.edg.com/
[9] http://www.cs.berkeley.edu/ smcpeak/elkhound/
[10] http://www.cs.berkeley.edu/ dsw/oink.html
[11] In general, this refers to compiler-specific and non-standard-compliant processing of program sequences.

header files are included and macros are expanded. The processed files are significantly larger than the actual program code.

The front-end already offers numerous output options, e.g. the output of an abstract syntax tree. The standard output of Elsa consists of a list of name-value pairs. It contains various information like control structures, declaration of methods and variables as well as their position in the source code. Elsa also distinguishes between ambiguous and unambiguous items. Different methods are implemented to resolve those ambiguities. The standard output can only be processed with difficulty due to the lack of computer-based structuring. Furthermore, Elsa also provides an XML output. However, this does not contain all information.

During the analysis of Elsa, repeatedly problems were encountered with newer versions of the C and C++ standard libraries. This is documented on the website of the project. Elsa is tested and approved for GCC 2.95.3 and GCC 3.4.x. The new version 4 is not supported.

The most valuable asset of Elsa is an open interface that allows the processing of internal data structures at different stages during translation. The data structure is called Elsa Parse Tree (EPT). The Visitor Pattern [GHJV09, pp. 331] is used to connect front- and back-end. This hides the implementation details of Elsa and offers a simple interface to access the information from the EPT. Existing back-ends can be found in another project named OINK.

Elsa meets all requirements. Additionally, it is open source and well structured, which significantly reduces the complexity of a self-written back-end.

Summary and Evaluation of Program Analysis Tools

The results of the study are summarized in Table 4.1. The table columns represent the required criteria, the table rows the analyzed programs. When a tool fulfills a requirement it is marked with a plus or minus sign (not satisfied). An empty field indicates, that this requirement is not suitable or can not be determined. Furthermore, no distinction is made between the system programs. They are grouped together.

Both the system programs and the debug-formats are based on object or executable files. Thus, they represent the wrong level of abstraction. At the level of binary or assembly language often major programming languages constructs are removed and optimized, due to this the preparation of a control flow graph based on the written source code is not possible.

Table 4.1: Summary of evaluated tools [WMP09]

	Line number	Symbol name	Decla-ration	Control-flow	API	C++-Std.
System Tools:	-	+	+	-	-	
Debug-Formats:	+	+	+	-	+	
SUN CC:	+	+	+	-	-	+
GNU GCC:	+	+	+	+	-	+
GCC_XML:	+	+	+	-	+	+
Sage++:	+	+	+	+	+	-
Elsa/OINK:	+	+	+	+	+	+
OpenC++:	+	-	+	+	+	-
XOGastan:	+	+	+	+	+	-
CPPX:	-	-	-	+	+	-

The results of the two compilers differ significantly. The reason is their respective licensing policy. Both compilers can output numerous information about the translation process, as well as the generated artifacts. However, these information are to be regarded separately and are not necessarily linked to each other. Both lack a simple interface for the development of integrated extensions and output formats. The implementation of such an extension for the GCC compiler is certainly possible, but it is accompanied with a lot of effort due to the complex internal structure. The source code of the SUN compiler is not available, so any changes are excluded.

A major problem of the investigated research projects (Sage++, OpenC++, CPPX), is that they are often not maintained. Usually they depend on a dedicated compiler version. Furthermore, they do not support all kinds of C++ language elements.

Only three projects fulfill most or all of the requirements. XOGastan is limited to C and GCC_XML examines method descriptions only. None of the tools can meet the requirements directly. Due to their open nature some could be adjusted in order to achieve the desired result.

To summarize, three tools can fulfill the requirements with a few adjustments: the Elsa/Elkhound project, the GNU-GCC and GCC_XML. The GNU compiler must be extended to include an interface, GCC_XML to investigate function bodies and Elsa needs an own back-end. Due to the clearly structured interface, Elsa is most appropriate and flexible for an extension. In addition, there are already Elsa-based projects available.

Finally it should be noted that the development of the Elsa parser was stopped[12]. In this context, the Clang compiler of the LLVM project[13] is an alternative and sophisticated approach. Compared with Elsa, it offers the same properties. Additionally it contains a preprocessor. This allows to solve many of the problems described in Chapter 5. Another important criterion is the further development of the LLVM project. All components are open source and currently subject to continuous development.

4.2 Description Languages

In scientific literature there are many examples and approaches which translate program code into other formats. The aim of these approaches is to prepare a machine-readable form of program code for program analysis or to create exchange formats between tools. Therefore, most of these approaches emerge from the software-reengineering environment. The main distinguishing features are the supported languages and the level of abstraction. The approaches range from control flow graph or abstract syntax trees to programming language-dependent descriptions.

Woods et al. [WOL+98] refer to these languages as Lanuage Independent Format (LIF). These often rely on abstract syntax trees and consist of language-specific components, such as control structures. Thus, the exchange format developed here is not referred to as language-independent, but as *annotated, platform-independent description*. In the following some of these formats are presented.

A Simple Exchange Format for Graph Transformations

A simple format for the exchange of graphs and graph transformations is defined by Valiente [Val00] and presented at the APPLIGRAPH in 2000 at the University of Paderborn. The aim was to create a basic format for a basic subset of graph transformation properties. The format is based on XML and consists of a description of the graph itself and a declaration of the transformation rules.

Especially the description of graphs, has greatly influenced the format developed here. Each graph consists of a set of nodes, which in turn have a unique name and a label. Additionally the edges have a unique name and define source and destination. They can be provided with a label.

---

[12] Now the parser is a legacy system.
[13] The LLVM project (http://llvm.org/) develops an infrastructure for compilers and tool chains with a focus on program translation.

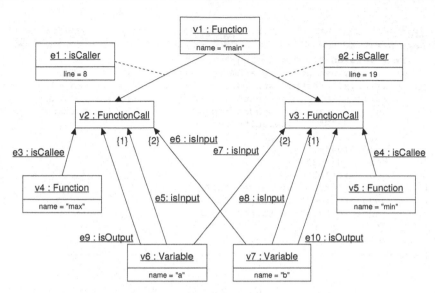

Figure 4.1: GXL Example by Winter et al. [WKR02]

Further information, which can be stored in this format, are the afore-mentioned transformation rules as well as information about the layout of graphs, e.g. coordinates, images or colors of nodes and edges. This data plays a minor role only.

GXL

GXL is designed by Holt and Winter [WKR02, HSSW12a] as a universal exchange format for reverse and reengineering tools. It was ratified on the Dagstuhl seminar for interoperability of reengineering tools as the standard exchange format [HSSW12b]. GXL has its roots in the Tuple Attribute Language (TA) [Hol02], the Graph eXchange Format (GraX) [EKW99, EKW00] and the file format of the PROGRES system [SW98]. All influencing formats as well as the development can be found in [HSSW12b].

GXL is based on XML and describes an attributed graph. It is build on the definition of UML class diagrams and distinguishes between schema and instance graphs. An instance is a concrete description of a graph, while the schema defines the structure (meta-level). Depending on the purpose, different schemata can be applied. In turn a schema itself is defined by a meta-schema. The meta-schema, as in the MDA, is self-describing. An example of a GXL graph is shown in Figure 4.1. Since not the entire UML

Listing 4.1: GraphML-Example of a structure description

```
1  <?xml version="1.0" encoding="UTF-8"?>
2  <graphml xmlns="http://graphml.graphdrawing.org/xmlns"
3      xmlns:xsi="http://www.w3.org/2001/XMLSchema-instance"
4      xsi:schemaLocation="http://graphml.graphdrawing.org/xmlns
5       http://graphml.graphdrawing.org/xmlns/1.0/graphml.xsd">
6    <graph id="G" edgedefault="undirected">
7      <node id="n0"/>
8      <node id="n1"/>
9      <node id="n2"/>
10     <node id="n3"/>
11     <edge source="n0" target="n2"/>
12     <edge source="n1" target="n2"/>
13     <edge source="n2" target="n3"/>
14   </graph>
15 </graphml>
```

---

class diagram is supported, e.g. inheritance, the authors provide a validator. It can validate both schema and instance. Furthermore, for various schemata Document Type Definitions (DTDs) are defined.

Using GXL, abstract syntax trees, class diagrams and control flow graphs can be mapped. It supports directed and undirected graphs, attributed nodes and edges as well as hierarchies.

GraphML

GraphML is an XML-based format for describing graphs developed by Brandes et al. [BEH⁺01]. It can be used to specify the structural properties of a graph. Furthermore it offers extensions to store application-specific data. It can handle directed and undirected graphs, hierarchies, arbitrary graphical representations and references to external data. For a GraphML an XML schema and a DTD for validation are available.

Specific data could be annotated to nodes and edges. Therefore, the <data>- and the <default>-element can be used. The structure of the format is described in the GraphML Primer [BEL12] in detail.

GraphML has the disadvantage that only one graph is described per file. If more than one graph is stored in a file, an application can decide to use the first graph or the union of all. It is not intended to distinguish the graphs. In Listing 4.1 line 6, it can be denoted that a <graph>-element has an identifier. However this is used as reference only.

Brandes et al. [BLP05] describe the possibility to transform in either direction between GXL and GraphML.

GraphXML

In 2001, Herman, Marshall and Scott [HM01] have published a predecessor to GraphML. The format specifies an XML-based description of graphs that can be validated by using a DTD. Later, the former two authors have contributed to the creation of GraphML. The similarities between the two formats are clearly recognizable (`<graph>`-, `<node>`- and `<edge>`).

Listing 4.2: GraphXML-Example

```
1  <?xml version="1.0"?>
2  <!DOCTYPE GraphXML SYSTEM "file:GraphXML.dtd">
3  <GraphXML>
4    <graph>
5      <node name="first"/>
6      <node name="second"/>
7      <edge source="first" target="second"/>
8    </graph>
9  </GraphXML>
```

Furthermore GraphXML can annotate application specific data to the graph, the nodes and the edges. The `<data>` element and for external reference the XLink standard [W3C01] is applied. This standard is also used for mapping hierarchies. Theoretically, individual graphs can be distributed via the Internet.

The JavaML-, CppML-, OOML-Family

The textual representation of programming languages is generally accurate and similar to natural language. It is a universal data format [Bad00]. The disadvantage of text is the processing by tools. In order to prepare the information stored in the text for machine processing, each tool needs a parser. Therefore, several research groups have initially defined XML descriptions for programming languages and for abstract syntax trees. The aim was to unify the development of exchange formats and tools.

Listing 4.3: JavaML-Example from [Bad00, p. 6]

```
1  <?xml version="1.0" encoding="UTF-8"?>
2  <!DOCTYPE java-source-program SYSTEM "java-ml.dtd">
3
4  <java-source-program name="FirstApplet.java">
```

```
5   <import module="java.applet.*"/>
6   <import module="java.awt.*"/>
7   <class name="FirstApplet" visibility="public">
8     <superclass class="Applet"/>
9     <method name="paint" visibility="public" id="meth-15">
10      <type name="void" primitive="true"/>
11      <formal-arguments>
12    <formal-argument name="g" id="frmarg-13">
13      <type name="Graphics"/></formal-argument>
14    </formal-arguments>
15    <block>
16      <send message="drawString">
17        <target><var-ref name="g" idref="frmarg-13"/></target>
18        <arguments>
19          <literal-string value="FirstApplet"/>
20          <literal-number kind="integer" value="25"/>
21          <literal-number kind="integer" value="50"/>
22        </arguments>
23      </send>
24    </block>
25      </method>
26  </class>
27 </java-source-program>
```

JavaML (Badros [Bad00]) is a definition for the Java programming language. The author examines several ways how to describe Java code using XML. The export of an abstract syntax tree is not sufficient, because it is too complex and contains more information than the author requires. Furthermore Badros simplified the description, e.g. by summarizing various types of loops into one single <loop> element. Comments in the existing program code will also be transfered into the XML description. For validation, the author offers a DTD. The created XML descriptions are validated by applying the transformation in both directions. The author generates the original program code using an XSLT transformation.

Next to JavaML, Mamas and Kontogiannis [MK00] use the same approach for the C++ language (CppML) and in general for object-oriented languages (OOML). The latter forms a superset of JavaML and CppML.

OOML is focused on the maintenance and migration of software. JavaML and CppML can be transformed into OOML with the loss of information. The aim of the authors, Mamas and Kontogiannis [MK00], is the establishment and the development of an Integrated Software Maintenance Environment (ISME). This maintains information about program code, documentation as well as control flow and call graphs. Other tools will use this data to aggregate it and visualize artifacts. For validation of the format in turn a DTD is available.

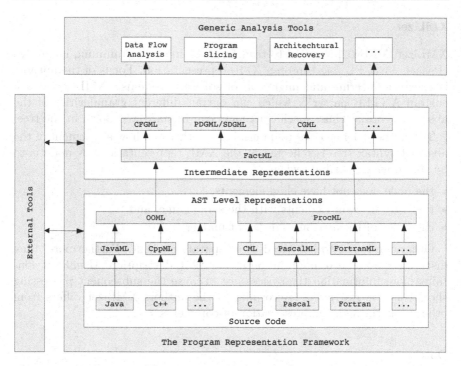

Figure 4.2: Architecture of the ISME [AEK05]

Based on the three languages above, Al Elkram and Kontogiannis [AEK05] developed further sub-languages. They are able to describe specific aspects of program analysis. Both, CPPML and JavaML, are still very close to the original language. Thus, tools need to maintain different implementations for the same analysis. Therefore a common abstract format should be provided for analysis tools.

The authors define formats at a higher level of abstraction to describe the control flow (CFGML), dependencies (PDGML) and call graphs (CGML). For each language in turn a DTD is defined. Additionally, all are derived from the FactML-model. FactML is a generic language, which defines all concepts required by the languages above.

In Figure 4.2 the general architecture of the languages is illustrated. Analysis tools should use it to work independently of the underlying programming language. Yet, there are no studies which analyze to what extent the information abstraction affects the analysis.

XMLizer

XMLizer [MMN02] is a tool to transform different programming languages (Pascal, Java, PL / IX) into an XML representation. Focus of the authors is the reengineering and migration of software systems. XMLizer uses a custom ANTLR parser[14], which can output different granularities of the abstract syntax. Thus, specific artifacts can be narrowed down in the tree.

The authors define rules to determine whether and how an element of the abstract syntax tree is reflected in the XML representation. A node is to be stored as an attribute when

- the node does not have child elements,
- there are no twin elements with the same name, and
- the order of the attributes does not matter.

Otherwise it has to be stored as a separate element. Furthermore, they discuss the amount of information in the XML description. Usually it contains more information than necessary because the subsequent processing should not be restricted. According to the authors XMLizer differs from other tools through the preservation of comments.

Datrix

The aim of the Datrix project (Bell Canada) is the analysis of program code in order to reuse and modularize components in the evolution of a system as well as to verify compliance with coding rules and standards.

Datrix itself is an interchange format [can00, LLL01] for the description of the results of a Java or a C++ parser. The underlying model is called Datrix Abstract Semantic Graph (ASG). It represents an AST, which is enriched with information such as types and declarations. The present study reuses the concept of annotated AST. The ASG is able to accommodate necessary information of different languages. Thereby the authors want to prevent a return to the program code. All program analyzes are based on the ASG and applicable to different languages.

The ASG can be exchanged between different tools with the help of the Datrix-TA-Format. It is built on a subset of the TA language developed by Holt [Hol02]. Amendments are described in Lapierre et al. [LLL01].

The ASG is similar to intermediate languages that are created during the processing of program code inside the compiler. The GCC uses this language to commonly describe optimizations and checks for all input languages.

---

[14] http://www.antlr.org/

Languages based on the Meta Object Facility (MOF)

The MOF is an UML-based description of meta-architectures (cf. Chapter 2.6) specified by the OMG. It was introduced to define the fundamentals of the UML. In addition, further languages are specified that influence the area of reengineering and program analysis. Usually they describe the mapping of language constructs at the model level. Two description languages, Knowledge Discovery Meta-Model (KDM) [Obj11b] and Abstract Syntax Tree Meta-Model (ASTM), emerged from the OMG-ADM project.

KDM: The KDM represents the core of the ADM initiative. It describes the initial meta-model to exchange data between tools, languages and platforms. Furthermore, KDM provides a summary of the application structure. It does not include any details and reaches down to the procedure level at maximum. Further packages for analysis, metrics and visualization are available.

ASTM: ASTM [Obj11a] is located below the procedure level. It represents individual statements in the program code. Based on ASTM different target languages can be created. Therefore a general and abstract meta-model of the syntax of the programming language is necessary. While the KDM gives a rough overview of an application, the ASTM extended this in order to fully describe an application.

EBNF in MOF: Wimmer and Kramler [WK06] implement a fundamentally different approach. They describe a method to map the Extended Backus Naur Form (EBNF) into the MOF on the meta-meta-model level. In general the grammar of a programming language is available as EBNF. Since the transformation to meta-meta-layer exists, a language can be described as meta-model and again by doing so a program can be described as model. The authors present a generic approach aimed at developing universal program analysis.

Another obvious possibility in the context of the OMG is the extraction of UML models from existing code. This procedure is discussed in scientific literature, e.g. Soley and Oara [SO06]. Many UML modeling tools offer the analysis of program code and the creation of UML models. This was further investigated by Steffen and Wagner [SWM10] for the application in Round-Trip-Engineering (RTE).

Meta-model for Java

Fuhr et al. [FHW10] describe a meta-model for the Java language in the context of the IBM Service-Oriented Modeling Architecture (SOMA) project. The aim was to read and analyze applications. The investigation includes the graphical interface as well as the functionality of the application. The authors detect specific class and interface names that have been determined in advance. The result is latter extracted and deployed into a web service.

Summary

The approaches listed here show an evolution from data format for programming languages or syntax trees to abstract descriptions for whole language families. In General a new level of abstraction is created to describe analysis and optimization in general and cross-linguistic. A major role is played by the definition of meta-models and the description of transformations.

Further papers describe the generalization of ASTs [CM08] or the description of the AST at OMG meta-model level, Reus et al. [RGD06]. Therefore the AST will be transformed first into a generic AST and afterwards into a UML model.

The approach developed in this book implements an exchange format between the Elsa parser and a modeling tool. The format is based on some attributes of Valiente, of GraphXML and the document structure of GraphML (see Chapter 5.5.1). A further definition of meta-models is not part of the study, because the currently used modeling tool does not possess an adaptable meta-model. The tool is being redeveloped. The next version is based on Eclipse Modeling Framework (EMF). Then it will be possible to use the meta-model mechanisms outlined above.

4.3 Reverse and Reengineering Tools

Columbus

The Columbus reengineering tool was developed in cooperation of the Universty of Szeged, the Nokia company and FrontEndArt. The tool combines different work packages of software reengineering. The aim was the analysis of large C++ software projects. Columbus has a powerful C++ parser and it defines a schema for the extracted data [FBTG02]. This contains the different elements of the programming language and the relationships between them in order to represent a system at a higher level of abstraction. The format itself is described as an UML class diagram. In addition, a common interface for reverse engineering tasks is provided. It enables the exchange of data between the front-end and various analysis and visualization tools.

Columbus can also include makefiles and project descriptions in the analysis. The preprocessor is able to analyze incomplete or defective code. The

Columbus system can be used on the command line, as pipeline or through a graphical interface.

Ferenc et al. [FBTG02] present different applications of Columbus. These include the reverse engineering of UML class diagrams, the detection of design patterns, the calculation of metrics in the FAMOOS project[15] and the data exchange with other tools such as GUPRO (see below) using the GXL [FB02]. Further export formats are CppML or Hypertext Markup Language (HTML).

In [FBTG02] Ferenc et al. present different requirements for the tool, the C++ front-end and the schema. The tool itself is based on the Columbus front-end CAN and a schema for C++. Furthermore it is extensible with a plug-in mechanism. The architecture and the process model are shown in [FBTG02] Figures 2 and 3.

Columbus consists of a front-end that analysis the data, a linker plug-in that combines data and a data export, providing different formats. For the implementation of extensions Columbus provides an API. A description of the linker or the export on an abstract level is not possible.

Main purpose of the tool is the extraction of facts from the analyzed source code. The approach is described in detail in [BFG05]. The authors prefer an incremental approach for program analysis and the processing of information. This is fundamental for the developed model-driven methodology (cf. [BFG05] Figure 1). Columbus does not exceed the extraction of information. It lacks a specific further processing for system migration.

Generic Environment for Program Understanding (GUPRO)

GUPRO is an environment that enables program understanding of heterogeneous software systems on different levels of abstraction [EKRW02]. It is based on the representation of the software as a graph (TGraph). Furthermore a query language (GreQL) and a meta-model (Gral) is necessary to analyze code. At first a graph database is created from an existing system. Information about the system are obtained with the help of queries.

A TGraph [EKW99] is a directed graph whose nodes and edges have both a type and attributes. Since the data format is closely related to GXL, the graph in Figure 4.1 represents a TGraph.

Gral is the TGraph specification language, Ebert et al. [EWD+96]. This is necessary to formally describe TGraphs and to adjust them to a particular project situation and target language.

---

[15] One outcome of the project is the book by Demeyer et al. [FBTG02] about patterns for the reengineering of object-oriented systems.

The declarative language GreQL is used [KK01] for the extraction of information from a graph structure. It is similar to a database query language and allows the selection of specific elements with defined properties as well as the specification of the output format. For the description of a query an API, a command line program and a graphical interface are available.

Further, GUPRO can differentiate between source code before and after the preprocessor. Additionally it has the ability to reproduce the original program code, also called unparsing.

The methodology developed here extends the idea of the query language for graphs, and defines a graphical notation that allows the extraction of information from a graph. Furthermore, the rebuilding of the original program code is essential for quality assurance and part of a back-to-back test (cf. Chapter 5.5.4).

Bauhaus

Bauhaus is a collection of static analysis tools for various programming languages. It includes C/C++ and is developed at the Universities of Bremen and Stuttgart [RVP06]. Bauhaus is based on the Rigi tool [KM10].

The analyzes subsumes the detection of programming errors, such as uninitialized variables, the improvement of code quality by identifying dead code, copy-and-paste sections, circular dependencies and the calculation of metrics. The second focus is application understanding, which is supported by the visualization of program code. Furthermore, it is possible to execute both control and data flow analysis.

In the first step, the Bauhaus tools transform the program code into an intermediate representation. Therefore the Intermediate Language (IML) [RVP06] and the Resource Flow Graph (RFG) [SB10] are available. The IML abstracts specific programming statements to general constructs, such as a while-statement to a loop-statement. This simplifies the cross-linguistic analysis of program code. The RFG represents an abstract view of a software system. It is defined as a hierarchical directed graph of which the nodes and edges are typed. The nodes contain relevant information such as methods, file names, types, and components of the system architecture. For further analysis a Graphical User Interface (GUI) (Graphical Visualiser (Gravis) [CEK+00]) is available. It can visualize different views of a system.

Different analyzes based on IML and RFG are described by Raza et al. [RVP06] in detail. The Bauhaus tools offer a wide range of program analysis. Approaches that use the obtained information for the migration of software are currently unknown.

Rigi

Rigi is a reverse engineering tool that was developed at the University of Victoria (Canada) by Kienle and Müller. The software package contains the extraction of information from program code, a data exchange format, different analyzes for transformation and abstraction of information as well as visualization in the form of directed graphs [KM10]. Rigi automates reverse engineering activities to enable the processing of large programs. According to the authors, Rigi was one of the first tools that visualizes software artifacts and their relationships. Additionally it allows the interactive manipulation of artifacts [Mü86].

The Rigi architecture consists of three components. The data extraction component analyzes the existing program code and creates a database. The second component extracts facts from the database. Those will be displayed in the third, the graphical interface. The analysis itself is described in a scripting language (Rigi Command Language (RCL)) to enable quick changes and extensions (rapid prototyping). Rigi uses the Rigi Standard Format (RSF) and it also supports the already presented graph formats like GXL or GraX.

Thus Rigi is comparable to the reverse engineering programs already mentioned above, but much older. Again, the aim is to improve the application understanding. It is possible to influence and adapt the analysis with the help of scripts as well as to visualize the results.

SLANG

An approach that does not exclusively run on code level, but attempts to expand the reverse engineering to model level, is described by Rugaber and Stirewalt [RS04]. They define a language called SLANG. It describes

- the application domain,
- the program to be analyzed, and
- a mapping of program constructs to the domain.

The authors hope to gain a better effort estimation, improving the quality and reducing the development risk in reverse engineering.

SLANG is a textual, declarative description of a system, the domain as well as the mapping between both. The approach differs from other approaches by utilizing only a single language for the description of different aspects. The language is implemented in a tool called Specware from Kestrel. SLANG is very similar to a scripting or programming language. For the development of the three models, the developers need to have a

huge amount of background knowledge. However the domain model has to
be created once (cf. [RS04, p. 52]).

This book defines a similar method and provides a single modeling language for code-models, analyzes and abstractions that works on the code-
models as well as their results. It is the advantage of this method that only
one modeling tool is necessary to cover different dimensions.

OMG-Architecture Driven Modernization (ADM)

OMG-ADM is a general approach and data model for modernizing legacy
systems. In 2003, the OMG established a working group for the development
of ADM standards. The first results KDM and ASTM were released in 2007
and 2009 (cf. Chapter 4.2).

The aim of the working group covers the definition of common data exchange formats, the description of program analysis, the calculation of metrics and the visualization for the reengineering of software systems. The
defined meta-models are based on already existing MDA[16] concepts.

In ADM a major role is played by the transformation of systems: From
a code-centric system towards the MDA and its model-driven development.
Unlike the present approach, which successfully implements this transformation, the ADM has no overall description of the process yet. First results
were presented by Reus et al. [RGD06] and Doyle et al. [DGGD06]. A modeling tool, which implements the basics of the ADM project is MoDisco. It
is explained in Chapter 4.6.

Summary

The tools or projects discussed in this chapter constitutes a small but representative set of existing tools. They were chosen because they summarize the state-of-the-art tools and techniques. Different aspects of the tools
have influenced the developed approach. Generally the tools differ in the
addressed reverse engineering problem, the used storage technologies, the
access method, the granularity of the program code as well as the analysis
and visualization techniques.

Further tools are Moose [SLT00], ArcStyler [RGD06] or the
GSEE [SFZ10]. An entirely different approach is presented by Murphy et
al. [MNS95]. A software-reflection model is calculated from manually created models and abstract descriptions of the program code. The reflection

---

[16] The acronym ADM is the reverse variant of MDA.

model illustrates differences and similarities. The authors use the approach to find violations of the software architecture.

4.4 Modeling Tools

The choice of the modeling tool Java Application Building Center (jABC) depends on the selected continuous model-driven development method XMDD (Chapter 3.3). The tool is implemented specifically for this method. Nevertheless further modeling tools are considered in the following. Hence it is possible to examine possible development paths as well as the transfer of the approach to other tools.

Java Application Building Center (jABC)

The authors of the XMDD method (Chapter 3.3) designed and developed a modeling tool to support the method and to demonstrate their suitability. In the following, the tool will be presented. In particular the development of process nodes and the plug-in mechanism are presented in detail.

The Java Application Building Center (jABC) allows the composition of process modules, applications and the development of new services. The process of software development is supported by rapid prototyping, animation, formal verification, debugging and code generation [MS09b]. A first predecessor of the program, the ABC [SM99], emerged in the mid-90s and was implemented in C++.

The tool provides a graphical interface for the modeling of process graphs. It includes a project administration, a library of process modules and various extensions, which define the semantics of models. Users can create and customize process graphs, also called SLGs. A process graph consists of building blocks named SIBs.

Figure 4.3 gives an overview of the surface of the modeling tool. It is composed of three components.

Project administration (A): The project tab contains a list of available projects. Each is composed of process graphs and process modules (SIBs). In addition to the project tab, The SIBs tab contains a list of all process modules. These are organized in a tree structure. The taxonomy is usually based on the Java package structure and the class name of a SIB. The taxonomy is customizable.

Inspectors (B): The properties of SLGs or SIBs are visualized and configurable on the bottom left of the main window. The inspector contains

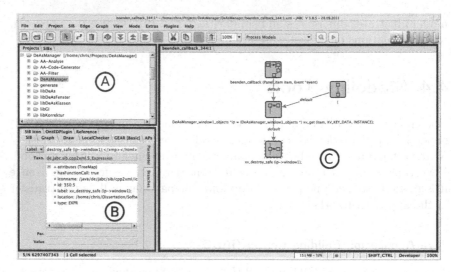

Figure 4.3: jABC – User interface

the name and parameters of a SIB. With the help of the inspector,
the entire model is configurable. Furthermore, appropriate inspectors
can be implemented.

Editor (C): The main window of the application can be found in the middle.
In the drawing area, the user can create and organize a process graph.
New process nodes can be selected directly from the SIB tree and
be dragged and dropped it onto the editor. Each process graph is
displayed in a new tab.

jABC: Service Independent Building Block (SIB) Implementation

SIBs can be grouped into two categories. The control SIBs allow the manipulation of the control flow of a business process. For example the Graph-SIB
enables the hierarchical structuring of models. The Graph-SIB contains no
execution semantics. It delegates the execution to the nodes in a sub-graph,
similar to a function call in a programming language.

The second category includes the actual process modules. For the application expert a process module consists of [MS04]:

- various parameters, which can be configured (via the inspectors),
- outgoing edges, which show the possible results of an execution,
- a symbol and a name to represent the SIB in the editor and

- a documentation of the node itself, its parameters and edges.

For the use of a SIB within a process graph the intended behavior is important for the application expert. The actual implementation is not necessary. For routine tasks, the jABC already offers a large amount of process modules, which are immediately available for modeling.

The processing nodes can communicate with each other via a shared memory, also called context. This is realized by the Blackboard architectural pattern [TMD09, p. 112]. The context consists of a hash table of name-value pairs. Each entry that is specified in the context has a unique name and a value. The latter can be represented by a simple data type or a complex object. Each SIB is able to read or write data from the context. The application expert is responsible for managing the key and the context.

The programming expert implements the semantic of a process node (Chapter 3.3.2) [MS04]. A SIB is represented by a Java class, which is marked by an annotation. The class contains a unique number to identify a node. All other features are optional, and can be implemented as follows:

Parameter: All public fields of a class represent the parameters of a SIB. They must be initialized with default values.

Edges: The definition of the outgoing edges of a node can be distinguished in fixed and variable edges. The former are defined by a non-varying, public array of strings with the name BRANCHES. The latter again uses an adaptable array (not final) to describe a variable amount of outgoing edges.

Icon: A default icon belongs to each process node. If this is to be changed every process node can define its own icon.

Documentation: To provide the parameters, edges and process nodes with documentation, a special method can be implemented.

Plug-in interface: Each processing node can support an arbitrary set of extensions. In general, an interface is implemented for each extension, which includes one or more methods. Standard plug-ins are the Tracer [SMN+07] to animate the SLGs or the aforementioned code generator project Genesys [Jör11].

The present case study uses the interface of the tracer to incorporate existing code into a process node. Other systems or programming languages can be integrated with the help of a wrapper (Chapter 2.5.2). While executing a process node, the implementation decides on the result and thus about the outgoing edge.

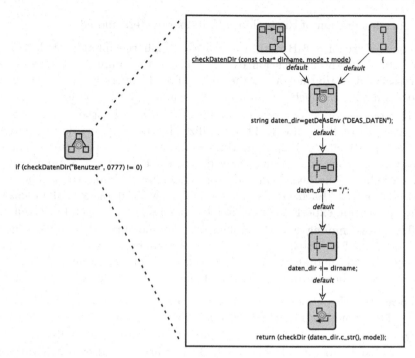

Figure 4.4: jABC – Modeling hierarchy

jABC: Service Logic Graph (SLG)

The formal basis of an SLG is shown in Chapter 3.3.2. The graph represents the control flow of an application. It provides an adequate abstraction for the conceptual modeling of processes. Furthermore, the SLG concentrates on one aspect of an application and hides the details about data structures and the architecture of the system [MS04]. It is recommended to equip each edge in the SLG with a name (label). The start node of a process graph is marked by an underlined SIB name.

The control flow graph can be simplified and refined by the definition of hierarchies. A hierarchy is shown in Figure 4.4. A SIB containing a sub-model is characterized by a circles with a dot in the middle of the icon. Like a function call in a programming language outgoing edges (model edges) can be defined at each node. The model edges represent the possible results of the execution of the sub-graph.

The jABC further distinguishes different types of execution semantics of sub-models. The default case is that a sub-model is treated as the current graph – both use the same context. The hierarchical separation is visualized on the modeling level only. A distinction between the contexts could be established with Graph- and Thread-SIBs. The former separates the context areas, which is very similar to a function call – each sub-graph has its own context. The Thread-SIB executes each sub-graph in a separate process.

The advantages of this hierarchical designs are mainly the reduced complexity during the modeling and the reusability of sub-graphs. Often, these hierarchies also represent the interfaces within an organization. This can lead to better communication with the stakeholders. The separation of modeling and code enforces a *separation of concerns*. The application experts focus on the process and IT experts on the implementation.

The meta-model is a formally defined transition system. Its implementation is fixed and can not be adjusted (see Chapter 3.3.2). This is in contrast to most of the modeling tools described below. To overcome this drawback, the next version of the modeling tool is developed with the Eclipse Modeling Framework (EMF).

Nevertheless the invariant meta-model is not necessarily a drawback. In the present case it simplifies the approach. Although the meta-model can not be modified directly, the abstract syntax can be adapted by new process modules. Furthermore, the domain expert can change the taxonomy, e.g. he can adapt SIB names and icons to the target domain. In addition, the semantics of the models can be changed with plug-ins.

jABC: Plug-in Implementation

Plug-ins extend the jABC with additional functionality to determine the semantics of a process graph. In general a flow graph semantics is assumed. New menus and inspectors are inserted into the graphical user interface to extend SLGs with domain-specific data. They allow a situation-specific execution of models. All plug-ins are working on the same model representation [MS09b].

The extensions are developed in Java. They implement a simple interface to be integrated by the jABC-core system. They have access to the graphical interface elements, the event system, project administration, as well as to process graphs and modules.

A new plug-in is developed for the model-driven analysis of source code and the migration of software systems. It controls and configures the transformation of the program code to code-models as well as their analysis. Further, two existing plug-ins are necessary: the Tracer [SMN+07] and the code generator Genesys [Jör11].

MetaEdit+

MetaEdit+ is a modeling tool developed by MetaCase in Finland. It focuses on the development of domain-specific languages and models, as well as full code generation [TPK07].

The meta-meta-model Graph-Object-Property-Port-Role relationship (GOPPR) [KLR96] forms the basis of the tool. Various meta-models (modeling languages) can be derived from GOPPR. Types of nodes and edges can be freely defined to represent the concepts, rules and notations of the domain. Further, a domain-specific code generator must be specified to map the model elements to program code.

Generally MetaEdit+ works with graphical models. It offers a graphical editor for the definition of the meta-model and its instances. Each model element in turn consists of an icon and various parameters. They are configured by the model and the code generator. For the description of the model notation, MetaEdit+ contains its own vector-based editor. Furthermore a debugger is available for the development of the code generator [TPK07].

Kelly [Kel04] compares MetaEdit+ with EMF (described below). He concludes that EMF requires more implementation effort. Further, he stresses that MetaEdit+ is much better suited for modeling by domain experts. In contrast EMF initially requires a tool expert who creates a modeling tool for the domain expert. Furthermore, the author refers to the build-in support of the evolution of models and meta-models in MetaEdit+.

Eclipse Modeling Framework (EMF)

EMF is based on the Eclipse development environment implemented initially by IBM. It allows the definition of modeling languages, the description of models and the generation of program code or other artifacts. It is based on the Ecore meta-meta-model, which is in turn derived from Essential-MOF.

EMF has the ability to import meta-models from different source formats. These include annotated Java classes, class diagrams that were created with Rational Rose or XML schema descriptions. Furthermore, a separate editor is available to manually describe the meta-model. Based on the described or on the imported model, EMF generates different libraries. They allow the access to the meta-model programmatically and to build a specific meta-model-dependent editor. The editor contains the elements and relationship as defined in the meta-model only. The instance of the meta-model, the model, is generated as a tree view in the editor. The generated libraries provide a further way to create a model. It can be instantiated in Java.

For the definition of graphical modeling languages the Graphical Modeling Framework (GMF) extension is available. Based on a described meta-model, it enables the implementation of a graphical notation. The GMF can enrich the editor with a graphical representation. This enables the advantages of graphical notations, listed in Chapter 2.6.3, to be used. Therefore a mapping of meta-model elements to a graphical equivalent is defined and in turn a separate editor is generated. The latter is a special Eclipse plug-in.

Different code generators create program code or other artifacts (e.g. XML documents) based on the EMF- or GMF-models. EMF contains the code generators JET (Java Emitter Templates) and XPand for the model-to-text transformation. Both are template-based [Jör11, p. 35].

From UML to Java and Back Again (Fujaba)

Fujaba is a modeling tool developed at the University of Paderborn [NZ99]. It is based on the UML notation and uses particular class, activity and collaboration diagrams to create a visual specification language. Their aim is to describe object-oriented systems and graph transformations.

A code generator processes the above mentioned UML diagrams and generates Java code. The class diagrams define the structure of the program code. The functionality is defined as an abstract description with the help of activity diagrams. The different activities can be implemented either in Java or described as graph transformations by means of collaboration diagrams. The developers refer to the combination of activity and collaboration diagrams as *story diagrams.*

Furthermore, Fujaba is also applied as a Round Trip Engineering (RTE) tool for Java systems. Nickel et al. [NNWZ00] describe the recovery of information from class structures as well as the creation of story diagrams from existing code. Thus, the purpose of the tool expands to the reengineering of Java systems. Based on Fujaba the tool Reclipse [DMT10] has been developed. It is a reverse engineering tool for statistical detection and evaluation of design patterns [DMT10].

Cadena

Cadena is an Eclipse-based modeling tool designed for the development of component-based systems [HDD+03]. It is developed at Kansas State University (KSU). The first version of the Cadena uses the CORBA Component Model (CCM). Through its architecture-centric approach it allows the refinement and reuse of architectural styles and the development of domain-specific modeling environments. The authors applied the tool for the development of product line architectures [HDD+03].

For further development the CCM of Cadena[17] was replaced by an abstract component model. All concrete models must be derived from the abstract model. The three-stages approach contains at the top-level a language with primitives to describe interfaces, connectors and a component model. In the second stage components and types are defined. In the last step a concrete scenario can be modeled. An extended type system forms the basis of the approach. It was developed by Jung and described in his thesis [Jun07].

Different types of plug-ins extend the functionality of Cadena. They enable analysis, synthesis and verification of component-based systems [HDD+03]. They operate at different levels and include code generators, editors, which offer the possibility to define temporal logic properties, and verification tools to test these properties.

Summary

In this section, the modeling tool jABC was discussed in detail and further modeling tools were presented. These differ in their development focus and flexibility in relation to the adaptation/configuration of meta-levels.

The EMF ranks among the approaches with the greatest flexibility. The approach developed here is not restricted to the jABC and can also be implemented with other tools. Specified interfaces and data formats between the individual process steps allow an exchange. Considering the reimplementation of jABC with EMF, this fact is particularly helpful.

4.5 Transformation Systems and Languages

Part of the present work is not only the transformation of program code into code-models, but also the analysis and abstraction of information. Even though the results are very different, both transformations operate on the underlying models. For this reason, several transformation systems and languages are examined in the following chapter.

---

[17] http://cadena.projects.cis.ksu.edu/

StrategoXT

The application of StrategoXT is the description and execution of program transformations [Vis04]. It is also referred to as a transformation system. Such a system consists of a transformation language, strategies for their application as well as a collection of tools [JVV01].

The textual transformation language XT operates at the AST of the source code. The grammar of the programming language is described with SDF [HHKR89]. A separate parser reads the program code and generates the AST. It is possible to define rules that rewrite this tree. The rules may contain dynamic elements that can be adapted to the specific context during runtime. A set of rules can be translated into an executable program, which can be used on the command line.

A special feature of StrategoXT is the introduction of strategies for the application of rules. A strategy can be executed in a specific phase or if a defined condition is fulfilled. StrategoXT renders the strategies explicit and controllable [Vis04]. Furthermore, transformations can be cascaded, gradated or run locally.

The transformation itself is organized as a data flow system [Vis04]. It deploys a pipeline architecture to link the components with each other. The format ATerm [BJKO00] is used for the data exchange between the tools.

StrategoXT is applied for source-to-source transformation, optimization of program code based on the AST, type checking, generation of documentation, beautifying of code and migration of programs by converting the grammar [Vis04, Chapter 12].

Turing eXtended Language (TXL)

TXL is a language for the definition of textual transformation rules. The aim is the transformation of programming languages, specification languages, database schemata, structured documents, the extension of programming languages with new features, the description of program analysis and the transformation (beautifying) of program code [Cor06b]. The three components are

- a BNF description of the structure to be transformed,
- a description of the language extension and
- the associated transformation rules.

The transformation language includes parameterized rules and a mapping for the application of strategies. In addition, rules can contain sub-rules. The execution of rules can be limited and bound to a certain context.

TXL was partly developed in the context of the Esprit project (see below). In software reengineering it has been used in program analysis, restructuring and remodeling of applications as well as in reverse engineering for the Y2K problem [Cor06a].

Kafka

Kafka was developed by Weis et al. [WUG03]. It is a rule-based, graphical transformation language. The authors focus on the MDA, in particular the transition from PIM to PSM. Each rule consists of three parts:

- a search for a specific pattern within the PIM,
- a search for a specific pattern within the PSM and
- a description of how the PSM must be adapted.

Once Kafka found a corresponding element in both, the PIM and the PSM, a substitution rule is applied. To determine the sequence of transformations, the authors use custom UML activity diagrams.

Query View Transformation (QVT)

In the context of MDA, the OMG standardized the language QVT [Obj11c]. It is part of the MOF and describes a model-to-model transformation textually. The core of QVT contains both declarative and imperative components. A transformation is similar to a program. Functions and variables can be defined. Access to the model elements and their attributes is given declaratively. In order to describe a transformation in QVT the metamodels of the source and target model are always necessary. They form the basis for the description of the transformation. Further, the language can be used for the validation of models.

Graph Repository Transformation Language (GReTL)

GReTL is part of an extension of the IBM SOMA project (see below) developed by Fuhr et al. [FHW10]. The project involves the transformation of legacy Java code in a service-oriented architecture. The TGraphs, already used in GUPRO, form the basis of the approach. Based on the graph specification, the authors defined the Graph Repository Query Language (GReQL) [BE08] and GReTL [HE11].

Transformations in GReTL are described in the Java programming language. They use the GReQL to extract information from the models and to map them to the target model.

UML-Object Diagrams as a Transformation Language

Milicev [Mil02] proposes a graphical transformation language, based on UML object diagrams, for creating output generators. The author argued that this should belong to any modeling environment, regardless of what it creates (text or other models).

UML object diagrams are extended by Milicev for specification of these generators. Through the use of diagrams, the advantages of visual notations become evident. In [Mil02] he describes the creation of object diagrams and the subsequent generation of C++ program code. With an additional level of abstraction, the author intends to split the code generator into a model and a programming language dependent component.

Atlas Transformation Language (ATL)

ATL is a language resulting from the ATLAS Model Management Architecture (AMMA) project. The aim is to describe the transformation of meta-models. The language should be compatible with QVT. As described in QVT, transformations are textual patterns.

Scalise et al. [SFZ10] apply this language for the reverse engineering and the extraction of information.

Summary

In general transformation languages can be divided into textual and graphical notations. The latter are of particular interest for the present approach. However, the developed approach is fundamentally different. It basically hides the technical details from the user, such as representation of rules, use of query language, pattern search and strategies. All necessary transformations are described as process model. The implementation is "hidden behind" the individual process node.

4.6 Projects in Software Migration

The migration of software is generally a complex and time-consuming activity which requires a variety of tools and a lot of manual effort. Various projects are presented in the following section. They specifically deal with the migration of software systems or components. A major part has been funded in the context of the research framework programs of the European Union (EU).

Renaissance

Aim of the Renaissance project was the development of a systematic approach for reengineering and software evolution. The focus was the efficiency and feasibility of methods in an industrial environment. To meet these requirements, the project partners developed an abstract process model for software evolution and software reengineering [War99, pp. 17]. This was tested on different systems. The model is oriented by industrial development principles and models.

Furthermore, it supports technical evolution as well as mechanisms for migration of programming languages (3GL to 4GL) or platforms/architectures, e.g. the transition from mainframe to client-server architectures. A further object of the project was the identification and assessment of cost models to enable appropriate evolution strategies, process planning and risk assessments. The developed methodology is based on an incremental evolution. The integration of existing legacy functionality is provided via distributed architectures.

The results of the project as well as two case studies are summarized by Warren [War99]. The Renaissance project approach represents a pattern for the model-driven methodology as well as their implementation. Unfortunately, the Renaissance process model could not be reused here since it is very generic.

Additionally the EU project Refine [KK02, p. 8f] should be mentioned. It specifically examines the recovery of business processes. Karagiannis and Kühn [KK02] applied the results to software systems.

MODELPLEX

MODELPLEX[18] was part of the Sixth EU Research Program. The target was similar to Renaissance, improving quality and productivity in the development and evolution of software systems. The central topic was the transfer of results into an industrial environment.

Part of the project was the development and application of a model-driven methodology [BBJ07]. This includes the development of tools, the design of methods, the analysis, synthesis, verification, and validation of models as well as the study of abstraction.

The original goal of the project, the development of software, has less in common with the migration of software systems. However, important

---

[18] http://www.modelplex.org/index.php

outcomes of the project are the development of a knowledge model similar to KDM, the ATL transformation language and the Eclipse tool MoDisco.

MoDisco

MoDisco[19] is an Eclipse tool, which emerged from the MODELPLEX project. It provides a framework to create model-driven tools for the modernization of existing software systems. The KDM already described above, is the meta-model for this approach.

The modernization of a system is described on the project website as

- the extraction of information,
- the understanding of these and
- the transformation into new artifacts to support the modernization.

MoDisco provides meta-models for the description of existing systems, *Discoverers* for the automatic creation of models and further tools for program understanding and transformation.

SOA Migration (SOAMIG)

The SOAMIG project is funded by the BMBF and examines the transformation of legacy systems to service-oriented architectures (SOA) [ZWH+11, FHW10]. The original functions are supposed to be preserved in order to expand the lifetime of the systems.

The project analyzes transformations of Cobol to Java source code and the associated creation of services.

Summary

The projects presented cover only a small subset of the research activities in the field of software migration. On the one hand it is clearly proven that this topic is research relevant, yet on the other hand it is shown that there are only very few useful tools. In general, the tool chain is adapted for each migration project.

Further examples that did not occur in the context of larger projects are the extraction of business processes in web applications by Zou et al. [ZLK+04], or the reengineering and the migration of telecommunication applications by Mosler [Mos09].

---

[19] http://wiki.eclipse.org/MoDisco

4.7 Analysis and Remodeling of GUIs

The analysis and remodeling of graphical user interfaces is a crucial component of the developed model-driven migration. Therefore, some papers from
scientific literature are presented in the following. In general, they focus on
the transformation of textual interface into modern graphical systems. The
techniques ranges from web standards such as HTML in combination with
a browser to graphical libraries.

Tucker und Stirewalt

[TS99] analyzed GUIs in the context of the MASTERMIND project. They
extracted three specific models [SR98]. The presentation model contains information and properties of the individual graphical elements. The dynamic
behavior of a surface is represented in the dialogue model. All accessible
and changeable elements are located in the application model.

The authors developed a *complexor* which combines the three models to
generate a new user interface. Subsequently the associated functionalities
have to be added to the interface manually.

Staiger

[Sta07a, Sta07b] examined the evolution of graphical user interfaces in the
context of the Bauhaus project. The goal was the analysis of manually
created GUIs and its migration into tools (GUI-Builder).

The authors used static analysis techniques, such as the calculation of
Def/Use-Sets. The objective is the detection of events to derive the architecture of the interface as well as the hierarchy of the windows. For the
presentation of results, various back-ends are developed, e.g. for documentation in HTML or to generate test cases.

Problems in concerning the amount of program code to be examined, the
development of efficient algorithms as well as the analysis of the program
code, which is complicated by pointers and language dialect, are identified
by the author.

Michail

[Mic02] improved the application understanding by analyzing the graphical
user interface. He extracted the structure and provided the user with a
browsing mechanism to find the application logic. The aim is to identify

callback routines. These represent the starting point of the functionality. The assignment is supported through the comparison of function names.

Michail highlights the method as a guide to get a system overview. Especially the training of new employees is to be facilitated hereby. The method itself limits the search depth and analyzed events. It ignores events which emanate from a mouse or a window. Furthermore, the method requires detailed knowledge of the GUI library and the programming language.

The browsing mechanism, as well as the identification of callback routines are re-used in the present approach. Graphical interfaces are analyzed and their structure is extracted. One difference to the approach of Michail is that not the program code, but already existing models are examined.

Chan

et al. [CLM03] used, in contrast to the methods above, a dynamic analysis. They recorded the behavior of a graphical interface at run time and created a database with the identified events. This data set is part of the application understanding. The system is designed to *replay* events that have been recorded. The authors have tested the approach with the text-based web browser lynx.

Merlo

et al. [MGK+93a] investigated the conversion of character-based user interfaces into modern systems. The goal was to create a client/server architecture as well as the automation of the process. Premise here is that the existing application may not be changed or adjusted. Therefore, they fit the new GUI on top of the existing one and defined a mapping between the graphical elements.

For this purpose, the source code is analyzed. The structure of the GUI is derived from the AST and is described in the Abstract User Interface Design Language (AUDIL). It forms the basis for new development. In [MGK+93b] the approach is expanded to user actions and system responses.

Stroulia

et al. [SERIS03] also transformed character-based interfaces. They developed a process called CELLEST. It contains different modeling and analysis components. The aim of the process is the transformation of existing interfaces into web applications. Therefore, the authors record the execution of an application. Thereafter, the most common paths are evaluated. Again, the existing application may not be adjusted. Based on the paths the surface as well as a *translation proxy* are developed. The latter translates commands and data between old and new interface.

Antoniol

et al. [AFMT95] are concerned with text-based interfaces again. Core of their work wa the evolution of PC-based legacy systems.

The authors examined GUIs that have been implemented in the programming language BASIC and migrated them to C++. At first an AST and a control flow graph are calculated. Afterwards the hierarchy of graphical elements is derived. This is the starting point for the new interface. A problem which is emphasized by the authors, is the localization of callback routines. These are required in order to bind the old functionality to the new system.

Summary

The graphical user interface is one of the core issues in the migration of software. The analysis and preparation of the interface could contribute to the application understanding process. One evident problem is the integration of existing functionality into the new GUI. Extra effort is required to reliably detect the callback routines.

The present study is mainly based on the ideas of Michail as well as Tucker and Stirewalt. The developed GUI analysis combines the presentation model and the application model. For a better understanding of the system, a browsing mechanism is implemented, which allows access from the interface to the callback routines. Thus, the maintenance engineer is enabled, starting from the user interface, to investigate and understand the associated functionality.

5 Case Study: DeAs

In this chapter the model-driven migration approach is applied to a mid-scale software system. The purpose of the DeAs system is the management of experiments and the control of a wind tunnel. The system was chosen due to the following aspects:

- It is a legacy system.
- The system is distinctly more extensive[1] than the usual examples from scientific literature.
- It is used in real, experiences and requirements of the users are based on daily operation.
- The project covers various areas of computer science: program development, scientific computing and control.

At First, the application area and the existing software system are explained. The latter includes a brief description of the operation as well as a representation of technical problems and further shortcomings.

Based on the current state of the DeAs system the software reverse engineering, the analysis of the program code and a prototypical migration of the system are described. Internal processes of the present wind tunnel software are remodeled with the help of the jABC modeling tool. The aim is to improve application understanding, to clean up the program code as well as to increase flexibility in the system architecture. Therefore process-related services are derived from the existing system and the corresponding program code is separated. The separation of the system based on the remodeling imposes a new, process-driven architecture on the system. Thus simple services can be exchanged, reused and/or new services are integrated. The result is much more flexible than its predecessor. The program code is generated entirely, applying different code generators.

The migration project was examined in terms of its applicability to a top-down as well as a bottom-up approach. It turned out that the first approach does not lead to the desired result (cf. Chapter 5.3). Therefore

---

[1] It contains more than 100,000 lines of code.

the development of a deeper understanding of the software using a bottom-up analysis (cf. Chapter 5.4) is required for the necessary changes.

The respective phases of model-driven migration (cf. Chapter 3.4) and the necessary developments are introduced in detail. These include an introduction of shared, expanded and reused tools, the description of the abstraction steps, the semi-automatic extraction of process models as well as the slicing of the existing system. Another focus is the support of the maintenance engineer, including application understanding, process control and remodeling as well as migration of the system.

5.1 Excursus: Operation of a Wind Tunnel

The German-Dutch Wind Tunnels (DNW)-Foundation is a consortium of wind tunnels of the German Aerospace Center (DLR) and the Dutch Nationaal Lucht- en Ruimtevaartlaboratorium (NLR). The organization is a service provider for experiments in the field of fluid mechanics. Twelve different experimental facilities in Germany and the Netherlands belong to the Foundation. Thus, a wide spectrum of measurements with different pressure, temperature and velocity ranges can be covered.

The case study software is used at different wind tunnels of DNW Germany. In order for it to be easier to classify the environment and thus the requirements as well as the functionality of a wind tunnel software, a wind tunnel is introduced briefly below. The foundation also is the main stakeholder of the DeAs software.

Experiments in a wind tunnel are often applied in basic research, e.g the validation of computational models, which were calculated for a certain body, as well as the certification of aerodynamic systems. These include aircraft components, trains, but also solid structures such as bridges. Usually prior to these experiments so called Computational Fluid Dynamics (CFD) calculations are performed, in order to find the optimal form for the expected natural conditions. The results are reproduced in the experiment and validated to verify the body. The wind tunnel must simulate certain parameters such as pressure, temperature and velocity very accurately in order to meet the expected conditions.

In the following the operation of the Transonic Wind Tunnel Göttingen (DNW-TWG) (cf. Figure 5.1) is explained. The DNW-TWG is a continuously operating wind tunnel, which means the air is circulating in the tunnel. The power unit has to compensate the losses caused by friction on

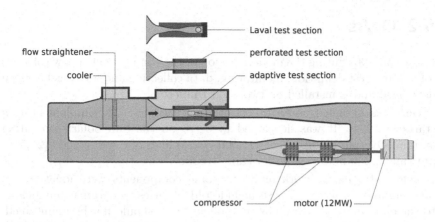

Figure 5.1: Transonic Wind Tunnel Göttingen (DNW-TWG)

the model and on the walls only. This form was developed in Göttingen and is therefore also called Göttinger Design[2].

The DNW-TWG has three distinct test sections (in Figure 5.1 shown above). They simulate different speed (Ma=0.3 to Ma=2.2) and pressure ranges (30 kPa to 150 kPa). The cross section of each test section is 1.0 m by 1.0 m. The flow is driven by an eight-stage compressor and a twelve-megawatt electric motor (Figure 5.1 bottom right). Additionally the wind tunnel has an external cooling system. The filters and rectifiers in the upper part intercept larger particles and enable a homogeneous flow in front of the test section.

Different Siemens Programmable Logic Controllers (PLCs) monitor and control the wind tunnel. They control certain set values (pressures, temperatures and position of the model). These are pre-defined in a measurement log and processed during an experiment. A software system developed by the German Aerospace Center (DLR) executes the definition of an experiment. It controls the set values and the data collection.

Through the further development of the measuring and computation technology, today's experiments are more complex and elaborate. This results in new requirements on the flexibility of the experimental equipment, measuring and control technology as well as associated software.

---

[2]   Named after the scientist Ludwig Prandtl (1875-1953).

5.2 DeAs

In the early 90s during the modernization of the wind tunnel, a new software for control, test definition, monitoring, data collection and analysis has been developed and is installed on two wind tunnels.

DeAs[3] is designed as an object-oriented system. The implementation starts in 1992. It was developed in C++ on the Sun Solaris operating system. Overall, it consists of 111,000 (76 %) lines of C++, 32,000 (21,5 %) of C and 2,200 lines (1,5 %) Fortran 77 code[4].

Before starting to work on DeAs some components were identified as obsolete and excluded. These include old libraries, programs that belong to the data analysis, as well as components that should not be maintained. Therefore the examined source code comprises 97,000 Lines of Code (LOC).

Currently DeAs version 3.6 is used on Solaris 2.6 and 2.8. For the evolution of the system the developer documentation for version 1.0 [GHK95, GHK00, Sac97] and the User's Manual for version 2.4 were available.

5.2.1 DeAs System Architecture

DeAs consists of 21 applications. All of them are developed around a monolithic core consisting of seven libraries (Figure 5.2). The core includes various functionalities like user interface, drivers for devices, data acquisition, and an interface to external processes.

For the evaluation of measured data small amounts were also developed in Fortran 77. This part is not considered in detail.

In Figure 5.2 the architecture of an application is illustrated. A monolithic core which is integrated as library in each application is in the center. In addition, further libraries are based on this core. Depending on the application, they can be additionally included. The libraries contain features for the graphical user interface, the storage of data, drivers for measurement equipment or data visualization and configuration.

Additionally with version 2.x, the core was extended with an interface for external processes (Figure 5.2 below). The file interface communicates via a file-based protocol with drivers for measurement equipment, the wind tunnel control or the visualization systems. This approach is especially advantageous with regards to the integration of customer systems: The core system does not have to be adjusted anymore.

---

[3] It is a German acronym and stands for Data Acquisition and Tunnel Control Software.
[4] The values shown were determined using the program `sloccount` (version 2.26).

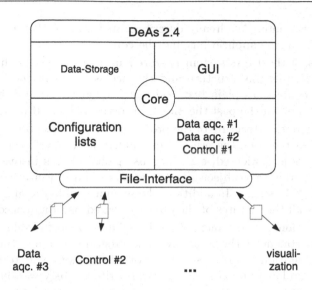

Figure 5.2: The monolithic core of the DeAs system

Problems within the Architecture

However, through the exchange of different measurement systems and the further development of the DeAs system has accumulated an unknown amount of dead code in the core libraries. Furthermore, the development of the vast majority of drivers has taken place in the system and within the department or alternatively was adjusted by external companies to the operating system. This concerns the communication with the PLCs. The driver was developed by Siemens and will not be updated.

The graphical interface is another critical point of the architecture. It is distributed over core and applications. The GUI is based on OpenLook developed by Sun Microsystems at the end of the 80s. OpenLook describes a guideline for the design of graphical user interfaces and has been implemented for the X Window System. The support for this library has been discontinued with version 2.8 of the Sun Solaris operating system. Since OpenLook is based on X, it is possible to execute OpenLook applications. A further or new development is no longer possible due to the lack of libraries. DeAs has been developed as a graphical application, so this limitation affects the entire system. The number of affected lines of code are very difficult to estimate. As already described above, the GUI functionality is distributed over the applications and the core.

The data of the DeAs system is stored in a self-developed hierarchical database. It uses the structure and the access rights of the file system. The files are stored as plain text and can be changed at any time by the respective users. In the past the manual processing has led to problems.

Furthermore the structure of the program code needs to be improved. In some parts of the code the original developers have developed procedural rather than object-oriented, e.g. they use global classes instead of global variables. At this time object-oriented analysis and object-oriented design were in the early stages. In addition, the compiler and system libraries did not support all the features of the object-oriented paradigm accordingly.

Modernization is furthermore exacerbated due to most developers having left the department or the company. The program code and the fragmentary documentation form the sole basis of information. Due to the lack of knowledge and low resources, a complete rewrite strategy was out of scope. The project goal, was a slow but steady migration of the DeAs system (cf. Chapter 2.5.3).

Classification as Legacy System

In summary it can be stated that DeAs fully meets the criteria for legacy systems defined in Chapter 2.3.2. In Table 5.1 the associated evaluation criteria are presented. The symbols +, – und o mean satisfied, not satisfied or partially met.

Only criteria KLS09 (cf. Table 5.1) is marked as not applicable. The DeAs versions on the two wind tunnels differ in their configuration, but not in their code base. Due to the above mentioned problems not all user requirements can be realized. Therefore KLS13 was classified as partially met. One of the original twelve developers is still working in the DLR (KLS03 partially met). In contrast, the obsolete documentation (KLS01) and the lack of test cases (KLS02) correspond fully to the criteria for legacy systems. DeAs is also relevant for business (KLS04). The maintenance of several components of the system (KLS05) is not longer performed by the manufacturers (Siemens and Sun Microsystems). The criteria KLS07 (unknown architecture), KLS08 (missing knowledge about the overall system), KLS10 (time-intensive maintenance) and KLS12 (duplicated code) result from the lack of knowledge. In turn this is due to poor documentation (cf. Chapter 5.2.4) and the developers are no longer available.

Table 5.1: Evaluation criteria of the DeAs legacy system

Criteria	Evaluation	Description
KLS01	+	outdated documentation
KLS02	+	missing test cases
KLS03	o	missing developers
KLS04	+	high business relevance
KLS05	+	expired maintenance contracts
KLS06	o	long time of translation
KLS07	+	unknown Architecture
KLS08	+	overall system not understood
KLS09	–	many versions
KLS10	+	time-consuming maintenance
KLS11	o	backlog of changes
KLS12	+	duplicated code

5.2.2 DeAs Applications and Libraries

An overview of all DeAs applications and libraries is given in Tables 5.2 to 5.5. This includes a description and the size in LOC.

Table 5.2: DeAs – configuration of wind tunnel and test object

Appl.	LOC	Description
An_an	1013	Creating tunnel: Creating a new wind tunnel or select an already existing for further processing.
An_be	4142	Edit tunnel: defines the structure of a wind tunnel. Generally, it contains different components (hardware) which are described by static and dynamic parameters and measurement values.
An_ko	3673	Configure tunnel: combines components into so-called configurations.
Mo_an	1310	Create or select a model (analog An_an)
Mo_be	4656	Edit a model (analog An_be)
Mo_ko	3668	Configure a model (analog An_ko)

Table 5.3: DeAs – configuration of the measurement technique

Appl.	LOC	Description
Mg_be	5344	Edit measurement values: managing of measurement equipment and calibrations.
Mg_se	3065	Edit sensor: is developed for certain sensors.
Mg_wa	4692	Edit balance: is specially designed for wind tunnel balances.
Me_ko	1054	Configure measurement values: variables of the model and the wind tunnel are grouped to configurations. They are measured in an experiment together.
In_an	1534	Creating instrumentation: Creating a new instrumentation or select an existing one for further processing.
In_be	246	Edit Instrumentation: assigns measurement values of tunnel/model to real measurement devices.
Vg_be	2157	Edit virtual devices: processed already measured data. These can be configured using Vg_be.

Programs belonging to the DeAs system can be divided into three categories: Applications of the first are responsible for the configuration of wind tunnel, model, instrumentation and measurement of project (Tables 5.2 to 5.4). They store their data in the hierarchical database. Furthermore the applications depend on each other. A measurement project can be created when the system, the model and the instruments are configured.

The second category includes just one application and is responsible for the execution of a real experiment. The application Ap_au (Table 5.4) executes the defined test plan step-by-step. It aggregates all configurations, sends all set values to the wind tunnel, records the measured data and stores it in a measurement protocol.

The analysis, evaluation and archiving falls into the last category (Table 5.4). These programs can be used during and after a measurement in order to evaluate and validate the measured data.

Table 5.5 describes seven libraries of the DeAs system. Only the first three are used by any application. All others are deployed to few DeAs applications only.

Table 5.4: DeAs – define and execute a test project

Appl.	LOC	Description
Mv_an	1857	Creating a test plan: Creating a new test or selecting an existing project for further processing. A test plan describes the whole experiment.
Ap_an	1249	Creating a measurement program: Creating a new measurement program or selecting an already existing for further processing. Different measurement programs belong to one experiment.
Ap_be	4546	Edit measurement program: divides a measurement program into several steps (run, polar and measuring point) and defines the set values (pressure, temperature, etc.) as well as the quantities of the values to be measured.
Ap_au	7205	Execute measurement program: is the actual execution of the experiment. The defined measurement program is executed and the data is recorded.
Ar_be	1160	Edit archive: archives the measured data and all configuration files of an experiment.
Aw_be	7294	Edit evaluation: evaluates the measured data.
Pr_aw	760	Select protocol: For each measurement point, a separate protocol is prepared. It can be selected with Pr_aw and viewed with Pr_as.
Pr_as	2508	View protocol, refer to Pr_aw.
DeAsManager	818	The DeAsManager is the central process instance. It combines all applications listed here. It represents the work flow of an experiment from configuration to execution and evaluation. Furthermore, it displays the selected configurations, tunnel, model and measurement project.
GPM	860	The device manager controls several processes (start/stop/send commands). It communicates via file interface with the DeAs system. Usually this is associated with data recording of different types of equipment.

Table 5.5: DeAs – system libraries

Appl.	LOC	Description
libDeAs	5405	The library is the basis for all DeAs applications and further libraries. It contains self-implemented data structures such as lists and general methods for error handling. It has the character of a standard library.
libDeAsFenster	4037	The library contains a collection of functions and components of the graphical user interface.
libDeAsKlassen	19774	The library contains classes for the persistence of configurations and measurement data.
libGI	709	The library contains the communication interface and management capabilities for devices.
libKorrektur	1982	libKorrektur is a library for the correction and analysis of measurement results.
libSPS	303	The library contains methods that ensure data exchange between PLC and DeAs.
libVGI	856	The library includes the communication interface and management capabilities for virtual devices.

5.2.3 Definition of the Measurement Program

The following section describes the functionality of DeAs. This includes the configuration of an experiment, of the wind tunnel and the model, the measurement equipment as well as the test plan. As discussed in the last section, a majority of DeAs applications is responsible for handling and maintaining this information.

The structure of an experiment consists of two parts. On the one hand the experimental setup (wind tunnel, model, measurement equipment) and on the other the experimental procedure. The latter builds on the configuration defined in the first step and divides the experiment into small work packages. To provide a better understanding, the relation of these components as well as the internal processes and the complexity of the software are shown below.

Definition of the Experimental Procedure

The configuration structure of system and model are identical. They are merely distinguished in order to create a clear separation between the *ex-*

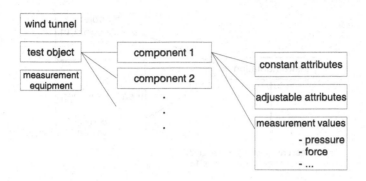

Figure 5.3: Properties of a wind tunnel model

perimental platform and the *experimental subject*. Therefore the model is discussed only.

The overall configuration of an experiment includes all properties of the wind tunnel, the model and the measurement equipment. These components do not change during a measurement program. Figure 5.3 shows the structure of these attributes. First, the attributes are grouped together into different components (component 1, component 2), e.g. an aircraft model consists of wing, body and nose.

In turn, each component has two different kinds of parameters. The static or constant attributes are always the same regardless of the experiment, e.g. weight, size or balance point. Furthermore there are elements in the model, which may vary during an experiment (flaps or flap positions). These are defined as changeable properties (adjustable attributes). All measured physical parameters (pressures, temperatures, forces) are stored in the third group, the measurement values.

The second part of the experiment configuration defines the sequences of the measurement program. This requires a completed description of the experimental setup. The configuration of the experiment is build on the instrumentation (Figure 5.4).

The instrumentation combines the defined measurement values with the real physics. That means each measurement variable is assigned to exactly one measurement value of a measurement device. The data are usually collected as electrical voltage. They are converted inside the system into another physical quantity, such as pressure or temperature.

The structure of the instrumentation is shown in Figure 5.4. The model and a measurement device are on the right side. The measurement device

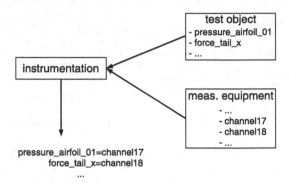

Figure 5.4: Instrumentation of measurement values

provides several data acquisition channels. Some measurement values have
been defined for the model (pressure_airfoil_01, ...). The instrumentation
associates the real physics with the model configuration, e.g. pressure on
wing 01 is associated with channel 17. Additionally for each channel a
calibration can be defined which converts a value into a physical quantity.

Description of the Experimental Procedure

The second part of the experiment configuration is the definition of a measurement project (cf. Figure 5.5). It includes an instrumentation and the
description of a sequence of steps that set the wind tunnel and the model
to defined states.

A measurement project always consists of measuring sections (run), measuring series (polars) and measuring points (measurement point). A measurement point is the smallest unit and defines the physical conditions in
the wind tunnel. During the execution of a measuring point, the DeAs
system transfers set values to the PLCs of the wind tunnel. These control the desired setpoints. Once they have reached sufficient accuracy, the
measurement engineer can start the recording of the measured data.

Measuring points which contain a constant physical value, e.g. speed,
form a polar. In Figure 5.5 the polar has a constant Mach number
(MA=0.65). The data points differ in the angle between model and flow. A
measurement section includes various polars. The run is finished once the
model or the wind tunnel has to be modified for a new configuration.

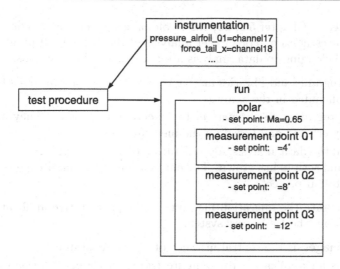

Figure 5.5: Configuration of a measurement mroject

5.2.4 Selection of the System Components

In the previous chapter it was been shown that several factors influence the development and migration of the DeAs system. Central problems are the monolithic core, the architecture and the lack of knowledge about the system. Furthermore, there is a lack of test cases and an obsolete documentation of design and program code for reliable development. The existing source documentation subsumes 43,000 lines (29 % of the total amount of LOC). 85% of these are allocated to the description of file and function headers (e.g. creation date, author, last modification). Usually the algorithms are not documented.

The major problems also include the outdated graphical system library OpenLook, the hierarchical database based on the file system as well as the proprietary communication protocol to the PLCs from Siemens.

Porting to a current Solaris operating system is not possible because some system components (implementation of the communication protocol) are not able to work on 64-bit systems. Further no developer libraries are supplied for OpenLook. In a first step the system should be understood and the system structure renovated. This contains the redocumentation and remodeling of internal processes.

As noted in Chapter 5.2, not the whole program code is considered in the present investigation. For further analysis of the system, all programs and libraries belonging to data analysis are ignored for three reasons:

- The programs and libraries are partly written in Fortran. This language is not included in the analysis.
- Most programs are not part of DeAs-core applications. They are additionally created and based on the measured data.
- Around the data analysis, a proliferation of different, proprietary applications and scripts has grown. The elimination of this landscape is another downstream project.

To illustrate the migration method, four representative applications are selected from the DeAs-core system:

DeAsManager is the central instance of the DeAs system.

An_an is an application to configure the wind tunnel. It was chosen to illustrate the algorithms and processes, because of its simplicity.

An_be is one of the larger and more complex applications of the configuration. It creates the components with the corresponding attributes for a wind tunnel or a model shown in Figure 5.3. It is chosen to prove the scalability of the approach.

Ap_au was chosen because it is responsible for the execution of an experiment. The program has the most LOC of all DeAs applications.

5.3 Top-Down Approach

The first analysis of the DeAs system starts with the `DeAsManager`. It is the central instance of all DeAs applications and the starting point for the configuration of experiments. Furthermore, the `DeAsManager` has a very simple and clear structure. Its functionality is to restore and to display the current configuration of a user. Starting from the graphical user interface (cf. Figure 5.6) all DeAs applications can be executed as external processes.

The approach consists of the following steps:

- remodeling the `DeAsManager` as a process model,
- linking these models with the implemented DeAs functionality,
- use of Java Native Interface (JNI) and adaptation of existing code,
- propagation of the approach to other DeAs applications and
- connection of DeAs libraries using JNI.

Figure 5.6: DeAsManager – user interface

Due to the top-down approach this application was modeled in jABC based on the structure of the graphical interface. Thereafter the existing functionality of the DeAsManager was linked to the process model.

For modeling, the program code was first manually examined and relevant process elements extracted. Figure 5.7 illustrates a process model that describes the start-up of the DeAsManager. At first the user is identified (UserDetection)[5]. If the user exists in the database, the current configuration is loaded (upper part: UserSettingsLoad). Thereafter the graphical interface of the DeAsManager is started. If the user is unknown, a new user is created in the database and a default configuration loaded (lower part: CreateUser and DefaultSettingsLoad). Any further applications of the DeAs system can be started via the graphical user interface (in the image on the right: Wind Tunnel, Model, Device and Experiment). These are organized in sub-models as indicated with Model.

In the next step, the developed model was linked to the appropriate functionality. The process model of the DeAsManager is supposed to be able, as its original, to launch the associated DeAs applications. Since DeAs applications are implemented in C++ it is not possible to directly access them. The Java language is necessary to connect process model and existing functionality. For this gap the suitability of the middleware system Common Object Request Broker Architecture (CORBA) and native execution using Java Native Interface (JNI) was investigated. CORBA requires a lot of effort due to the necessary client and server implementation. Therefore it was postponed. However a JNI implementation is considerably less expensive.

---

[5] Internally, the standard UNIX/Linux system variable $USER is used.

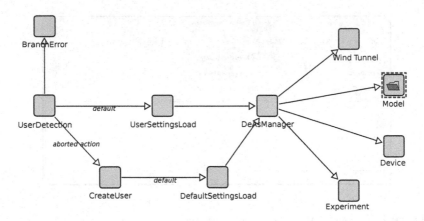

Figure 5.7: DeAsManager – process model (start of application)

```
    Listing 5.1: main-Function of DeAs application

1  /*
2   *   main for project Ap_an
3   */
4  int
5  main (int argc, char **argv)
6  {
7     Icon  base_frame_image;
8     Benutzer hilfBenutzer;
9     ...
```

Certainly the conversion of data types and the management of the build process must be taken into account.

Linking with the Existing Source Code

Prerequisite to call a DeAs application via JNI, is the replacement of the main function by a generated JNI function (ll. 4-5 in Listing 5.1 and Listing 5.2). The following are necessary:

- Definition of a Java class,
- generation of a C++ header definition that contains the method name and parameters of the interface described in the Java class using the program javah and

---

Listing 5.2: DeAs application with the replaced `main`-function

```
1  /*
2   *  main for project Ap_an
3   */
4  JNIEXPORT jstring JNICALL
       Java_aero_dnw_prototype_deas_apan_Ap_1an__1C_1Ap_1anImpl
5  (JNIEnv *env, jobject myclass)
6  {
7    Icon base_frame_image;
8    Benutzer hilfBenutzer;
9    ...
```

- inclusion of header file and replacement of the function in the original program code.

A detailed description can be found in Gordon [Gor98, pp. 8, Fig. 2-1].

Translating the C++ source code proves to be rather challenging: At run time JNI can only reload one shared library. Reason for this is that JNI can not resolve C/C++ symbols that are located in another library. Therefore the entire DeAs application with all dependencies must be translated into one library. These respective libraries can exceed 50 MB.

Furthermore all `exit` functions in the DeAs code must be replaced by `return` statements. Since the C++ instance runs in the process of the modeling tool, the call of a function `exit` causes the termination of the whole process.

The original `DeAsManager` created separate processes for all started applications. Thus it was possible to work in parallel with multiple programs. However, the implementation chosen here excludes multithreading, because the call of DeAs application will block the entire modeling environment[6].

Except for the lack of concurrency, the modeled `DeAsManager` has an identical be[7]. The `DeAsManager` is illustrated as central instance and all DeAs applications are arranged in a circle around.

Expansion of the Remodeling

Subsequent to the modeling of the `DeAsManager`, the top-down approach is to be applied to all other applications. However, they are much more

---

[6] The used jABC version 1.6.1 did not have the ability to remodel concurrent processes in the process model. This issue was fixed with a later version.
[7] Model is presented in German.

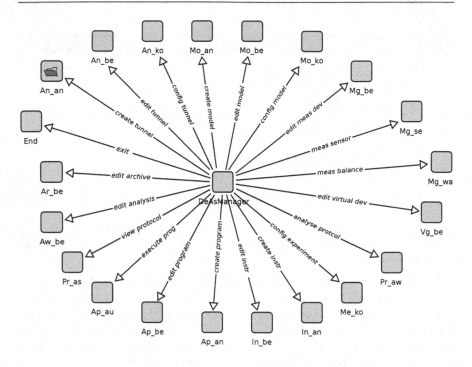

Figure 5.8: `DeAsManager` – process model (start of DeAs applications)

complex and reuse the functionalities of the DeAs libraries to a large extent. To remodel the applications, each method of the DeAs libraries are made available using JNI. Now they can be used as a building block for the process of remodeling in jABC.

Such an approach does not correspond to the model-driven idea, since programming is shifted to the model level. The problems outlined above with the native execution of C++ program code impede their use: For each class within the libraries a JNI representation was created and translated. Both, the size of the libraries as well as the required time for translation, make the approach impractical. The translation process lasts 30 minutes for 60 classes with 500 methods.

Based on the libraries, other functionalities of the individual applications were remodeled and transferred into the process model. Again a manual analysis of the program code using a debugger was necessary. The program was executed step-by-step and the process model was developed in parallel. This procedure is less effective for larger systems and the created models are

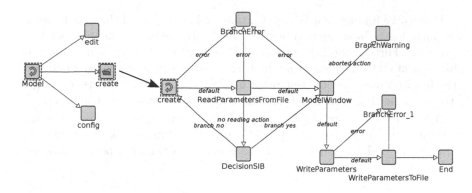

Figure 5.9: Modeling – definition of a wind tunnel

not complete. This is due to the debugger only following one path - and that path being depend on the inputs and parameters - within the application.

Figure 3 shows a model that describes the creation of a wind tunnel. On the left-hand side, the model can be created, edited or configured. The right-hand side illustrates the individual process steps for one item: create. This includes loading the current model configuration, opening a window for editing, and storing the data.

Using the SIBs derived from the libraries, the process models are supplemented by an implementation. This approach proved to be less feasible. A central problem represented the conversion of data types: The data types of parameters and return values can not be exchanged between process blocks. Instead, only the memory addresses are passed. The receiving DeAs function casts the memory address back to the appropriate data type. This solution is not practical for larger applications. It completely removes the type safety of programming languages.

Evaluation of the Top-Down Approach

The top-down approach demonstrates both technical and conceptual problems. Therefore, it is classified as partly useful. A very profound understanding of the system is required for remodeling an application on the one hand as well as for integrating the created SIBs into the process.

Usually an application includes 1,000-7,000 lines of code. They must be modeled and linked to an implementation. The model consists of both the SIBs already derived by the DeAs libraries as well as further additional developed process modules.

Due to the finding that the application understanding of the maintenance engineer has to be supported by extensive tools, the top-down approach was canceled. Furthermore, the question arises whether it is really necessary to implement all DeAs libraries methods as SIBs. In summary, the gap between the libraries and the first generated models (manual analysis) is too large. To overcome this, a thorough understanding of the system is necessary.

Alternatively, a bottom-up approach has been chosen. It extracts information from the source code and supports the maintenance engineer in application understanding. The focus is on remodeling the process models.

5.4 Model-driven Migration with DeAs

In the previous section as well as in the fundamentals (cf. Chapter 2.4) the necessity of a deep application understanding for extensive changes was already motivated. Based on the bottom-up approach defined in Chapter 3 (Figure 3.2) the application of the designed method is described in the following section. The DeAs system is transformed and migrated to a new platform (cf. Figure 3.4). Therefore necessary preliminary work, the applied and developed tools, the performance of the methods and problems encountered are described.

Primarily the focus is the concrete realization in the context of model-driven migration (cf. Chapter 3) and the described method fragments. The realization highly depends on the software system to be migrated. The programming language, for example, determines what tools are to be applied for the analysis of source code. Furthermore, the possibility for abstraction is coupled with the interface and libraries.

Starting from the definition of model-driven evolution (cf. Chapter 3.4) the following chapters are divided into model-driven reengineering (Chapter 5.5) and model-driven migration (Chapter 5.6) of the DeAs system. The main focus are the method fragments:

- Adjustment of a suitable analysis tool,
- the description of a data exchange format,
- the adaptation and application of a modeling tool,
- the development of various transformation languages for the analysis and abstraction of program code,
- the development and adaptation of different code generators as well as the prototypical migration of the system.

5.5 Model-Driven Reengineering

In model-driven reengineering the C/C++ program code of the DeAs system is analyzed with the help of the Elsa parser and translated into an annotated, platform-independent format (Chapter 5.5.1). Afterwards it is transformed into a control flow graph and processed in the modeling tool jABC (Chapter 5.5.2). In order to improve the application understanding, metrics and dependencies of the existing application are calculated in Chapter 5.5.3. The last step in model-driven reengineering contains the validation of the generated code-models using a code generator (Figure 3.5) and a *"Back-to-Back Test"* procedure (Chapter 5.5.4) .

5.5.1 Reverse Engineering

Figure 3.8 illustrates that the reverse engineering consists of small, consecutive steps. The result is the transformation of the program code into an annotated, platform-independent description. This is the basis for the subsequent analysis and abstraction phase.

Woods et al. [WOL+98, p. 57] use the term *Language Independent Format* (language-independent description), but language independence is not the aim in the present approach. Rather, the machine readability and the amount of maintainable information are in the focus.

In Chapter 4.1, various program analysis tools have already been investigated regarding their suitability for the code-model creation. For the present approach the Elsa C++ parser is applied. It is extended with a back-end to generate the annotated output format. The approach is based on the tool chain according to Arnold as well as Favre et al. (cf. Figure 3.7). The advantage of such an intermediate format is the decoupling of program analysis and information extraction.

Preparation of DeAs Source Code

The program code of the DeAs system had to be adapted in a few places during the project in order to optimize the processing or to correct errors. The modification is described below briefly. The semantics of the program code has not changed.

The C++ language has the ability to define specific methods within a class as `inline`. Corresponding markers are treated separately by the compiler to improve the performance of a system. These methods are not implemented in the C++ file, but already within the class definition in the header file. Since the analysis focuses on the code – due to performance and complexity reasons –, these definitions have been removed from the header and are copied into the C++ file. Otherwise they would not be available for the analysis of the system.

Furthermore, all macros (2 macros with 34 occurrences in the whole system) have been replaced. The Elsa parser requires as input C++ files that have been processed by a preprocessor. All comments are removed and header files as well as macros are replaced by their implementation. Without the manual substitution of macros, problems with the labeling of nodes occur during the transformation into a control flow graph. The nodes are named after the source line from the associated C++ file. The correct term can only be assured if no differences exist between the original and the preprocessed code. This step is essential for the code-model generator. The generation process is based on the label of each node.

Thirdly, various `extern` definitions have not met the C++ standard [KR90, p. 224]. `Extern` definitions are used in C/C++, to define the characteristics of external/global functions or objects. During compilation, objects defined as `extern` are integrated through libraries or further source files, respectively are defined globally in a system library. In combination with the Elsa parser, errors occurred when declaring objects or methods. As a result of wrong `extern` definitions various interprocedural analyzes are distorted because some objects are incorrectly linked or could not be found.

The only adjustment of program code, which also changes the semantics, concerns the evaluation of measurement data. In a few sections DeAs accesses Fortran routines which are not considered in detail. For a comprehensive analysis these have been replaced by stubs (function without implementation/behavior).

Development of an Elsa-Parser Back-End

The Elsa parser package includes a parser front-end for the languages C/C++ and different simple back-ends. The front-end is generated by the Elkhound parser generator and provides an annotated parse tree (AnST) for further processing. This tree is exported into a new output format with the help of a self-defined back-end. This chapter gives an overview of the design and implementation of the back-end.

Processing of Program Code by the Elsa Parser

The Elsa parser requires an already preprocessed C/C++ file, which is analyzed with the help of the ccparse program. Depending on the application, the parser can output data on various phases (parsing, type checking, semantic analysis). The format is simple text or structured text. The back-end TypedAST creates a textual representation of the abstract syntax tree. The output for the assignment b = 3; is exemplified in Listing 5.3.

Listing 5.3: Elsa – Extract from the AnST for statement b = 3;

```
1  user@host: > ccparse -tr printTypedAST File.i
2     ...
3  stmts[4] = S_expr:
4    succ={ 37:2 }
5    loc = test.cpp:35:2
6    expr = FullExpression:
7      expr = E_assign:
8        type: int &
9        target = E_variable:
10         type: int &
11         var: int b, at test.cpp:34:6
12         name = PQ_name:
13           loc = test.cpp:35:2
14           name = "b"
15       op = =
16       src = E_intLit:
17         type: int
18         i: 3
19         text = "3"
```

The example represents an expression of type S_Expr (l. 3). The assignment (l. 7) is composed of a variable (ll. 10-14) and a constant of type integer (ll. 17-19). Name and declaration of the variable (Test.cpp file, l. 34, col. 6) are also included. Furthermore, in line 4 the address of the next statement can be found.

This output contains information about the control flow as well as detailed information about individual program lines. Later, these are necessary to represent program code on model level. However, the standard output of Elsa is unstructured and requires much effort for processing due to the complex structure (depending on the number of blanks). Therefore a self-describing format was chosen.

Access to Elsa Internal Data Structure

The Elsa parser offers a well-structured interface for access to the internal data structures. It uses the visitor pattern [GHJV09, pp. 301][8] to encapsulate operations that work on the elements of the syntax tree. This interface includes two methods for each type of a node. The `visit` method is called when entering a node and the `postvisit` method when leaving.

To implement an own back-end a generic visitor class is available. This is part of an inheritance hierarchy which implements all necessary methods. Therefore, a fine tuning to specific items or information in the syntax tree is possible. Elsa has a total of 68 `visit-` and `postvisit` methods.

Structural Basis of the Code-Models

Following elements of the syntax tree are central:

TranslationUnit is the top element of the tree and represents a processed file. A `TranslationUnit` contains one or more `TopForm` nodes.

TopForm: Each `TopForm` element represents a function, a method or a name space. It contains name and path of the file being parsed and represents an independent syntax tree.

Function describes a function in the classical sense. The element contains parameters, return value and exception handling.

Statement: A statement represents a construct of the language. These elements are further subdivided into loops, branches, assignments and expressions. Each of them has specific attributes. In general, a statement includes further sub-elements such as an `Expression`.

Expression is an expression [McP12].

PQName is a fully qualified, distinguished name.

The structural basis of the code-models are the following elements: `TranslationUnit`, `TopForm` and `Statement`. Therefore, the `TopForm` element for functions and a loop statement of the type `S_for` as well as their properties are considered in detail.

The TopForm Element

The `TopForm`-element forms the root of the syntax tree. The structure for `TF_Func` is shown in Figure 5.10. It is derived from a generic `TopForm`

---

[8]   The visitor design pattern is used to group operations on object structures in external
       classes. This allows to add new operations without changing the object structure.
       This external class is called visitor class.

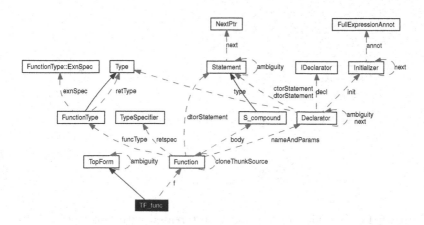

Figure 5.10: Overview of the `TF_func` object (created with Doxygen)

class (directed solid line). Furthermore, parameters and all associated elements are illustrated.

`TF_Func` has the parameter f (outgoing dashed line). It points to an object which contains further information relating to a particular function. The object includes the parameters (`nameAndParams`) as well as the return value (`retspec`) and a reference to the function body (`body`). The latter is a generic statement (`S_compound`). `S_compound` symbolizes an opening and a closing brace in C/C++. The element includes a list of all source lines of the method body (cf. [Str98, pp. 863, 868]).

The Statement Element

There are 22 characteristics of a statement. Each has general and specific statement attributes. The former include the location within the source code, the address of the successor nodes and the type of a statement. Depending on its classification further properties are added.

The localization is based on the scheme: `file:line:column` (cf. Listing 5.3 (l. 5)). Additionally, each statement is uniquely marked because line number and column are not duplicated. In Listing 5.3 (l. 4) the successor of the statements is given in the same notation. Since a statement can not span multiple files the file name is redundant.

A `For` loop is illustrated in Figure 5.11. It is derived from an abstract class and has various statement specific attributes. This contains initial-

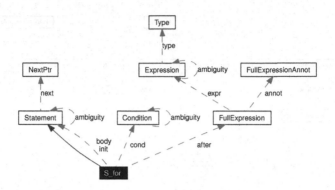

Figure 5.11: Overview of the For loop (created with Doxygen)

ization (init), loop body (body), termination condition (cond) and loop counter (after).

Analogously, this applies for branches (S_if). They include specific attributes like a condition (cond) and the two branches (then, else).

Construction of the New Data Structure

On the basis of Elsa's internal representation the back-end is based on a new tree structure. The leaves are represented by statements. Therefore the AnST is cut off after the statement nodes. All elements that are below a statement in the tree structures, are assigned to the leaf nodes as attributes, e.g. in Listing 5.3 starting from FullExpression (ll. 6-19).

In addition, a list of edges is calculated. This will support the subsequent transformation into a control flow graph (cf. Chapter 5.5.2). The details of the successors of the respective statements are necessary for the list of edges. The succ element (cf. Listing 5.3) contains one or more entries. Their assignment is done according to the statement type. Thus, e.g. the successors of a branch can be distinguished in then and else.

The result is a reformatted AnST which contains a high density of information on each statement. Later these data can be used in data flow analysis, for optimization or for dependency analysis (cf. Chapter 5.5.3).

The back-end uses the Decorator design pattern [GHJV09, p. 199] to generate the data format described in the next section. Each element of the tree has a decorator. It can describe the item in the notation specified by the data format.

As lookahead, a reference to the XML output in Listing 5.4 is given. It is illustrated that the Decorator for `E_assign` processes different data than the Decorator for an `E_variable`. The latter includes information from type check, such as the declaration location of the variable (`refersto`).

Listing 5.4: Elsa – XML output

```
1  <expr_kind kind="E_assign" operator="="/>
2  <expr_kind kind="E_variable" type="int &amp;"
3     var="int b" refersto="test.cpp:34:6" />
4  <pqname pqname="b" loc="test.cpp:35:2" name="b"/>
5  <expr_kind kind="E_intLit" type="int" value="3"/>
```

Test and Performance of the Back-end

The developed Elsa back-end has been tested with various files. The Elsa parser itself provides 880 test files. They are included in the project. Furthermore, the test suite of the GCC for C/C++ was used. Overall, the back-end has been tested successfully with 1,200 test files.

Difficulties are primarily tests that lead to an expected error in the Elsa front-end (syntax errors or type check errors). These were eliminated, because they have no influence on the back-end. Furthermore not all test cases from the GCC test suite could be reused. This is due to the reason that most tests correspond to the error handling in the front-end. Therefore the result is an expected error or that certain characteristics of the GCC compiler, which are not covered by the standard, are evaluated. In most cases, this is documented in the test cases themselves, and they were excluded.

With the help of the test cases, it was possible to optimize the memory usage and processing of individual elements of the AnST.

Furthermore, an already integrated profiling mechanism could be reused for the back-end to evaluate the performance. It measures the time required by the parser during different phases. The results are available for each processed file.

Listing 5.5: ccparse – Program output

```
1  user@host: > ./ccparse ./in/AsciiDatei.C.i
2  typechecking results:
3    errors:   0
4    warnings: 0
5  XML output Back-end
6  XML output Back-end - end
7  parse=278ms tcheck=190ms integ=9ms elab=111ms backend=2682ms
```

Listing 5.5 represents the time required in the individual phases (syntax, type check, back-end, etc.) of the parser. The back-end developed here (Listing 5.5 marked with `backend`), requires the majority of the resources for the transformation of the internal data structure.

Description of the Intermediate Representation

A platform-independent format has been defined for the exchange of data between the Elsa parser back-end and a modeling tool. It was not possible to determine the precise requirements on such a format at the beginning of the project. Different existing formats for the representation of program code or graphs are discussed in Chapter 4.2. They serve as template. The separation of node and edge descriptions was reused to simplify the creation of the control flow graph in the phase of modeling.

The defined data format is based on the XML description language to achieve a maximum tool and platform independence. It is strongly influenced by the GraphXML format introduced in Chapter 4.2. It was preferred in this particular case, because composition and structure are significantly less complex. Both the structure of nodes and edges are separate descriptions. Additionally various attributes (numbering of the graphs, nodes and edges) are applied.

Description of the Graphs in the Intermediate Format

Below a brief example for the defined format is presented. A meta-description in the form of DTD can be found in Appendix A.

Listing 5.6: Extract from the annotated intermediate format

```
1  <graph id="3">
2   <graph_attr type="Function"
3     loc="test.cpp:9:5"
4     fnname="main"
5     qualifiedname="_global_ _definition_ int main(int argc, char
         **argv)"
6     suc="{ 11:2 }" >
7   <params>
8     ...
9     <typespecifier loc="test.cpp:9:10" id = "int"/>
10    <declarator context="DC_D_FUNC" var = "int argc" type = "int
         "/>
11    <pqname pqname="argc" loc="test.cpp:9:14" name="argc"/>
12    ...
13  </params>
14  <return>
```

```
15    <typespecifier loc="test.cpp:9:1" id = "int"/>
16    </return>
17    <![CDATA[int main(int argc, char *argv[])]]>
18    </graph_attr>
19    ...
20  </graph>
```

An excerpt of the format is illustrated in Listing 5.6. A new graph starts with the <graph> element (l. 1). The attribute id is an incremented counter, which provides each graph with a unique number. This reflects both the number of TopForm elements within a TranslationUnit and also the amount of analyzed methods.

A general description of the present function follows after the <graph> element. It is initiated by the <graph_attr> element and consists of different attributes and three sub-elements. The attributes contain information about the location (l. 3), the function name (l. 4, fnname), the fully qualified name (l. 5) and the address of the first statement (l. 6, usually a compound statement, cf. Listing 5.6) of the function body. The three sub-elements are divided into:

<params>: A description of the parameters of the function. The first parameter of the main function is shown in Listing 5.6 (ll. 7-13).

<return>: The return value of the function is illustrated in Listing 5.6, lines 14-16.

<![CDATA[...]]>: The original line from the program code is localized and stored in a CDATA section (l. 17). This section can contain any character data. It is not evaluated by the XML parser. A conflict between reserved symbols in XML and constructs of the programming language (&, <,>) is avoided.

Localization of the Source Code

The localization of the code within the existing sources is complicated by different programming styles. Use of macros can lead to incorrect results. As already described in the introduction, the Elsa parser uses preprocessed code as input. Hence, all macros are already expanded. However, the localization of the source line must be done on the original, non-preprocessed sources. But the parser defines the source line always relative to the preprocessed file and not to the original one. Usually the preprocessed file is much larger than the original file, since all #include statements are replaced and copied into the file. Thus the original program code slips to the end of the file. However, the parser does not calculate the offset between the original and preprocessed file. In the present example the offset has an average of more than 50,000 lines.

Due to performance reasons, a time consuming search in the preprocessed file is to be avoided. Therefore all macros must be replaced in advance by the appropriate program code.

Listing 5.7: Pseudo-code – Extract a source line from code

```
1  program: readSourceLine
2  parameter: filename, linenumber, columnnumber, statement type
3      // a new line of source code will be read from file
4      sloc = getLineFromFile(linenumber);
5
6      // trim string on left side - with columnnumber
7      sloc = sloc.substr( column-1, sloc.length() );
8
9      // check type of statement and source line
10     if ( type == "Statement_COMPOUND" )
11          findBracket(); // find left brace
12     if ( type == "Statement_DOWHILE" )
13          findWhile(linenumber);
14     if ( type == "Statement_TRY") {
15          findTryCatch(linenumber);
16     if ( type == "Statement_EXPR" || type == "Statement_DECL" ||
17          type == "Statement_FUNCTION" || type == "Statement_RETURN
                  " ||
18          type == "Statement_NAMESPACEDECL" || type == "
                  Statement_BREAK" ||
19          type == "Statement_GOTO" || type == "Statement_CONTINUE")
20          findSemiColon(linenumber);
21     if ( type == "Function" || type == "Statement_IF" ||
22          type == "Statement_FOR" || type == "Statement_WHILE" ||
23          type == "Statement_SWITCH" || type == "
                  Statement_COMPUTEDGOTO")
24          findParenthesis(linenumber);
25     if ( type == "Statement_CASE" || type == "Statement_RANGECASE"
                  ||
26          type == "Statement_DEFAULT" || type == "Statement_LABEL")
27          findColon(linenumber);
28
29     return sloc;
```

The pseudo-code in Listing 5.7 provides a general procedure for the programming languages C/C++. The algorithm reads the corresponding source line from the file and removes leading and trailing spaces (ll. 4 and 7). In the next step the algorithm searches, depending on the type of the statement, a terminating character. A loop or a branch is closed by round bracket (ll. 21-24). Further symbols are terminated by colon (for multiple branches), semicolon or curly braces. Furthermore, a source line may also extend multiple lines within a file (e.g. parameter lists or complex boolean expressions). The algorithm reads further program lines until it detects an appropriate terminating character.

Description of Node Properties

All statements within a method are defined using the <node> element. Comparable to the <graph> element, it has a number that is locally unique within a method. The identification of the node is derived from the location of the statement and is composed of the row and column number (row:column).

Listing 5.8: Node description and associated attributes

```
1  <node id="35:2">
2    <node_attr type="S_expr" loc="test.cpp:35:2"
3      line="35" column="2" succ="{ 37:2 }" >
4      <expression>
5      <expr_kind kind="E_assign" operator="="/>
6      <expr_kind kind="E_variable"
7        type="int &amp;" var="int b"
8        refersto="test.cpp:34:6" />
9      <pqname pqname="b" loc="test.cpp:35:2"
10        name="b"/>
11      <expr_kind kind="E_intLit" type="int"
12        value="3"/>
13    </expression>
14    <![CDATA[b=3;]]>
15    </node_attr>
16  </node>
```

In Listing 5.8 a node is illustrated which describes the statement b = 3;[9]. Similar to the <graph> element all attributes that are assigned to a statement can be found in the <node-attr> element. Each statement contains a fixed set of data. These include the following properties (ll. 2-3):

Type is the type of the statement (loop, branch, etc.).

Loc corresponds to the address in the source file.

Line and column represent row and column in the source file.

Succ contains a list of successor nodes.

In addition to the fixed data set more statement-specific attributes are available. For example, a branch contains the additional attributes then

---

[9] Listing 5.3 shows the same statement in the Elsa output format.

and else. They refer to the respective child nodes and are addressed by the known localization schema row:column. This is especially helpful for the construction of a control flow graph (cf. Chapter 5.5.2).

The compound statement includes, for example, the number of units inside the compound as a specific attribute. This attribute is used by the developed code generator for the transformation of the code-models from a flow into a block structure (Chapter 5.5.4).

Furthermore, the <node-attr> element contains any number of sub-elements that describe the statement in detail, e.g. expressions in Listing 5.8. The XML tag name is identical with the type of the node in the Elsa syntax tree. The attributes of the sub-elements are in turn dependent on the type of the element itself. They contain all information which are available in the Elsa parser.

The structure of the <node> element as well as the CDATA section (l. 14) are illustrated in Listing 5.8. The statement is an expression (l. 4), which in turn consists of an assignment (l. 5), a variable (ll. 6-10) and a constant (ll. 11-12). These descriptions can be arbitrarily complex.

Description of the Edge Characteristics

A separate list of the edges is stored at the end of the file. The separation of node and edge description offers advantages for the later usage. A list of all edges is established in parallel to the processing of the node. Therefore the loc as well as the succ attribute of each statement are processed.

Listing 5.9: XML edges with source and taget

```
1  <map id="3">
2    <edge id="" source="34:2" target="35:2"/>
3    <edge id="" source="35:2" target="37:2"/>
4    ...
5    <edge id="" source="64:2" target="71:2" cyclic="1"/>
6    ...
7  </map>
```

Listing 5.9 presents an excerpt of the edge description. It starts with the <map> element, which in turn has a unique number. The number is identical to the number of the corresponding <graph> element.

The <edge> element may have up to three attributes (ll. 7-8). Source and target of the edge are mandatory. The third, the cyclic attribute, is optional. It specifies whether the edge initiates a circle, e.g. in a loop. The values of all attributes contain the well-known localization schema. They always address statements.

The Elsa parser inserts additional edges for so-called dummy statements. Those dummy statements do not exist in the source code. Each branch has both: a `then` and an `else` branch, even solely the `then` part is implemented. These dummy statements are generally ignored.

5.5.2 Modeling

In the next step of model-driven reengineering the XML description is imported into a modeling tool and visualized as a control flow graph at model level. In Chapter 3.3.2, it has been described that the jABC modeling tool is well suited for the elaborated method. It is designed for continuous, model-driven development, and successfully applied in this area.

Graphical Representation of SIBs

A notation and a corresponding graphical representation of the symbols must be defined for the representation of the models. The notation is based on the node type of the Elsa parser and thus the C/C++ grammar [Str98]. For each statement type an own icon with appropriate graphical representation is created.

Figure 5.12 gives an overview of the created icons. The name of the nodes correspond to the names used in the Elsa parser. They start with the prefix S_ and ends with the type of the statement. The notation includes the usual programming language elements branch, loop, expression, statement, declaration and compound. Not included are the symbols for the declaration of namespaces, assembler instructions as well as goto and label statements. Due to their very rare use they have a standard icon.

To improve the readability of the graphical notation, a pictogram was added to each element (cf. Figure 5.12). This illustrates graphically the role of the node in the control flow. In Figure 5.12 bottom right the function element must be highlighted: It represents the start node of each code-model and contains the parameters as well as the return value. In contrast, S_Function represents a function call within a method. The design of the icons was based on the principles of Moody [Moo09, p. 764] and Agrawala et al. [ALB11, p. 63]. They suggest, among other things, to use typical symbols of the domain and to represent them as pictures or pictograms.

Import of the Code-Models

For the import and the creation of the code-models an extension for the jABC (hereinafter called plug-in) has been developed. This domain- and

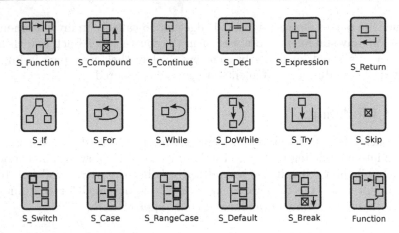

Figure 5.12: jABC – SIB elements of the C/C++ grammar

and user-specific plug-in defines the semantics of the underlying transition system (see Chapter 3.3.2). In the present case of a CFG in C/C++.

The intermediate, annotated description is read with the help of an XML parser and converted into the corresponding graphical model. Elements and attributes in the XML description are transformed as follows:

Function: A function in the XML description (<graph>-element) is represented by a SIB graph. For each method a separate model is created. The model name is composed of the input file name and the address of the method. The data in the <graph_attr> element is stored as a parameter on the model itself. The model parameters include file name, path and name of the graph. Furthermore, a Function-SIB (cf. Figure 5.12) is created. It defines the start node of the control flow graph. All further attributes (parameters, return values) are stored in the parameter attribute of the SIB.

Statement: Analogous to the <graph> element, for each statement a SIB is created according to its type. The associated parameters from the <node_attr> element and its sub-elements are stored as attributes of the node. These are organized in a tree structure (tree map). The information is stored as key-value pairs. The key is always formed from the Elsa type name plus a sequential number. Using a tree structure offers advantages regarding the storage of variable data, in concerning understandability and extensibility.

As an example, the already introduced assignment (b = 3;) is shown in Figure 5.13. In the field Name (upper part) the type of the

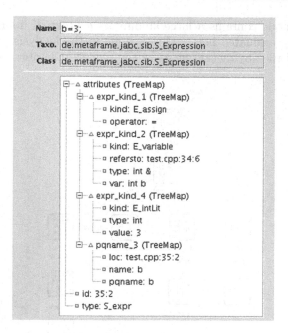

Figure 5.13: jABC – SIB attributes

node (S_Expression) is recorded. In the sub-trees all elements are listed, which determine the expression in more detail. This includes the assignment (E_assign) and the two corresponding operators (E_variable, E_intLit). They consist of a fixed value and a variable. Additionally the address of the statement itself (parameter: id) is visualized.

Edges: After the creation of the nodes, the edges are connected to form a control flow graph. The list of edges can be found at the end of the XML file. The edge list contains the source and the destination address of the node to be linked. One can imagined that the separation of node and edge definition is very helpful because it ensures that all nodes have already been created.

In a subsequent processing step, all edges are labeled. The common label is default. Nodes that affect the control flow, obtain an alternative label. The outgoing edges of a branch have the labels then and else. Loops are marked with body and default. Figure 5.14 illustrates a switch-case statement and a do-while loop.

Now each node contains a large amount of contextual information that is not initially evaluated here. This is done in the analysis phase (Chapter 5.5.3) and the abstraction phase of the models (Chapter 5.6.1).

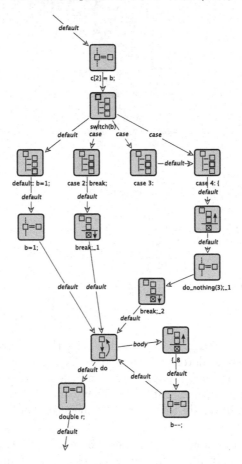

Figure 5.14: jABC – Excerpt prepared a code-model

Layout of the Code-Models

After creating the control flow graph, it is converted into a readable form. Therefore an existing jABC graph layouter plug-in is applied. It provides three different layouters: Sugiyama [STT81], GEM [FLM95] and Fruchtermann-Rheingold [FR91].

After various experiments, which have been compared with regard to the performance and the quality of the results, the Sugiyama layouter is applied. Based on the computation time, it is better classified as, for example, the Fruchterman-Rheingold layouter, but does not deliver the best results in all situations (e.g. in the allocation of the number of nodes or overlapping edges). Due to the amount of processed graphs a compromise between computation time and adequacy of the models had to be found. the inhomogeneously distributed nodes and edges across the code-models (from three up to more than one hundred nodes) are one reason for partially fluctuating results. This aspect is covered later in the analysis.

During creating the code-models in the modeling tool, no information is filtered or omitted in order not to restrict subsequent analyzes.

Linking of Code-Models

After the control flow graphs are created and designed, the models are inspected for functions. The aim is to find all function calls and to link them to each other. Therefore the jABC offers the opportunity to interrelate models with so-called Graph-SIBs. This simplifies the analysis of the code-models. The result can be compared with a code-browser.

During the transfer of the XML description into a graphical notation, a database of previously analyzed functions is setup. Each entry consists of a unique fully qualified name, the name of the source file and the code-model, its unique number as well as the associated path (cf. Figure 3.9).

For the linkage of code-models the attributes of each node are investigated for function calls. Sub-trees in the tree map which start with a S_Function introduce such a call. It contains a qualified name as well as the source file where the function is declared. These two pieces of information are necessary to find the corresponding model in the database. Source and target model are linked with the help of the unique identification numbers of each model. Figure 5.15 shows the relationship between the database and the models to be linked.

In the analysis of nodes, it is not unusual that several S_Function elements are in one statement. The source lines are constructed according to the scheme objectA.MethodB.MethodC.MethodD. The separation of function calls and the creation of an intermediate model is essential (cf. Figure 5.15 below). Each function call is then represented, in compliance with the correct call sequence, in a new sub-control-flow-graph by a separate node. The separated components can now be linked according to the described process.

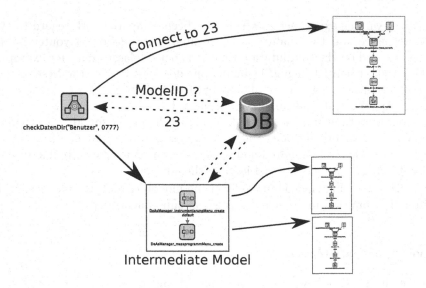

Figure 5.15: Linking of Code-Models

jABC Plug-in

To support the maintenance engineer, the steps above and the functionality were summarized in a plug-in for the modeling tool jABC. Figure 5.16 shows the menu structure of the extension (C++ -> jABC).

The plug-in supports the user in the configuration of the project, the conversion of the existing source code, the import into the modeling tool and in the linking of the imported models.

Various parameters of the project can be adjusted via the Options menu. Figure 5.17 presents all configurable properties. These include the call parameters, and the program files of the preprocessor as well as of the adjusted Elsa parser (-Binary and -Options), furthermore the source- and the project directory and the location of the database created during import. The file extensions for program and for preprocessed files can also be defined.

The maintenance engineer can execute the transformation of the program code directly from the plug-in. Therefore the menu items Convert C++ -> SLG, Convert I -> SLG and Convert XML -> SLG are available. The first item performs a three-step process. First, the program code is processed by the preprocessor, then the Elsa parser creates the corresponding XML representation and in the last step, the representation is imported into the

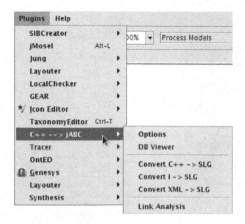

Figure 5.16: jABC – Structure of the developed jABC plug-in

jABC. If one of the intermediate formats already does exist, the other two menu items are available.

At the start of each transformation, the user can limit the files to be processed by means of a path and file selection dialog.

The contents of the database created during the transformation can be inspected; DB Viewer (Figure 5.16). For each imported function the database contains its name, a fully qualified name, the file name of the created jABC-graph as well as of the original C/C++ file, a unique model number as well as an additional column that contains the count of function calls (not shown in Figure 5.16).

The last menu item – Link Analysis – executes the hierarchical linking of the code-models. Again, the maintenance engineer has the option to limit the amount of files to be processed at the beginning of the process.

During the execution, the plug-in provides different information about the status and the progress of the transformation. Information about the performance of the individual phases can be found in the next section.

Evaluation of the Performance of the Method

The performance of the developed method fragments is determined and evaluated in different phases. The focus is on the required time and the use of resources. The correctness of the generated code-models is validated in Chapter 5.5.4 separately.

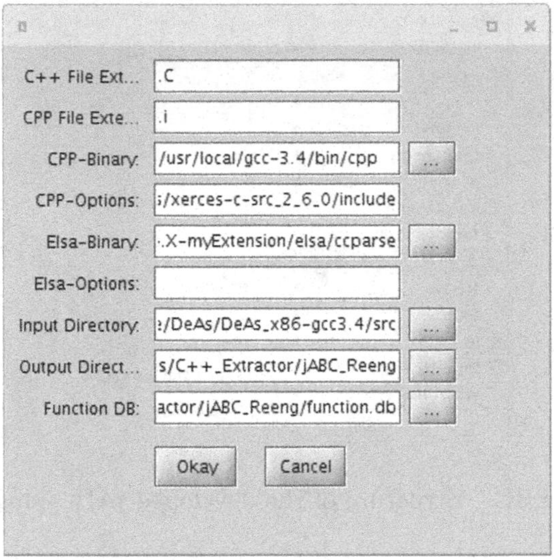

Figure 5.17: jABC – Configuration of the plug-in

Each phase – from the application of the preprocessor through the linking of the code-models – is analyzed. A Linux system with 3 GB main memory and a 2-core processor with 2.5 GHz is available. The analysis focuses in particular on the magnitude of the measured values. Therefore, no special arrangements for the time measurement, in order to improve the accuracy in the range of milliseconds, are taken. In order to ensure comparability each measurement is performed several times and the average is calculated. Further, each test is always bound to one core of the processor.

An overview of the results in tabular form is located in Appendix B of this book. The following section summarizes the results and explains relevant data in detail.

The first two steps, the preprocessing and the creation of platform-independent descriptions, are not executed by the modeling tool jABC. Instead, a simple test class is used. This reduces the software stack and the amount of memory needed considerably, and hence enabling more accurate measurement results.

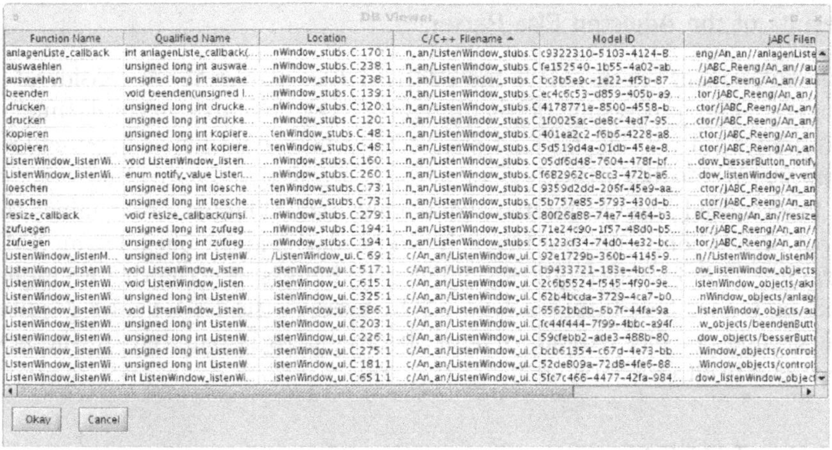

Function Name	Qualified Name	Location	C/C++ Filename ▲	Model ID	jABC Filen
anlagenListe_callback	int anlagenListe_callback(...	...nWindow_stubs.C 170: 1	...n_an/ListenWindow_stubs.C c9322310-5103-4124-8...	...eng/An_an//anlagenListe
auswaehlen	unsigned long int auswae...	...nWindow_stubs.C 238: 1	...n_an/ListenWindow_stubs.C fe152540-1b55-4a02-ab...	...jABC_Reeng/An_an//au
auswaehlen	unsigned long int auswae...	...nWindow_stubs.C 238: 1	...n_an/ListenWindow_stubs.C bc3b5e9c-1e22-4f5b-87...	...jABC_Reeng/An_an//au
beenden	void beenden(unsigned l...	...nWindow_stubs.C 139: 1	...n_an/ListenWindow_stubs.C ec4c6c53-d859-405b-a9...	...tor/jABC_Reeng/An_an/
drucken	unsigned long int drucke...	...nWindow_stubs.C 120: 1	...n_an/ListenWindow_stubs.C 4178771e-8500-4558-b...	...ctor/jABC_Reeng/An_an/
drucken	unsigned long int drucke...	...nWindow_stubs.C 120: 1	...n_an/ListenWindow_stubs.C 1f0025ac-de8c-4ed7-95...	...ctor/jABC_Reeng/An_an
kopieren	unsigned long int kopiere...	...tenWindow_stubs.C 48: 1	...n_an/ListenWindow_stubs.C 401ea2c2-f6b6-4228-a8...	...ctor/jABC_Reeng/An_an
kopieren	unsigned long int kopiere...	...tenWindow_stubs.C 48: 1	...n_an/ListenWindow_stubs.C 5d519d4a-01db-45ee-8...	...ctor/jABC_Reeng/An_an
ListenWindow_listenWi...	void ListenWindow_listen...	...nWindow_stubs.C 160: 1	...n_an/ListenWindow_stubs.C 05df6d48-7604-478f-bf...	...dow_besserButton_notify
ListenWindow_listenWi...	enum notify_value Listen...	...nWindow_stubs.C 260: 1	...n_an/ListenWindow_stubs.C f6B2962c-8cc3-472b-a6...	...dow_listenWindow_event
loeschen	unsigned long int loesche...	...tenWindow_stubs.C 73: 1	...n_an/ListenWindow_stubs.C 9359d2dd-206f-45e9-aa...	...ctor/jABC_Reeng/An_an
loeschen	unsigned long int loesche...	...tenWindow_stubs.C 73: 1	...n_an/ListenWindow_stubs.C 5b757e85-5793-430d-b...	...ctor/jABC_Reeng/An_an
resize_callback	void resize_callback(unsi...	...nWindow_stubs.C 279: 1	...n_an/ListenWindow_stubs.C 80f26a88-74e7-4464-b3...	...BC_Reeng/An_an//resize
zufuegen	unsigned long int zufueg...	...nWindow_stubs.C 194: 1	...n_an/ListenWindow_stubs.C 71e24c90-1f57-48d0-b5...	...tor/jABC_Reeng/An_an/
zufuegen	unsigned long int zufueg...	...nWindow_stubs.C 194: 1	...n_an/ListenWindow_stubs.C 5123cf34-74d0-4e32-bc...	...tor/jABC_Reeng/An_an/
ListenWindow_listenM...	unsigned long int ListenW...	.../ListenWindow_ui.C 69: 1	...c//An_an/ListenWindow_ui.C 92e17299-360b-4145-9...	...n//ListenWindow_listenM
ListenWindow_listenWi...	void ListenWindow_listen...	...istenWindow_ui.C 517: 1	...c//An_an/ListenWindow_ui.C b9433721-183e-4bc5-8...	...ow_listenWindow_objects
ListenWindow_listenWi...	unsigned long int ListenW...	...istenWindow_ui.C 325: 1	...c//An_an/ListenWindow_ui.C 62b4bcda-3729-4ca7-b0...	...nWindow_objects/anlag
ListenWindow_listenWi...	void ListenWindow_listen...	...istenWindow_ui.C 586: 1	...c//An_an/ListenWindow_ui.C 6562bbdb-6b7f-44fa-9a...	...listenWindow_objects/au
ListenWindow_listenWi...	unsigned long int ListenW...	...istenWindow_ui.C 203: 1	...c//An_an/ListenWindow_ui.C fc44f444-7f99-4bbc-a94f...	...w_objects/beendenButt
ListenWindow_listenWi...	unsigned long int ListenW...	...istenWindow_ui.C 226: 1	...c//An_an/ListenWindow_ui.C 59cfebb2-ade3-488b-80...	...dow_objects/besserButt
ListenWindow_listenWi...	unsigned long int ListenW...	...istenWindow_ui.C 275: 1	...c//An_an/ListenWindow_ui.C bcb61354-c67d-4e73-bb...	...Window_objects/control
ListenWindow_listenWi...	unsigned long int ListenW...	...istenWindow_ui.C 181: 1	...c//An_an/ListenWindow_ui.C 52be809a-72d8-4fe6-88...	...Window_objects/control
ListenWindow_listenWi...	int ListenWindow_listenWi...	...isten_ui.C 65: 1	...c//An_an/ListenWindow_ui.C 5fc7c466-4477-42fa-984...	...dow_listenWindow_object

Okay   Cancel

Figure 5.18: jABC – Database view of the plug-in

Results of the Preprocessor

For the preprocessing of the code the preprocessor cpp is used in version
3.4.6. It belongs to the GNU Compiler Collection (GCC). In Table B.1
the results of the first phase are summarized. It is illustrated that the
parsed code consists of 97,000 lines, which corresponds to a total volume of
3.87 MB. After the processing of all files, the size of the program code has
grown to 500 MB (150-times increase).

The explanation for this steep increase is the header structure within the
project. Any DeAs application includes a few header files called collection
header. These include a variety of class definitions and further declarations of global variables or structures. Each DeAs library provides such a
header file. They contain all library classes and functions. This approach
offers advantages during application development, because no distinction
is made between individual and necessary dependencies. In contrast, the
preprocessor must copy the collection header including all the further dependencies therein. The dependencies are resolved, regardless of whether
they are needed or not. In summary, the enormous increase is caused by
the DeAs #include-structure.

Therefore the header files are excluded from analysis and transformation.
Instead an emphasis is put on the existing source code. The processing of
all files by the preprocessor requires almost 47 seconds (cf. Table B.1).

Results of the Adjusted Elsa Parser

The subsequent execution of the adapted Elsa parser takes considerably longer. The processing of the program code requires a total time of 26 minutes (cf. Table B.2). Here, the memory consumption is reduced from 500 MB to 125 MB.

The reduced size has limited significance only. The parser examines the program code only (but not the included header) and the output is an XML format. This format requires significantly more space than conventional text or binary-based approaches[10]. On average the Elsa parser requires 4.5 seconds per file. About 75 % of the resources is required by the new back-end itself (cf. Table B.2).

Results of jABC Import

The Elsa parser creates 430 XML descriptions which contain 5,589 methods with 63,000 nodes. The import into the jABC requires 12 minutes (cf. Table B.3). The conversion to the internal data structures and the layout of the generated code-model takes 0.13 s on average. On average each imported function contains 11 nodes. Furthermore, in Table B.3 it is illustrated that the jABC internal data format requires 5 times more space (674 MB). This is mainly due to additional information such as coordinates of the node, interpolation points for curved edges and one icon per node.

Analysis Results of the Imported Models

Furthermore, the number of methods per file and the number of nodes per code-model have been calculated while importing the XML descriptions. These analyzes permit a first impression of size and complexity of the overall system. Table 5.19 shows a histogram. It compares the number of methods per file (x-axis) with the sum of all files with the same amount of methods (y-axis). The peak is expected near the origin of the coordinate system.

More than 50 % of the code files have less than ten methods per class. 80 % own less than 23 methods. The amount of files with many methods is reduced in an increasing number. Two top classes have 108 methods. A comparison of the two using the program diff came to the conclusion that they are identical. Hence duplicated code could be found and removed quickly and efficiently.

---

[10] In general, XML formats can be compressed to reduce the memory consumption. A compression was omitted.

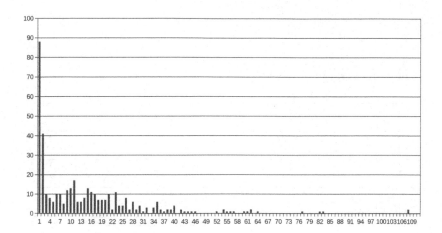

Figure 5.19: Number of methods per XML description

A second analysis examined the number of nodes per method. The aim is to find further evidence for complex methods that can lead to problems in the subsequent migration. Figure 5.20 illustrates the spectrum.

The x-axis shows the number of nodes per method. The y-axis shows the number of methods, which contain the same amount of nodes. The expected peak is again close to the origin. Almost 50 % of 5,589 methods have less than five nodes per method, 80 % less than 15 nodes (11 nodes on average). 250 methods (4.5 %) own more than 50 nodes. The top method communicates with the PLCs of the wind tunnel and has 247 nodes.

Result of the Code-Model Linkage

In the last step, all 63,000 nodes are examined for function calls (Link Analysis, cf. Table B.4). This phase requires 48 minutes. On average 22 nodes are processed per second. The analysis found 18,100 function calls and linked the corresponding models together. The vast majority of function calls is expected in the DeAs libraries. Surprising results were obtained by the application Aw_be. It has 1,300 function calls, most of the DeAs applications. This may be the first indication of high dependencies inside the application.

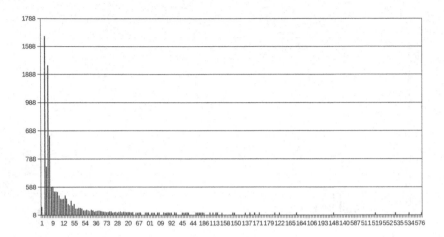

Figure 5.20: Number of nodes per method (for better visualization all values are increased by 15 points.)

Application of the Tool Chain to the DeAs System

The following two tables summarize the results of the processing of DeAs libraries (Table 5.6) and DeAs applications (Table 5.7). The execution of the Elsa parser, the modeling and the linking of the models in jABC are being considered. For the first step (preprocessing) it is assumed that it is error-free because the DeAs source code is available and can be translated[11].

A hook in the table means error-free execution of all associated files. If the hook is additionally provided with a clamp, a few minor problems have been encountered. They are explained below.

All DeAs libraries were converted into an XML description and imported in jABC. During the analysis of the control flow graph problems emerged in the libraries libSPS and libKorrektur.

The problems in the libSPS occur due to the lack of a PLC system driver. Hence the function calls could not be assigned to the corresponding code-models. The difficulties regarding libKorrektur are similar. Here Fortran routines are called from C/C++ program code. Since Fortran was not analyzed the associated models are missing. For the two interfaces, a

---

[11] except the system drivers for network communication with the PLCs by Siemens

Table 5.6: Conversion of DeAs libraries into code-models

Libraries	Elsa parser	jABC import	Create hierarchy
libDeAs	✓	✓	✓
libDeAsKlassen	✓	✓	✓
libDeAsFenster	✓	✓	✓
libKorrektur	✓	✓	(✓)
libSPS	✓	✓	(✓)
libVGI	✓	✓	✓
libGI	✓	✓	✓

skeleton was implemented for each of the missing methods. These methods are replaced syntactically.

Furthermore, one method in `libDeAsKlassen` uses a function pointer. Since this is only evaluated at runtime, the function could not be assigned.

The transformation of DeAs applications provided similar results. Again, no problems occur at the creation of the XML specification and the code-models. In the following analysis phase, several errors were found. The errors in `Ap_be` and `Ap_au` are related to incorrectly assigned static methods. `Aw_be` calls Fortran methods from `libKorrektur`. The difficulties in `Mv_an` are based on an unspecified behavior of the Elsa parser. The affected method uses a composite data type (`struct`) as return value. The data type contains a serial number which is provided by the parser. Since there is no match between the numbers regarding the function call and the function declaration, the method could not be found in the database.

An unexpected result is the large discrepancy in the number of source lines. The program `sloccount` determined 97,000 lines but the number of nodes is 63,000 only. It was expected that both would be very close. The deviation is partly generated by the control flow graph. Closing brackets are not instantiated as a node (and therefore they are not counted). Although this does not explain the gap of about 30 %. The reason is the programming style-dependent counting of `sloccount`.

`Sloccount` counts each line that is not part of a comment or empty. Therefore source lines which are extend over multiple lines are counted several times. This is not the case in the control flow graph. Here, it is irrelevant how the code was originally formatted. Listing 5.10 and Listing 5.11 illustrate this behavior. In the first case, the call to the function `methodA` is in a row, the latter is spread over several lines. The calculated values of

Table 5.7: Conversion of DeAs applications into code-models

Program	Elsa parser	jABC import	Create hierarchy
An_an	✓	✓	✓
An_be	✓	✓	✓
An_ko	✓	✓	✓
Mo_an	✓	✓	✓
Mo_be	✓	✓	✓
Mo_ko	✓	✓	✓
Ap_be	✓	✓	(✓)
Ap_au	✓	✓	(✓)
Ap_an	✓	✓	✓
Aw_be	✓	✓	(✓)
DeAsManager	✓	✓	✓
In_an	✓	✓	✓
In_be	✓	✓	✓
Mv_an	✓	✓	(✓)
Mg_be	✓	✓	✓
Mg_wa	✓	✓	✓
Mg_se	✓	✓	✓
Pr_as	✓	✓	✓
Pr_aw	✓	✓	✓
Vg_be	✓	✓	✓

`sloccount` are indicated at the top. The second listing has two lines more than the first example.

5.5.3 Model-Driven Analysis

The aim and the perspective of the designed *model-driven analysis* approach primarily supports the process of application understanding and enables the maintenance engineer to find complex and problematic code. For the first time a model-driven approach is used in software reengineering. It includes in particular the definition and documentation of analyzes, the reusability of components and the associated flexibility and adaptability.

Basis of this method is the modeling of the analyzes as XMDD process graph. The process components (cf. Chapter 4.4) were newly developed or existing ones could be reused. Using the model-driven approach, the maintenance engineer can adjust the analyzes to the project requirements.

Listing 5.10: Sloccount == 6	Listing 5.11: Sloccount == 8

```
1 void methodeA ( int param1,
      int param2, int
      param3 ) {
2 }
3
4 void testMethode (void) {
5   int param = 0;
6   methodeA (param, param,
      param);
7
8
9 }
```

```
1 void methodeA ( int param1,
      int param2, int
      param3 ) {
2 }
3
4 void testMethode (void) {
5   int param = 0;
6   methodeA (param,
              param,
              param);
7
8
9 }
```

Existing techniques for program analysis can be transferred to the model-driven approach. Thereafter these techniques are applicable to code-models, e.g control and data flow analysis or the calculation of metrics. Hereafter the calculation of the number of source lines as well as the Cyclomatic Complexity are discussed. Both give an overview of the possibilities and the broad range of the model-driven analysis.

Furthermore the integration of external tools as well as the creation of data formats are shown. The analyzes are modeled by the maintenance engineer. They can be immediately tested in the modeling tool. Thereafter fully executable program code can be generated. Hence these analyzes are available outside the modeling environment as an executable program.

Due to the amount of available information, the annotated code-models offer various options. The generation of test classes or test skeletons, the detection of anti-patterns and the generation of documentation similar to programs such as JavaDoc[12] or Doxygen[13] are not further considered here.

Software Metrics

Various calculation methods exists for the mathematical classification of source code. They fall into different categories: product, expense or com-

---

[12] http://www.oracle.com/technetwork/java/javase/documentation/index-jsp-135444.html

[13] http://www.doxygen.org

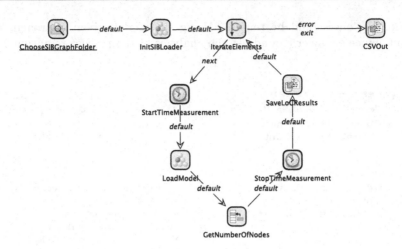

Figure 5.21: Process graphs for the calculation of LOC metric

plexity metrics. In general, these data are used in combination with historical information and experiences to determine the status and the quality of software. In the following product and complexity figures are calculated for the DeAs system.

Lines of Code

The LOC metric belongs to the group of product metrics and provides the simplest software metric. Its calculation is supported by the basic structure of the code-models. Since each node represents a row in the source code, it is easy to determine the set of nodes per model.

Figure 5.21 shows the process graph to calculate the LOC metric. The start node (ChooseSIBGraphFolder) has several parameters. A file or a folder containing code-models can be chosen. Additionally, sub-folders can be searched recursively. Depending on the configuration the start node creates a list of all code-models and stores them in the context (internal memory model) of jABC. The next node (InitSIBloader) prepares the internal data structures for instantiating the code-models. In the subsequent loop (IterateElements) each model is loaded (LoadModel). Furthermore its associated set of nodes (GetNumberOfNodes) is determined. Together with the time period (StartTimeMeasurement, StopTimeMeasurement), which is required for loading and reading of the value, the results are stored in a data structure (SaveLoCResults).

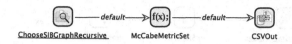

Figure 5.22: Coarse-grained process graph to calculate the McCabe metric

The result includes the name of the graph, the number of nodes, and the time necessary for analysis. After processing the loop, the result is stored in a comma-separated list (CSVOut). The file name is a parameter of the node. The processing of Comma-Separated Values (CSV) files can be ensued easily with further tools, such as spreadsheet software.

Applied to the entire DeAs system, 63,000 lines of code are calculated. The measurement corresponds to the determined value of nodes while importing the code-models (cf. Table B.3). Hence, it confirms the accuracy of the measurement.

Calculation of the Cyclomatic Complexity

The cyclomatic complexity belongs to the complexity measures. It was developed by McCabe [McC76] and determines all independent paths within a function. The author states that too many paths will complicate the application understanding. The calculation is based on the control flow graph and contains the number of nodes and edges. M is mathematically defined as

$$M = E - N + 2P,\qquad(5.1)$$

where E is the number of edges, N the number of nodes and P is the amount of studied control flow graphs. Since only one graph is considered ($P = 1$), the formula simplifies to

$$M = E - N + 2.\qquad(5.2)$$

To calculate the McCabe metric two different process models are shown below. They illustrate the flexibility of the approach, and the difference between coarse- and fine-grained modeling.

Figure 5.22 shows the coarse-grained process model consisting of three components. The first node opens a file dialog (ChooseSIBGraphFolderRecursive). The user can select files or directories to be analyzed. They are placed in the jABC context. The second node (McCabeMetricSet) calculates the cyclomatic complexity for all selected

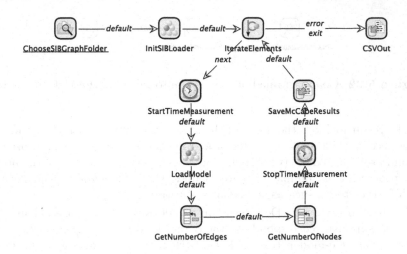

Figure 5.23: Fine-grained process graph to calculate the McCabe metric

code-models and stores the result into the context. This data contains the calculated metric as well as additional information on the duration of the calculation. The last node has already been introduced in the previous process model. It converts the results to a comma-separated list and stores it into a file. Furthermore the start node can be replaced by a SIB without graphical interaction. This is especially helpful for batch processing.

The benefits of a fine-grained modeling are explicit in the second process model (Figure 5.23). It also calculates the cyclomatic complexity. However, in comparison to Figure 5.22, it is modeled on a higher level of detail. The node McCabeMetricSet is remodeled. Now, the steps of the calculation, including performance measurement, are recognizable.

The process model for determination of the LOC metric is reused and slightly adapted. One node is added (GetNumberOfEdges) and the node to calculate the result (SaveMcCabeResults) is replaced.

Existing analyzes can be adapted to a new target by small extensions or changes. The maintenance engineer must decide on the granularity of the created process graph. In the first case, the process model is compact, but less adaptive. The second example has been developed from an existing one with very little effort and documents the procedure in detail.

A common benefit of process modeling is the descriptive documentation of the analysis steps. In contrast to programming techniques both the content and the method are readily apparent.

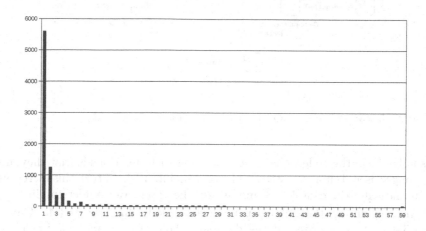

Figure 5.24: Results of McCabe metric

Figure 5.24 illustrates the results of the DeAs system. The majority of methods, 98.9 %, has a complexity below 10. According to McCabe, this value defines the limit at which a function is considered too complex and should be adapted. This boundary leads to an improved understanding of the application and it limits the complexity of test cases: The higher the score of the McCabe metric, the more complex are tests, that aim at a complete path coverage.

The highest complexity was measured with 59. This is due to one weak point of the cyclomatic complexity: The method consists of a switch-case statement, which includes nearly thirty case paths. Due to the nature of the statement, each case represent a path and is therefore counted separately.

The results of the cyclomatic complexity have to be critically reflected. Beyer and Fararooy [BF10] for example, summarize the problems and develop alternative ideas.

Analysis of Dead Code

Dead code is defined here as a function which is not used (called) in the entire system. These often arise due to maintenance work. Usually a big picture of the overall system is missing for the exchange or replacement of functions (cf. Chapter 2.2). Therefore, the function which is replaced is

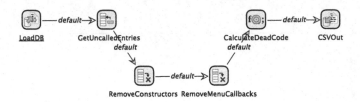

Figure 5.25: Process model for the detection of dead code

usually left in the code. The disadvantage of such functions is that they are no longer used, but also tested and further maintained. In turn this increases automatically the complexity and affects the application understanding.

Already during the linking of models to model hierarchies (cf. Chapter 5.5.2) it is recorded in the database, how often a method is called. Assuming the entire program code is analyzed, this data can be used to identify dead code. However, the analysis of two special cases is necessary.

First, the database contains the `main` functions as well as constructors and destructors. In general, a `main` function will never be called within a program. Therefore it is not considered further. Constructors and destructors are not marked in each case as a function call by the Elsa parser, e.g. when declaring variables with a default constructor. Therefore they are not captured in the linking phase and not considered here.

The second problem are function pointers. Usually they are applied for the invocation of callback functions, e.g. for graphical interface elements. This is also known as *Inversion of Control*. Function pointers could neither be resolved nor found when reading the models. Therefore the function which is linked to the pointer appears as dead code. Two different strategies are used to resolve this issue:

Firstly, the function name is analyzed. If it contains the string `callback`, it is not considered further. Secondly, a fixed number of menu `callbacks` of the graphical interface exists within the DeAs system. They are reflected in all applications. These were collected and sorted out.

Detection of Dead Code

The process model in Figure 5.25 explains the individual process steps. First, the previously created database including the descriptions of all methods is loaded (LoadDB). The next step identifies all methods with an empty call counter (GetUncalledEntry). The result is filtered according the rules described above (RemoveConstructors, RemoveMenuEntries). The final list

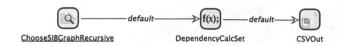

Figure 5.26: Process graphs for the determination of function calls

of process models is instantiated to determine the number of source lines. The process node (CalculateDeadCode) is a sub-model, which is indicated by the circle with a dot. The sub-model is a reuse of the already known process graph to determine the program lines (LOC, cf. Figure 5.21). Finally, the data is stored as a comma-separated list again.

The result is 990 methods with 9,000 lines of code that are classified as unused. This represents 14 % of the overall program code of DeAs.

Visualization of Dependencies between Components

The calculation and visualization of dependencies between program components is useful for the estimation of maintenance impact. In the following, two different approaches are presented which analyze and prepare the provided data for external tools. The BundleView tool [BTD11, Hol06] developed by the Hasso Plattner Institut (HPI) Potsdam and the Graphviz package are applied for the visualization of graphs.

The aim of the analysis is to document the dependencies between DeAs libraries as well as between libraries and DeAs applications. Furthermore, it should be proven that no dependencies between DeAs applications exist. The latter point is crucial for the migration of the system. It specifies whether a system can be migrated application-by-application.

BundleView Tool

Two different files need to be generated from the existing code-models. The first contains a list of all function calls, consisting of a unique model number of caller and callee. The second file corresponds the model number to the function name and the project path of the C/C++ function.

Figure 5.27 shows an excerpt of the result for the program An_an. The visualization illustrates that the application requires three DeAs libraries only. The outer rings are divided into the application and the libraries. The inner ring represents the individual source files. The edges illustrate function calls between the application An_an and the libraries. The more often a function is called, the greater the contrast of the line.

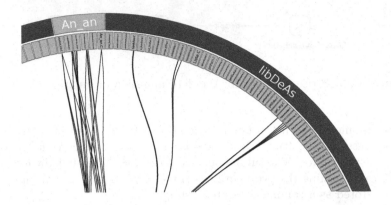

Figure 5.27: An_an – Overview of function calls

For a better overview, Figure 5.27 shows an excerpt of the results of the BundleView software only. The application itself, the libDeAs library as well as some fragments of function calls are visualized.

A complete overview of the visualization is shown in Figure 5.28. It presents the analysis of function calls between the DeAs libraries. Five libraries were selected (outer ring). All function calls are visualized, which invoke the functionality of the libDeAs or vice versa. The tool is interactive, so that each library may be examined by selection. In Figure 5.28 the libDeAs is highlighted.

The direction of a function call is visualized as gradient in Figure 5.28. The source of the function call is brighter and the target darker. It is evident that almost all DeAs libraries, except libVGI, use libDeAs. However, a closer examination results in this library only being used by others. Therefore it has no external dependencies[14].

The BundleView program could not be integrated into the process model shown above. The reason for this is that only a Windows version was available, but the modeling tool is developed under Linux. Therefore, all the necessary data is generated, transferred to the Windows platform, and analyzed separately.

Graphviz Tool

A second analysis examined dependencies at different levels. For a given function, all dependent source files are to be identified. Furthermore all

---

[14] This is not visible in detail, due to the resolution of this visualization.

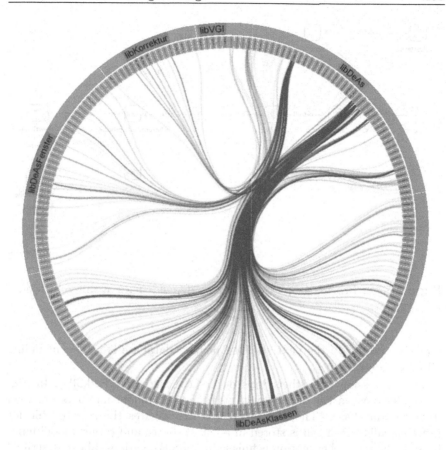

Figure 5.28: Result of the BundleView software for DeAs libraries

outgoing function calls are to be visualized as a graph. The former is necessary to identify which source files are relevant for application understanding. The latter, the analysis of the function calls, presents relationships and
dependencies. Due to the linking of the code-models, this information is
already available. The representation in this case is much more compact
and easier to analyze. In Figure 5.29 the process graph is shown, which
enables the various analyzes.

The process model starts with the selection of the to be analyzed code-
model (FileChooserSIB). In order to limit the complexity of the graph only
one can be selected. Otherwise, the information value would lead to rapidly

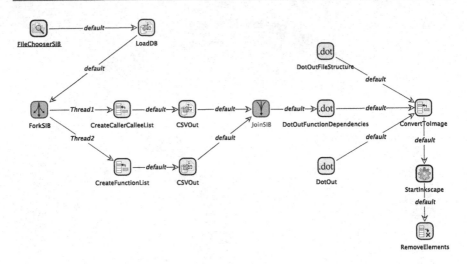

Figure 5.29: Process graph to determine dependencies at different levels

growing graphs. In the next step the project database is loaded including all function calls.

The processing of further steps occurs concurrently (ForkSIB). In Figure 5.29 below, a list of all functions and their model numbers are read from the database. The second process investigates the selected file for function calls. Each call is stored in a list of source and target model numbers. If the parallel execution is finished (JoinSIB), various, above described analyzes, are available. Three of these blocks are shown in Figure 5.29:

The DotOutFileStructure node scans the list of all function calls. It generates a tree structure which contains all source files belonging to function calls. Thus, the maintenance engineer obtains a well-structured overview of all associated fragments. Figure 5.30 presents an example of all program files and function calls associated with the file An_an.C.

The DotDependencyStructure node calculates the call graph of the selected function. For this purpose the function calls originating from the method are analyzed. The corresponding graph is shown in Figure 5.31. The functions called from the main function are easy to identify. The node DotOut combines the two analyzes in one visualization.

By changing the outgoing edge of the JoinSIB the different analyzes can be performed. Of course there is also the opportunity to use all calculations in parallel.

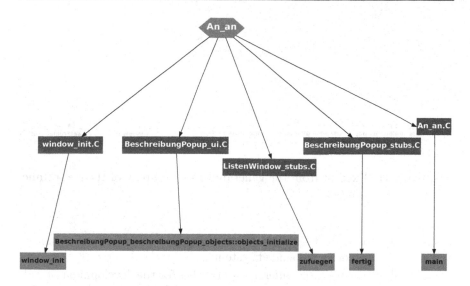

Figure 5.30: Files that are related to the `main` function (excerpt)

The process nodes use the dot format to describe the data to be visualized. The next nodes generate a vector-based format (ConvertToImage), in this case the Scalable Vector Graphics (SVG) format. This can be processed by Inkscape[15] to present and edit the graphs (StartInkscape).

5.5.4 The Code-Model Generator

To validate the generated code-models a code generator is applied. This approach, described by Rugaber and Stirewalt [RS04, p. 46], has already been motivated in the definition of the method fragments (cf. Chapter 3.5.4).

The validation itself is divided into two phases: At first the developed code-model generator will restore the original source code line by line. Thereafter the source code is compiled. In the second step the newly-generated program code undergoes a second model-driven reengineering step including the application of the code-model generator. Both generated sources (from first and second step) are supposed to be identical.

The generation and the comparison of results from two different sources is also referred to as *Back-to-Back-Test*. Stürmer et al. [SCDP07] describe

---

[15] http://inkscape.org

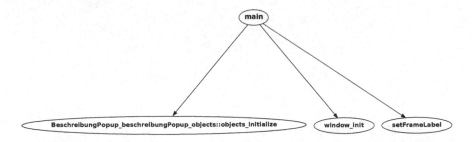

Figure 5.31: Excerpt from the generated call hierarchy of the `main` function

a similar approach for the validation of simulation and code generation in the area of automotive embedded systems.

Generally there are three different approaches for the development of code generators: rule-based transformation, template-based methods and string concatenation. For the code-model generator, the focus is on the transformation of a flow into a block structure. Therefore the string concatenation method is used to assemble the source code.

The generator itself is developed according to the XMDD principles. Therefore, it was possible to reuse the already existing process modules from a corresponding project for the development of model-driven code generators [Jör11].

Development of the Code-Model Generator

The code-model generator consists of three process models: the initialization, the main model and the code generator.

Process Model: Initialization

Figure 5.32 illustrates the necessary steps for the initialization of the generator. At first the input model (SetRootModel) is defined. In general, this is the `main` function of an application. In the following, various parameters are configured: These include the model path (ModelPath), the output directory for the generated program code (output Directory), the instantiation of process models (InitSIBLoader), an object which acquires the generated source lines and sorts them by file (an extended concatenation, (createStringAppender)) as well as a stack which contains all to be processed

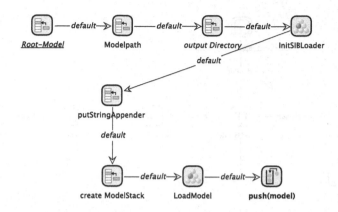

Figure 5.32: Initialization of the code generator

sub-models (create ModelStack). At the end the input model is loaded (LoadModell) and is put on the model stack (push(model)).

Process Model: Main Model

The main model of the generator is shown in Figure 5.33. The start node initializes the generator (previous model, Init-Code-Model-Generator). The loop iterates over all elements in the model stack (GetNextModel) and passes them to the actual code generator (CodeModel2String).

First the model parameters file name and path of the original source file are read from the code-model. The SIBs GetFilename and GetDirectory are reused from the corresponding project for model-driven development of code generators[16]. Subsequent each file name is added to a FileAppender. This is an object that receives the source lines and assigns them to the corresponding output files, e.g. two methods that belong to one class should be in one file.

Once all models are processed, the output files will be created (writeFiles). In addition, a so-called beautifier improves the readability (format code). It formats the source code according to certain guidelines. These include indentation as well as the position of brackets and function parameters. At

---

[16] All process modules reused from this project are marked by a triangle with circles.

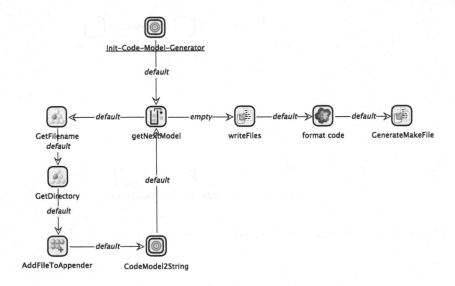

Figure 5.33: Main model of the code generator

the end, a customized Makefile (generateMakefile) for the translation of the code is created[17].

Process Model: Code Generator

The code generator model in Figure 5.34 transforms the control flow graph into a block-oriented, textual description. The implementation is more complicated than expected. Complexity is in particular increased by nested loops and branches.

In the first step, the start node of a code-model is determined (GetStartSIB). Subsequent the header of the original file will be investigated. Therefore all #include statements are inherited (AddOrigHeaderToFile) from the original. This is necessary since only the program code, but not the header information, is analyzed. In this context, the next step copies (CopyHeaderFiles) all C/C++ headers located in the directory of the source file into the directory of the generated source code.

---

[17] A makefile automates the translation of source code. Usually it is used in C/C++. It consists of a set of rules, a lists of dependencies, search paths and libraries that are necessary to compile and create the executable program file.

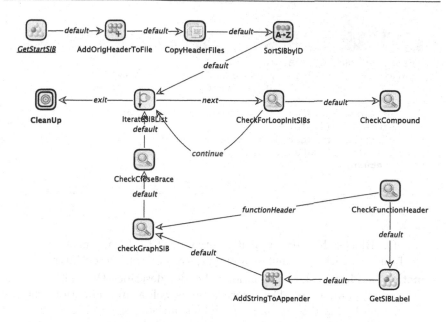

Figure 5.34: Code generator: transformation into a block structure

Afterwards all existing nodes are sorted by their position (row: column) in the original program file (sortSIBbyID). As discussed in Chapter 5.5.1, the localization is unique. All closing parenthesis are missing in the control flow. They have to be recalculated to generate a correct output.

The subsequent loop processes the sorted nodes and calculates the source line based on the name of the respective node (cf. Chapter 5.5.1). Here, different special cases have to be addressed. These include For loops (CheckForLoopInitSIBs), Compound statements (CheckCompound) and function headers (CheckFunctionHeader).

For-loop: For the initialization of the For loop, an own node in the control flow graph is created by the Elsa parser. This is represented by one SIB in the model. Since the generated source code already contains the full loop statement, the initialization must be ignored to avoid duplication (CheckForLoopInitSIBs, continue edge).

Compound statement represent a block and thus an opening parenthesis. Furthermore the statement contains a list of all source lines belonging to the block. These are necessary for the calculation of closing brack-

```
1  program: CheckCloseBrace
2  parameter: currentCell, compoundCounter, contextStack
3      locationStack, sibListIterator, stringAppender
4
5      // remove id from top list in locationStack
6      removeSIBId(sibID);
7      // return if locationStack is not empty
8      if ( !locationStack.peek().isEmpty() ) {
9          return;
10     }
```

ets. Blocks that are implicitly introduced by Elsa, e.g. for loops or branches with one single statement, are not considered further.

Function header: So far, a functional header describes the method name and all parameters. The return type as well as an indication whether the method is able to change variables of the class (const declaration at the end of the method), are not yet available. These properties are read out from the attributes. They are added to the source line. The further execution of the model is abbreviated (headerFuncion-edge).

All other nodes are processed with an uniform method. The label of each node is read (GetSIBLabel) and added to the output code (addToStringAppender). Furthermore each node is examined for sub-models (checkGraphSIB). If it contains one or more function calls, they are added to the model stack. To avoid duplicates it is checked in advance whether the code-model has been processed or is part of the model stack.

Calculation of the Closing Brackets

The last step of the loop (CheckCloseBrace) checks whether one or more closing brackets must be inserted into the source code. Based on the information from the compound statement and the analysis of the control flow, the calculation of the closing brackets is possible.

To illustrate the problem and the complexity, a description, pseudo-code (cf. Listing 5.12 to Listing 5.15) and small examples of each problem are given in the following.

The method CheckCloseBrace requires six parameters for the calculation of the brackets (ll. 2-3). The compoundCounter indicates the level of

Listing 5.13: Pseudo-code – Calculation of the closing brackets (part 2)

```
11    // check iterator if hasNext -> end of method
12    if ( !sibListIterator.hasNext() ) {
13
14        while(!locationStack.isEmpty()) {
15          LinkedList<String> locations = locationStack.pop();
16          if ( locations.isEmpty()  ) {
17             compoundCounter--;
18             contextStack.removeLast();
19             outputString = indentText()+"}";
20             appender.addToCurrentFile(outputString);
21          }
22        }
23      return;
24    }
```

the nested block – the location of the current SIB (currentCell). Each opening brace increases the counter and each closing decrements it.

The contextStack indicates the context of the statement. In general, this corresponds to a loop or a branch. The distinction is necessary since loops merely require one closing (bracket), branches however can call for up to two closing parentheses.

The list of elements, taken from the Compound statement, is stored in the parameter locationStack. Once a node has been processed, it is removed from the stack (l. 6). Since Compounds are often nested, the locationStack is designed as a stack of lists. Each new Compound list is put on the stack. If the last element has been deleted from the current locationStack, the check for a closing parenthesis can begin (ll. 8-10).

The parameter (sibListIterator) is necessary to detect the end of the method. It contains a list of all previously sorted nodes of the control flow graph. The stringAppenders is able to add text to the actual output.

The second part (Listing 5.13) checks whether all nodes of the code-model are processed (l. 12, sibListIterator). If this is the case, the algorithm adds one or more, depending on the height of the locationStack (l. 14), closing braces (l. 20). Furthermore it updates the associated data structures (ll. 17, 18). The function indent() adds blanks in front of the parenthesis (l. 19). The amount depends on the size of the compound counters. Figure 5.35 illustrates part 2 of the calculation.

The While loop is located at the end of the method. A termination depending on the number of outgoing edges will fail, because the edges

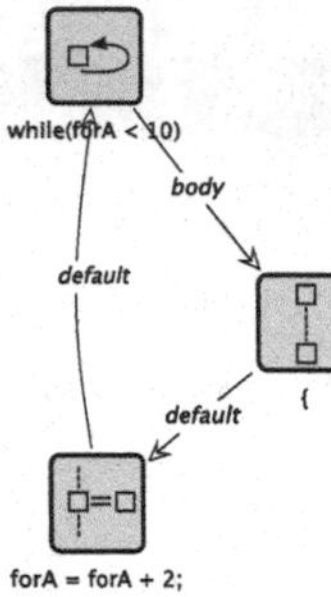

```
1  void testWHILEEndInLoop(void) {
2      ...
3      while(forA < 10) {
4          forA = forA + 2;
5      }
6  }
```

Figure 5.35: While loop at the end of a function

point back to the loop. The program code in Figure 5.35 on the right side illustrates that two closing brackets are required in this case.

Listing 5.14: Pseudo-code – Calculation of the closing brackets (part 3)

```
25   // if a SIB has no outgoing egde
26   if ( outgoingEdge.length == 0 ) {
27       printBrace(environment, appender);
28       return;
29   }
30
31   // SIB has one outgoing edge
32   if ( outgoingEdge.length == 1 ) {
33       SIBGraphCell nextCell = outgoingEdge[0].getTargetCell();
34       // if targetCell has 2 or more  incoming Edges
35       SIBGraphEdge[] nextCellIncomingEdges = nextCell.
               getIncomingBranches();
36       if ( nextCellIncomingEdges.length >= 2 ) {
37           printBrace(environment, appender);
38           return;
39       }
40   }
```

The third part of the algorithm (Listing 5.14) examines the outgoing edges of the current SIB. If it has no outgoing edges a closing parenthesis is added (ll. 26-29). The printBrace method adds the bracket to the output string (cf. context and locatonStack in Listing 5.13). In addition, it checks if further brackets must be inserted. Therefore the locationStack is evaluated. Each empty stack corresponds to one closing bracket.

If a SIB has exactly one outgoing edge (l. 32), the number of incoming edges of the successor is checked. This part of the algorithm searches for nodes where the control flow is reunited. At least one closing bracket must

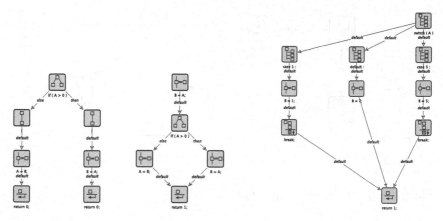

Figure 5.36: Variations of a reunited control flow

be set. These include the execution of `then` and `else` branches. Several variants are shown to in Figure 5.36.

An example without outgoing edges is illustrated in Figure 5.36 on the left. After each leaf node a brace is necessary. On the right, a converging control flow is shown with a multiple-branching statement (`switch-case`). A bracket has to be set in front of the convergence (ll. 35-38) in each case.

If a node has more than one outgoing edge (not presented in pseudo-code), additional care has to be taken for each edge to be examined as to whether it is directed towards a loop. A loop usually has several incoming edges – therefore the closing bracket would be put in the wrong place.

Listing 5.15: Pseudo-code – calculation of closing parenthesis (part 4)

```
41   // end of loop: for, while, dowhile
42   // compoundStack == LOOPTYPE, incomingEdge == default, source
         == LOOPTYPE
43   if ( "LOOPTYPE".equals(contextStack.getLast())
44          && "LOOPTYPE".equals(outgoingEdge[0].getTargetCell().
                getSIB().getSIBParameter("type") )) {
45       printBrace(environment, appender);
46       return;
47   }
```

The last section in Listing 5.15 examines the occurrence of the closing parenthesis in loops. The current context is queried (this must match to one of the loop types `While`, `For`, `DoWhile`, l. 43). Furthermore an outgoing edge of the node must point back to the loop (l. 44). If these

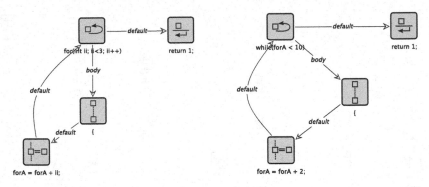

Figure 5.37: Different loop types

two conditions are met, the last statement of the loop is reached and a parenthesis is set (l. 45) (cf. Figure 5.37).

The transformation of a flow into a block structure is a complex challenge, and in a few cases it can not be achieved. Figure 5.38 shows a comprehensive example. Listing 5.16 presents the program code as well as the shortened code-model (statements 2 and 3 are missing). In addition, the generated code is shown in Listing 5.17.

Listing 5.16: Original code	Listing 5.17: Generated Code

```
1  int testCaseReturn(void) {
2      int A = 0;
3      switch ( A ) {
4      case 1 :
5          B = 1; return 0;
6      case 5 :
7          B = 5; return 1;
8      default :
9          B = 7;
10     }
11     return 1;
12 }
```

```
1  int testCaseReturn(void) {
2      int A = 0;
3      switch ( A ) {
4      case 1 :
5          B = 1; return 0;
6      case 5 :
7          B = 5; return 1;
8      default :
9          B = 7;
10         return 1;
11     }
12 }
```

The listing on the left illustrates that the `return` statement is not part of the `default` section (compare to the right side, l. 10 after the generation). A `case` statement does not contain a list of the associated program lines (`Compound` statement). Hence, it is not possible to determine how many nodes the `default`-section is to contain. Therefore, the final `return`

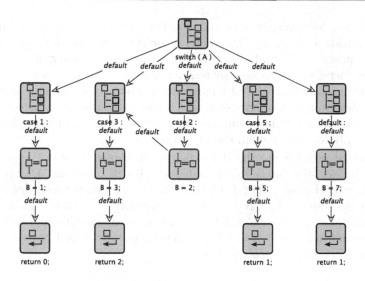

Figure 5.38: case-statement with five branches

statement migrates into the multiple branching statement. The generated code is not equal, but at least semantically equivalent to the original.

Translation of the Generated Code

After the code generation, the following section discusses the translation of the four selected DeAs applications. All steps which are necessary to translate the generated program code are described. In advance additional manual adjustments are necessary for the creation of an executable program.

These can be divided into three general problem classes. The aim is to automatically generate executable source code. This could only be achieved partially by modifications.

Problem Classes

The first problem class contains missing header files. Each DeAs application has at least one header file that defines the dependencies, objects and variables. Since the parser initially analyzes the program code only, these are entirely missing. They must be transferred from the original code into the target folder of the generated code (cf. Figure 5.34, CopyHeaderFiles).

Global or local variables as well as `extern` declarations are usually defined outside a function. Thus they can be resolved manually only (second class of problems). Usually they are defined at the beginning of a source file and are therefore not covered by the code-models. One option would be not to limit the analysis of the Elsa parser to functions. The missing definitions can be determined in combination with a data flow analysis, which examines variables that are declared outside of a method. This was not implemented due to only few locations in the program code.

Function pointers are the third class of problems. Within the graphical user interface, they are applied to define callback functions. Compared to the analysis of dead code (cf. Chapter 5.5.3) function pointers are not visible in the source code. It is therefore necessary to examine all interfaces and functions in advance to identify them. One possible approach is described and implemented in Chapter 5.6.1. The developed procedure does not entirely solve the problem class.

Translation of DeAs Applications

The entire process chain is to be assessed by the transformation of the existing program to models and back to source code. The processing of source lines using the Elsa parser revealed weaknesses that need to be remedied. These included, e.g. to hide comments that are located within a multi-line statement, the correct processing of `do-while` loops and pointers.

DeAsManager: The `DeAsManager` could be transformed from the model into source code in 1.5 s. During translation the problem classes two and three occur. In the `main` function, the global definition of an icon, a global variable and a function declaration were missing. These were taken from the original file.

The generated code amounts to 1,107 lines. After elimination of the mentioned problems, the size grew to 1,145 lines. Inconsistencies due to function pointers (class three problem) can only be detected when creating the executable (linking). The graphical interface of the `DeAsManagers` includes different callback routines which start the individual DeAs applications. Altogether 21 functions with a total volume of 146 lines were missing. Thus, the total amount of source lines rises to 1,291 lines. 184 (17 %) are manually added.

An_an: The preparation of the 1,245 lines of program code takes 1.3 s. The definition of the icon, three variables and a method that is declared within an `extern` definition are manually appended.

The linker starts out with 1,310 lines of source code to create an executable program, but the callback routines are missing again. Commonly, the implementation of the callback functions within all DeAs applications consists of two files. The developers separated the callback, starting out from a graphical element, from the actual, underlying functionality. The implementation of the user interface part is a file that has the extension _stubs.C. These files were copied from the existing project and added to the Makefile for translation. The actual implementation of the callback and the methods called from it, a total of twelve functions, are added manually. The program comprises 1,701 lines of code. Thus it is augmented by 37 %[18].

An_be: A similar picture emerges for the application An_be. The code with 38 files and 2,305 lines is generated in 2.7 s . Again, the icon, as well as eight global variables are missing. Thus, the source grows to 2,315 lines. Additionally, six _stubs.C files (1,420 lines) and eight implemented callbacks need to incorporated. Due to the global definitions and the function pointer, the program code was increased by 1,550 (67 %) lines. The vast majority of those contains the GUI-side implementation of callback routines in the _stubs.C files.

Ap_au: The most complex DeAs application involves 12,486 lines after generation (duration: 13.8 s). The program icon, different methods and global variables, with a total volume of 331 lines are added manually. Furthermore, three _stubs.C files and 64 functions that are directly or indirectly dependent on the implemented callbacks are missing. The total volume of source code is 14,718 lines (plus 15 %).

It is possible to automate the above described manual reworking in some cases. For doing so a significant amount of effort is necessary. Their implementation, such as the incorporation of global variables and extern definitions, is planned for subsequent projects.

An advantage of the proposed way of generating code is that the maintenance engineer does not have to face the entire system. Solely, the program code necessary for the application perspective is generated. The focus are the relevant parts of an application. The extensive investigation of the source code and an incessant jump between libraries and program is omitted. Furthermore, the maintenance engineer can familiarize him-/herself directly with the translation and by doing so starting to recognize the first implementation aspects.

For the DeAs application An_be the amount of source lines is reduced from 32,200 lines (program and DeAs libraries) to 3,855 lines (12 %). The

---

[18] Of the 456 lines of code 202 (44 %) already account for the copied _stubs.C files.

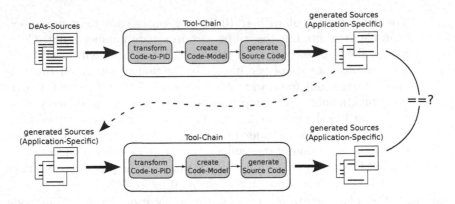

Figure 5.39: Structure of the back-to-back testing

advantage of the approach is a significant reduction of complexity, which is particularly helpful during for the migration phase (cf. Chapter 5.6.3).

Validation of the Tool Chain

The validation of the tool chain is performed by a Back-to-Back Test. This method originated in the development of safety-critical software, e.g. in the aerospace or automotive industry. A software product is created by different development teams using different methods. The results are compared against each other to test the implementations of the given specification.

In the present case, the Back-to-Back Test is adapted at two points:

- The different development teams are replaced by the tool chain developed here and
- the result is checked for identity.

The process chain receives input data from different sources. The aim is to demonstrate that it always creates an identical result. Figure 5.39 illustrates the general procedure for a Back-to-Back Test. The program code is generated from two different sources. The results are compared to each other. Input sources are the existing DeAs source code and the source code generated from a DeAs model. The tool chain (code transformation, modeling and code generation) is applied to both. This results in a validation of the entire process chain – including all developed tools – from importing into the modeling tool back to the program code.

The DeAsManager is subjected to this test method. He is representative for all DeAs applications. The first step, the application of the process chain to the existing program code, is explained in the previous chapter. The generated and manually adapted source code excerpt from step one is the input for the second part of the Back-to-Back Test.

The code is again transformed by the preprocessor and the Elsa parser into code-models and thereafter retranslated into a textual block structure with the help of the code generator.

In each case this results in 17 program files with 1,107 lines of code. A comparison of the two generation steps using the `diff` program prove their identity. Therefore, the entire tool chain is validated successfully. Naturally, the same problems are experienced in the translation of the code as with the previously generated variant (step one).

5.6 Model-Driven Migration

Phases and steps of the model-driven migration have already been discussed in Chapter 3.6. In the following the applications `DeAsManagers` and `An_an` are prototypically migrated. The aim is the creation of process models as well as the manual transformation of individual process sequences to remodel the capabilities of the selected application.

To migrate a system, the generated code-models are not sufficient. Due to their information density and the associated complexity they are inappropriate for manual processing.

The existing amount of information which is hidden in the code-models, initially has to be abstracted by *filters* in order to extract the interesting aspects. At first, the developed API-based abstraction is applied. It is built on top of the structure of the graphical interface (see Chapter 3.6.1).

The transformation of code-models into an abstract description is itself defined as a process model (XMDD). According to scientific literature this approach is referred to as *Fact Extraction* [BFG05].

The next steps comprise the separation of the existing source code, being mainly supported by the preceding focus on the necessary program code (cf. Chapter 5.5.4), and the remodeling of the application's process model.

Based on the remodeled process models, an executable program is created and translated in the last step. This application can be a combination of migrated components and existing code. Furthermore, it has been proven that the more applications have been migrated, the higher the level of reuse.

5.6.1 API-based Abstraction

The API-based abstraction is the basis of the developed abstraction step. It
is used for remodeling and migration of existing software systems. To create
an abstract description of source code at a higher level, various information
must be extracted from the code and be linked together. The code-models
serve as source of information.

For the remodeling and migration of software systems, the following
points are important:

- The identification of the specific functionality which must be remodeled.
  This includes all actions, also called process sequences, which can be
  triggered by a user or another external mechanism.
- Their partial or complete mapping on process sequences and
- the definition of an abstraction mechanism (filter), which extracts the
  components of this functionality from the source code, and represents
  them in a new model. If possible, this model is supposed to contain
  additional references.

Below the API-based abstraction is presented using the graphic library
of the DeAs system. In graphical user interfaces it can be assumed that the
user can trigger all process sequences of an application. As a consequence,
it can be concluded that it is possible to determine all possible actions by
analyzing the GUI. The result is a complete set of process sequences.

Stirewalt and Rugaber [SR98, p. 178] defined three model types for the
analysis of user interfaces: The *presentation model* contains information
about the interface, the *application model* focuses on the displayed and
variable data and the *dialog model* describes the dynamic behavior. The
model-driven migration creates a combination of presentation and application model. The dynamic aspects are immaterial.

The definition of a filter corresponds to Kühne's (cf. Chapter 2.6.4) abstraction function β. Here, the difference to the analysis ($\beta = id$) introduced
in Chapter 5.5.3 is clearly illustrated. The API-based abstraction is characterized by a specific classification of information.

To extract the set of process sequences from the DeAs applications the
components of the graphical user interface are examined. Therefore the
code-models are analyzed, the components extracted and related to each
other. The analysis is based on the programming interface (API) of the
XView library. The library defines which GUI elements exist and if they
contain actions, that trigger process sequences. The name API-based abstraction is derived from this idea.

XView-API

The XView interface can distinguish between visible (window, input fields) and invisible elements (servers, screen fonts). For the creation and manipulation of these elements XView [Van93, p. 6] provides six functions:

xv_init() Provides a connection to the X server, initializes all the necessary resources and accepts the parameters of the command line. The X server receives, for example, mouse and keystrokes events and sends them to the active window for processing.

xv_create() creates an object of the graphical interface.

xv_destroy() destroys an object of the graphical interface.

xv_find() searches an object according to certain criteria if it does not exist, it is created.

xv_get() reads an attribute of an object.

xv_set() sets an attribute of an object.

Each element of the graphical user interface is created with the xv_create or xv_find methods. The parameter list of the functions specifies the type and other properties. Each created object has a unique number. Therewith it can be accessed at any time.

Usually GUIs are organized as a tree. The topmost window includes different sub-windows, which in turn contain buttons, text boxes and labels. The creation of objects is always starting from the root up to the leaves. For assigning an object to a window, the *father* element is also passed on at the creation.

Listing 5.18: Creation of **Panel**-Elements with various parameters

```
1  Panel_item panel_item;
2  panel_item = xv_create(panel, PANEL_CHOICE_STACK,
3                  XV_WIDTH, 50,
4                  XV_HEIGHT, 25,
5                  PANEL_LABEL_X, 100,
6                  PANEL_LABEL_Y, 100,
7                  PANEL_LABEL_STRING, "Open File"
8                  PANEL_CHOICE_STRINGS, "Append to file",
9                  "Overwrite contents",
10                 NULL,
11                 NULL);
```

In Listing 5.18, the creation of an XView Panel is illustrated. The xv_create method as well as the descriptive attributes are illustrated. The first parameter defines the predecessor element, which is assigned to the Panel. All other parameters form a variable list. This is a peculiarity

of the languages C/C++. If the number of parameters to be passed to a
function can not be defined, a variable list of parameters may be applied.
It is recommended that each parameter is of the same type.

The second parameter specifies the type of the graphical element, here a
list (`PANEL_CHOICE_STACK`). All other properties are divided into name-
value pairs (cf. Listing 5.18). The first part describes the attribute, the
second the value. Moreover it is to be noted that the value can also consist
of a list of items (ll. 8-10). The end of such a list as well as the end of the
parameter list itself is marked by a `NULL` value (ll. 10 and 11).

Listing 5.19: Initialization and start of the graphical interface

```
1  void main (int argc, char* argv) {
2    Panel panel;
3
4    xv_init (XV_INIT_ARGC_PTR_ARGV, &argc, argv, NULL);
5    Frame frame = (Frame)xv_create (NULL, FRAME,
6                            FRAME_LABEL, argv[0],
7                            XV_WIDTH, 200,
8                            XV_HEIGHT, 100,
9                            NULL);
10
11   xv_main_loop (frame);
12   exit(0);
13 }
```

The XView interface is initialized by the `xv_init` function (cf. Listing 5.19, l. 4). It must be called prior the creation of any interface element.
The function `xv_main_loop` (l. 11) draws the GUI and assumes control
regarding inputs and actions. The source code between these two points
describes the static and the dynamic behavior of the user interface.

Therefore, this section is the focus of the analysis and the abstraction of
DeAs applications. All `xv_create` calls are examined between the initialization and the start-up of the interface. The structure of the graphical user
interface is, in combination with a data flow analysis, modeled.

Listing 5.20: Generating of a button with associated callback function

```
1  Panel_item button;
2  button = (Panel_item)xv_create(panel, PANEL_BUTTON,
3                       PANEL_LABEL_STRING, "Quit",
4                       PANEL_NOTIFY_PROC, quit,
5                       NULL);
```

Another above-defined objective is the enrichment of the created models
with further information. This includes, e.g. the linkage of action elements

with the implemented functionality. The model corresponding to the trigger, is linked to the element and describes the action in detail. Therefore a special parameter – PANEL_NOTIFY_PROC – is evaluated. The accompanying parameter value is a function pointer which points to the appropriate callback routine; illustrated in Listing 5.20, l. 4.

Listing 5.21: Pseudo-code for finding callback functions

```
1  program: searchNotifierEndpoint
2  parameter: notify, modelPath[], progname
3    LinkedList<String> resultList = new LinkedList<String>();
4    // check all files in project dir to find the corresponding
         function
5    for(int ii=0; ii<modelPath.length; ii++  ) {
6      // find all files containing notify string
7      if ( modelPath[ii].contains("/"+notify+"_") ) {
8        resultList.add(modelPath[ii]);
9      }
10   }
11
12   // make a guess
13   // at first program name + notify
14   String guess = "/"+progname+"/"+notify;
15   for(String tmp: resultList) {
16     if ( tmp.startsWith(guess) ) {
17       return tmp;
18     }
19   }
20
21   // next guess
22   // use first part of XV_HELP_DATA
23   // pathname contains first part and function name = notify
24   String xvHelpData = (String) sib.getSIBParameter("xvHelpData")
         ;
25   for(String tmp: resultList) {
26     if ( tmp.contains(xvHelpData) && tmp.contains("/"+notify+"_"
         ) ) {
27       return tmp;
28     }
29   }
```

Function pointers have led to problems in the first code generation phase (Chapter 5.5.4). Now, a multi-stage algorithm has been implemented to detect the callback routines. Therefore the algorithm uses the database created while importing the code-models.

Listing 5.21 describes the algorithm as pseudo-code. The algorithm has three different levels to find the corresponding function. In the first, the algorithm searches the database for all functions. The name of the function

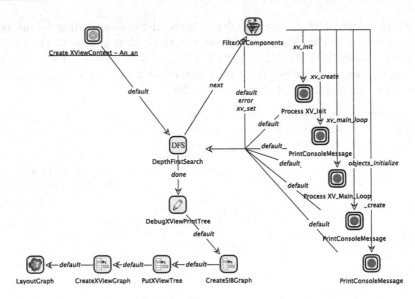

Figure 5.40: Process model of a filter

must exactly match the value that is specified in the PANEL_NOTIFY_PROC attribute. The result is accumulated in a list.

The next two steps attempt to derive the appropriate function from the list. The second stage limits the functions to the source directory. In general, the callback routines are implemented in the same folder. For more complex GUIs with multiple windows the implementation of this function can also be associated with the name of a window. Therefore, in addition the XV_HELP_DATA parameter is used. It comprises the name of the containing window.

In every studied DeAs application the algorithm identifies all function pointers and links them to the corresponding code-models.

Description of the Process of Abstraction

Based on the analysis of the xv_create calls a model of the graphical interface is created. All elements that can trigger an action are connected to the associated code-model. Figure 5.40 illustrates each step of the filter.

The start node **CreateXVContext** is connected to a sub-model. It initializes all parameters and data structures. These include, the starting model, usually the `main` function of the application, a list of all models which have already been processed and the output path for the model to be created.

A depth-first search (`DepthFirstSearch`) is used to run through the code-model layer of the application. Additionally, the search order depends on the labeling of the outgoing edges. Basically the first edge of a loop is the `body`-edge and second the `default`-edge. Furthermore the DepthFirst-Search node examines each statement regarding function calls. If one is found the processing is continued with the new function.

All nodes are analyzed with regard to XView elements (FilterXvComponents). The search ends when the already introduced `xv_main_loop` function is found.

The determined XView elements can be classified into different categories. For each group, the FilterXvComponents node has outgoing edges:

xv_init initializes the user interface. The return value of this function reflects the root node of the interface structure. All subsequently created windows are related to this.

xv_create creates an arbitrary element of the graphical user interface. The parameters include the father element and the type of GUI component.

xv_main_loop completes the analysis of the program.

objects_initialize is a method that is used in DeAs to perform the initialization and grouping of several related elements.

_create The `_create` methods are interesting for data flow analysis. Often, the creation of individual elements is outsourced in a separate function. In the analysis the parameters are important.

Once all associated models have been analyzed, the generated tree can be printed optionally (DebugXViewPrintTree).

In the next step, a new SIB model is created (CreateSIBGraph). Thereafter a tree representation of the XView elements is prepared. The next node (CreateXViewGraph) performs a data-flow analysis to link the information of the found GUI elements. It starts with the return value of the `xv_init` function. Furthermore, all `xv_create` calls, which have been assigned to its father node, are examined in order to interrelate them. The tree in Figure 5.41 describes the analysis process and the relationships between the elements.

For better visualization the created model is layouted. In this case, the GEM layouter of jABC calculates the best results. The result is a tree that represents the structure of the graphical interface elements. Certain types of items are examined for callback routines, e.g. buttons and menu structures.

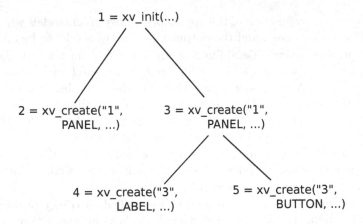

Figure 5.41: XView element tree starting from `xv_init`

The corresponding parameters and the resolution of function pointers are described in the previous section.

Create Tunnel: `An_an`

In the following the migration results for the program `An_an`[19] are discussed. By way of comparison, Figure 5.42 and Figure 5.43 display the original user interface.

The main window is displayed on the left side. The menu structure in the middle presents the actions a user can perform, e.g. these include modifying or creating a new wind tunnel. On the right side the associated input mask is shown. Each tunnel has a name and a description.

Figure 5.44 illustrates the result of the abstraction process for `An_an`. The structural model consists of 32 nodes. Each visible GUI element is additionally characterized by a pictogram. This simplifies identifying its type. Furthermore all elements that are able to trigger process sequences are highlighted by a circle with a dot. This suggests that a sub-model (code-model) is linked to the node.

The result includes the set of all possible process sequences including the associated code-models. This is the starting point of the manual remodeling of the software (Chapter 5.6.3).

---

[19] The user interface of DeAs is available in German only.

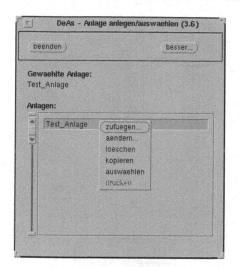

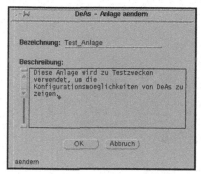

Figure 5.42: Main window   **Figure 5.43:** Editing window

Advantage of the approach is that the maintenance engineer does not have to identify all graphical elements manually. Additionally a link to the corresponding implementation is created. The link structure of the code-models enables the browsing of the graph. Therefore the user is able to collect information about the functionality. The relationship between the structure of the interface and the code-model is presented for one user action in Figure 5.45.

In detail, a section of the menu structure is shown below. The Figure contains the original menu structure. The dots indicate sub-models. For illustration the Select tunnel menu is linked to a chain of underlying models.

The presented transformation language extracts XView components from the program code. In a second step a model of the user interface elements is created. The static aspects were singled out in particular, since they are essential for process modeling. Likewise, the study of the dynamic aspects is possible. They are described using the xv_get and xv_set methods as well as their parameters.

This abstraction step has been applied to all applications of the DeAs system. The most complex model with 395 elements is presented in Figure 5.46. It is the result of the Ap_au application. The analysis takes 19 s. Several cloud patterns are easy to recognize. Each spot represents an individual window which in turn contains many GUI components (high density). Related sub-windows can be identified as part of a sub-tree.

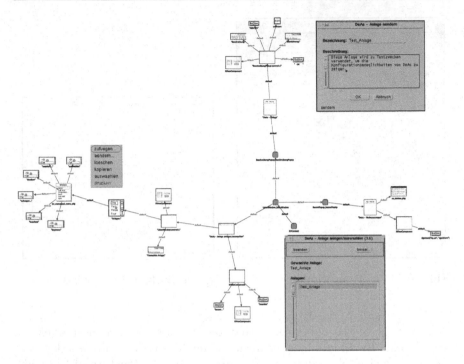

Figure 5.44: An_an – Structure of the graphical interface

5.6.2 Preparing to Migrate

On the basis of remodeling, the DeAs system should be split up. The aim is to provide the required functionality through interfaces. In this section, the applied technique is described. The specific approach as well as an example is the subject of the next chapter.

The DeAs system in combination with the modeling tool jABC requires information exchange among different platforms at any rate. The communication between the programming languages C/C++ and Java can be ensured with the help of a communication layer like CORBA.

Common Object Request Broker Architecture (CORBA)

Figure 5.47, according to Henning and Vinoski [HV99, p. 17], provides a general overview of the CORBA architecture. It consists of a server as well as multiple client applications that invoke the functionality of the server. Both are not necessarily implemented in the same programming language.

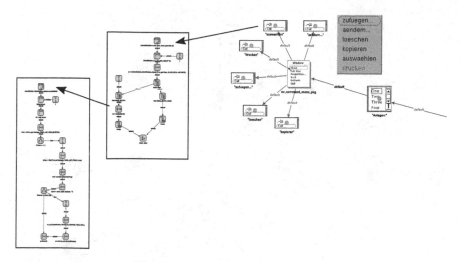

Figure 5.45: An_an – Linking of code-models with process sequences

Central elements of CORBA are the Interface Description Language (IDL) and the Object Request Broker (ORB). All functionalities offered by a server are described using the IDL in a C++-like syntax (cf. Listing 5.22). The IDL compiler generates the appropriate source code for client and server in the target language. Additionally this code contains functions for packing and unpacking of a function call, the corresponding parameters and return values. The IDL compiler generates a stub on the client side, which serves as a representation of the object located on the server. For the server a skeleton is generated that contains the implementation of the functionality (cf. Figure 5.47).

Both on server and on client side, the ORB controls the actual communication. The communication takes place via a local network or via memory (client and server are on the same machine). This is opaque to the caller. The ORB wraps function calls on the client side and provides them to the server. On the server side, the ORB instantiates objects, delivers the function call and forwards the response to the client. The ObjectAdapter is responsible for the instantiation (Figure 5.47, right). It has different policies to create a new object, e.g. once for each call or once for a session.

Two additional functional blocks are illustrated: DII and DSI. They are necessary for the dynamic remote calls (without IDL) and are not relevant.

Figure 5.48 is also according to Henning and Vinoski [HV99, p. 55]. It represents the present scenario of a C/C++ server and a Java client. Both

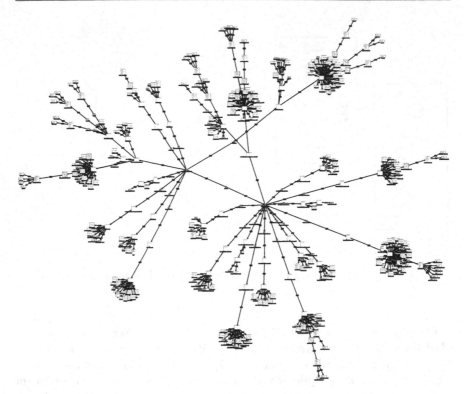

Figure 5.46: Ap_au – Structure of the graphical interface

use the same interface description. The appropriate stubs and skeletons are generated by an IDL compiler, which is available per language.

In the present approach, the open-source CORBA implementation OmniOrb[20] is used for the server. The CORBA client is already included in the Java standard library.

To facilitate the identification of services offered by the server, CORBA provides the possibility to set up a name service, containing the references to all existing objects. In order to reduce the dependencies, this mechanism is applied in the project.

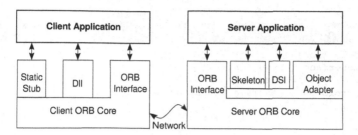

Figure 5.47: CORBA – Construction of the communication layer

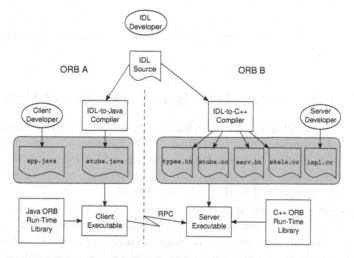

Figure 5.48: CORBA – C++ Server and Java Client

CORBA in the Context of DeAs

In Listing 5.22 an excerpt of an interface description for the DeAs class
Benutzer is presented. The interface C_Benutzer and the methods for
loading and storing the user settings are shown in ll. 2-6. Several descriptions can be collected in a module (module libDeAs_Corba, l. 1). These
form a namespace to separate the DeAs libraries.

In the IDL description, the declaration of constructors with one or more
parameters is not possible. For this purpose, a proprietary method must
be defined. The Factory pattern [GHJV09, pp. 107] is applied here. It

---

20 http://omniorb.sourceforge.net/

Listing 5.22: IDL – Description of the class **Benutzer** (excerpt)

```
1 module libDeAs_Corba {
2   interface C_Benutzer {
3     // set Anlage
4     void putEineAnlage(in string name);
5     // get Anlage
6     string getEineAnlage();
7   };
8 };
```

describes a method that accepts all parameters. It instantiates the object and returns it.

5.6.3 Create Process Models and Migration of DeAs

Based on the structure of the graphical interface, the prototypical migration of two DeAs applications is described. This includes the DeAsManager, which is also used in the top-down approach (cf. Chapter 5.3), and the An_an application. The technique for the integration of existing functionality has been explained in the previous chapter.

In general remodeling and migration of applications is a manual task. The analysis results from Chapter 5.5.3 and in particular the results of the abstraction process support the maintenance engineer. The abstraction contains the entire amount of process sequences to be remodeled. With the help of the analyzes, shown in Chapter 5.5.3, the dependencies and correlations in the system itself are examined. All in all this facilitates the process and illustrates the advantages of the selected approach.

5.6.4 Remodeling of the **DeAsManagers**

The existing DeAsManager is already shown in Figure 5.6 (p. 159). On the top, the menu bar with the sections for the configuration of an experiment is shown. All DeAs applications can be executed by the menu. Below, the current user configuration (wind tunnel model, measuring projects, etc.) can be found. Furthermore, the window contains a command line.

The remodeling of the DeAsManagers starts with the abstraction process of the graphical interface. The result of the first step is illustrated in Figure 5.49.

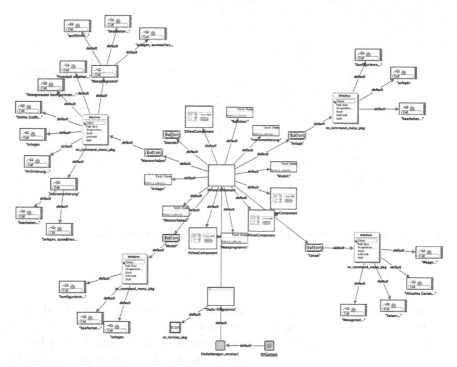

Figure 5.49: DeAsManager – Structure

The start node (root node of the window structure) is arranged bottom in the middle of the image. The next nodes are a general container (DeAsManager_window1) and the actual window titled DeAs - Programme. The latter contains further components that in turn contains all elements of the window. The graphic elements which display the user settings are easy to recognize. This includes the buttons of the menu bar (cf. Figure 5.6). They in turn are menu elements (except the Exit button) with different items. These represent the leaf nodes of the tree. The latter are usually linked with a code-model.

Figure 5.50 illustrates in what manner the maintenance engineer is supported by the modeling result. The associated code-model and the corresponding functionality contain a system call for a DeAs application. The code-model in Figure 5.50 is directly linked to the anlegen (English: create) menu. The system call is shown on the left (labeled with A).

Based on the current state, a complete list of all process sequences as well as their implementation in form of models is accessible. Both form the

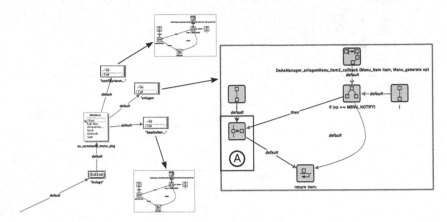

Figure 5.50: `DeAsManager` – Menu with code-models and system call

starting point for the next step – the remodeling. Specifically with reference to the `DeAsManager`, 21 menu items that trigger process sequences as well as six text boxes, to be filled with the current configuration, belong to it.

The initialization of data objects for the graphical interface can not be derived directly from the result of the abstraction. For the investigation of this initialization, the start node of the interface model was linked to the `main` function of the application. Thus, the maintenance engineer can examine the corresponding source code to identify and migrate the necessary objects (cf. Figure 5.51, the generation of user object is marked with A).

The result of remodeling is shortened in Figure 5.52. The model contains the menu Anlage (English: Wind Tunnel) only. All other menu items can be considered to be analog.

The remodeled DeAsManager starts to load the user settings in the node LoadUserSettings. For testing purposes, the stored data can be printed. The actual functionality is hidden in the ChooseApplication-SIB. It displays the user settings and allows the user to launch further DeAs applications. The node has several outgoing edges. Each of them represent various actions of the program. The edges are named after menu entries or buttons. The next nodes are from the jABC basic set. They execute an application on command line.

Thus, the remodeled `DeAsManager` behaves similarly to the original version. Furthermore, it is able, as opposed to the first version (top-down method, cf. Chapter 5.3), to launch multiple applications in parallel.

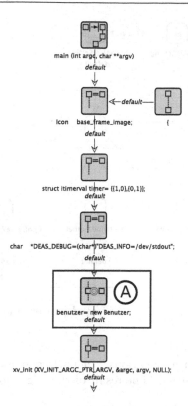

Figure 5.51: DeAsManager – main function with Benutzer object

In addition, the user configuration can be updated at any time (reload edge and the LoadUserSettings SIB). This feature was not available in the original version and represents an extension.

For the loading of the user configuration the existing functionality is accessed via CORBA. Therefore, a CORBA server is created that describes the interface of loading and saving of user data. On the part of the jABC, the LoadUserSettings-SIB is implemented as CORBA client. It receives the data and provides it to other process components.

Figure 5.53 presents a prototypical interface of the new DeAsManager. Below the user data, two lines with different buttons are illustrated. At the top, the reload of the user settings (Reload...) or the termination of the program (Exit) can be found. In the second line, the original Anlage (English: Wind Tunnel) menu is represented by three buttons. They can

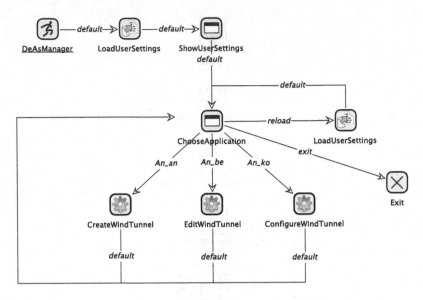

Figure 5.52: DeAsManager – migrated process model

launch the associated applications. In particular an ergonomic graphical interface has been omitted. The result of the migration was the main issue.

Evaluation of the Results

The remodeling of the DeAsManager process model as well as the integration of the existing functionality only caused little effort (6 h). The result is a process model with nine nodes. The description of the IDL interface comprises 18 rows containing 15 methods. The CORBA server has 860 source lines of which 730 are generated and further 130 lines are necessary for the implementation of the interface. Additionally, three process nodes were implemented. Together with the connection to the CORBA client an overall size of 724 lines of code (420 generated from the IDL description) is the result.

For comparison: After the code-model based generation the DeAsManager has a size of 1,291 lines of C/C++ code.

Overall, after remodeling 434 lines of code are manually implemented. Not included are the reused functionalities from the DeAs libraries. For the class Benutzer (English: User) 150 lines have to be added.

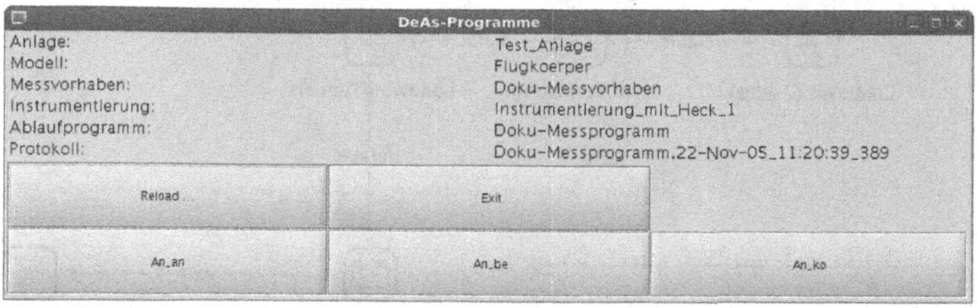

Figure 5.53: `DeAsManager` – GUI of ChooseApplication-SIB

Through the completion of the process model to all DeAs programs, the program code would change marginally. The graphical interface in ChooseApplication-SIB must be adjusted to display the appropriate buttons. In the process model itself, separate process nodes are necessary for each program that executes a DeAs application.

The remodeling process illustrates the core functionality of the `DeAsManager` (display the user configuration and launch DeAs programs). This is extracted from the source code and mapped on the model level. Where necessary, references are made to the corresponding existing functionality. This process supports a step-wise migration. Here the process sequences are in the foreground. The persistence, or the data structures are not considered. These aspects can be adjusted in a further step.

Additionally, it is possible to generate fully executable program code from this model. Therefore, a code generator (XMDD-Code-Generator, cf. Chapter 3.6.4, p. 103) is implemented in the modeling tool. A model-to-code transformation is applied to the SLGs. An executable is created that is completely independent of the modeling tool.

The proposed validation method (cf. Chapter 3.5.4) that compares the outputs of the original program and remodeled application is not necessary here, since the `DeAsManager` merely has read-only access. Hence, it was successfully checked whether the remodeled application can start the same DeAs programs as the original.

5.6.5 Remodeling of `An_an`

The application `An_an` is the second example. It is based on the results of the migration of the `DeAsManager`. Focus of the first migration was the graphical user interface (Figure 5.42 and Figure 5.43) as well as the abstraction step (Figure 5.44). The aim of this chapter is therefore the remodeling of the application.

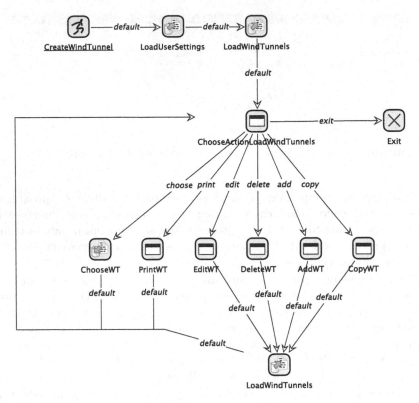

Figure 5.54: An_an – migrated process model

The migrated process model is shown in Figure 5.54. It illustrates that reuse is a major advantage of this approach. The second node (LoadUserSettings) was developed for the migration of the DeAsManager. It can be reused without modification. In contrast the next node is developed here. It loads the complete list of all defined wind tunnels.

The ChooseActionLoadWindTunnels-SIB is central. It represents the main window of the original application, shown in Figure 5.55. The outgoing edges describe all possible user actions. A wind tunnel can be selected, created, edited, deleted, printed or copied. Some of these actions may result in a change to the overall wind tunnel list. Therefore, the list is reloaded after each change.

The implemented interface in Figure 5.55 contains the selected tunnel, a list of all tunnels and, at the bottom, various buttons which can trigger

Figure 5.55: An_an – GUI of ChooseActionLoadWindTunnels-SIB

Figure 5.56: An_an – edit tunnel user interface

an action. If a tunnel is edited or created, the window in Figure 5.56 will appear. Both the name and the description of a tunnel can be adapted.

The graphical interface elements and the possible user actions can be taken directly from the structural model shown in Figure 5.44. This includes the input fields as well as the buttons and menus. With the help of the related code-models (Graph-SIB) the related functionality can be inspected very quickly. Usually a maximum depth of two to three model levels is sufficient for this purpose.

All DeAs functionalities are connected to the process node using CORBA. Hence the same advantages apply as described in the example above. The data exchange between the processing nodes is done via the context of the modeling tool.

For the DeAsManager as well as for the An_an application one functionality was not considered in detail. The besser (English: better) button is not migrated, since the users did not accept the idea. The original idea was that a user can store improvements or enhancements belonging to DeAs applications in his profile. The button opens a text field which can be used to describe new requirements. Any DeAs application contains such a besser-button.

Evaluation of the Results

The overall developed source code for the migration comprises 886 rows. 16 lines were necessary for the extension of the CORBA interface definition. The adaptation and implementation of the server skeletons involves 116 lines. On the client side, eight SIBs are created with a total of 766 lines. The time for the migration was less than one day.

For comparison, the generation of program code based on the code-models for this application has a total amount of 1,701 lines (cf. Chapter 5.5.4). The remodeled process model contains twelve SIBs.

The method, comparing the program output, described in Chapter 3.5.4 has been successfully applied to validate the functionality as well as the correct execution of the original and the migrated software. The file-based hierarchical database supports this approach. Changes can be easily tracked using a text editor or the diff program. After executing an user action in both programs, a comparison of the data sets is done. Similarly to a blind test both were indistinguishable.

5.6.6 Rules for Process Modeling and Migration

During the migration process of the DeAs applications, different aspects about the separation of software could be identified and generalized. For the following explanation, the individual categories are sorted according to quality and relevance from strong to weak.

Structural Separation based on Folders and Filenames

The separation of program code based on the file and directory structure represents a very simple but effective way. Requirement is that the structure of the overall system is not yet completely eroded. Furthermore the developers should have the separation of algorithms, program logic and data taken into account.

In this case, this approach was very effective. By separating the application and the libraries the maintenance engineer can easily determine by perusal of code-models, whether he is still within the application or already in the library. It has proven beneficial to use the transition as an interface to the outside.

Mixture of Program Code

This item summarizes code sections containing different types of source code. These include, e.g. a few lines of program logic, which are located between statements belonging to the graphical interface.

These sections should be considered carefully. Usually interfaces can be derived directly. Inside the DeAs system a mixture of program logic and graphical interface is present. A strict separation of both is missing. To find the relevant code areas – the actual program logic and not the logic within the GUI (e.g. enabling or disabling of buttons) – the classification of code is very helpful.

Avoid unnecessary Complexity within the first Migration Phase

For the first remodeling of the application as well as the migration of functionality it has proven to be beneficial, to keep the jABC process models as simple as possible. This is accompanied by the introduction of only a few interfaces to the existing system.

This procedure prevents the existing program code being analyzed too deeply, and by thus avoid the emergence of too many unnecessary interfaces. In this case, the process model is composed of the components of the graphical interface. Additionally, the data that is displayed in the interface is necessary. The focus on these elements has meant that for each process sequence one or two new interfaces into the DeAs system were introduced only. Thus the complexity remains manageable.

Read or Write the Data Methods

Building on the previous point, a procedure for methods which read or write the data is defined. The DeAs data base system was not considered in detail in this phase of the project[21].

The maintenance engineer should not define an interface that directly accesses data. This could be a hint for the analysis having been too deep and a more general interface is necessary.

When using such interfaces in a very early stage of migration, it is possible that in addition to the program logic, the data needs to be migrated. This additional complexity is of little help. In a further step of the migration this issue can be addressed by refining the process models.

---

[21] For complexity reasons, the data storage has not been studied, although it is one of the weak points of the system.

Error Handling

Among other things, the consideration of error handling may help when designing the interface. Two interesting aspects arise: on the one hand, the error handling can be encapsulated by the interface or on the other it can be part of the process model. The decisive criterion is whether this error will affect the process.

An error occurs if an algorithm is not working properly or can not be executed. Errors are to be distinguished in function and process errors. The former involves checking whether a function has been executed correctly. In general, the function errors are mainly handled very deep in the core of the system, e.g. to check whether a file is opened correctly.

The second category contains errors that affect the process. Inside the DeAs system, an example would be to check whether the user has selected a wind tunnel before it can be configured.

The two classes are not easily distinguished. An indication is the processing of the error. These aspects can be differentiated into functional (first category) and process errors (second category).

Minimization of Interfaces

The interfaces to the existing system should be limited as much as possible to avoid unnecessary complexity. This is done automatically by the modeling approach and the process model. The remodeled nodes are implemented and thus only the necessary functionality is linked. Furthermore, these can be reduced to a few interfaces by combining function calls and parameter lists to a few interfaces.

Leaf Node of an Inheritance Hierarchy

Classes, which are a leaf node in an inheritance hierarchy provide a key criterion for the definition of interfaces. Through the inheritance they include a large amount of the implemented functionality. Usually, due to their position within the hierarchy, they have a major role.

An example in the DeAs libraries is the class Benutzer (English: User). It inherits from the class Bezeichner (English: Identifier), and this in turn from the class Speicher (English: Memory). The two upper classes contain methods for persistence. It is not very logical to provide the intermediate level with an interface. The Benutzer class combines the functionality and provides a qualified interface.

Summary

It is to be noted that the points above are no strict criteria. They should be regarded as indicators that present meaningful interfaces or avoid complex code in the first phase of migration. Furthermore, it has proven helpful to limit the search depth of the code-models to be investigated to three. In general, the analysis of two model levels is sufficient to develop the functionality and to determine the appropriate interface.

In the present approach, no methods have been developed which automatically implement the mentioned points. For this, the use of empirical/statistical methods is required. In subsequent projects this issue should be examined more closely.

5.7 Results of the Case Study DeAs

In the present case the model-driven evolution of software systems could be successfully applied. Various tools have been selected and extended to implement the required method fragments for the methodology.

Two different migration strategies have been investigated. It was shown that a top-down approach has not yielded the desired results. The subsequently developed model-driven approach (bottom-up concept) helps to analyze a software in detail. Thus the application understanding is improved. Furthermore, the developed API-based abstraction focuses on the relevant parts of an application for the remodeling and migration. Furthermore the complexity of an application is significantly reduced by the code generator which is working on the basis of code-models. This is due to only the necessary program code being generated.

The modeling tool jABC as well as already included plug-ins and libraries of process nodes have supported the development of the analysis, the abstraction process and the code-model generator. In particular the existing code generator, the layouter and the programming interface of the modeling tool are extensively used.

The remodeled DeAs applications are validated against the original ones. The method was proposed in Chapter 3.5.4 according to Rugaber and Stirewalt [RS04, p. 46]. They propose the comparison of program outputs. This was successfully tested for the programs DeAsManager and An_an.

In subsequent migration steps, the presented case studies can be refined and further developed at the model level (e.g. persistence functionality). Thus, the model level is the only necessary development artifact. The executable code is always generated on this basis. More functionality of the DeAs system can be incorporated or exchanged via a CORBA layer.

This proves that there is presently no distinction between development and operation/maintenance of software. The DeAs system is transformed into a continuous development process and evolution of the system.

6 Further Applications

In this chapter further applications of the developed approach to model-driven evolution of software systems are discussed. Of interest are the portability as well as the reusability of the existing tool chain. Focus is the model-driven reengineering. This includes

- the generation of code-models,
- the analysis and
- the subsequent regeneration of program code.

These three steps are the basis for the abstraction and migration phase. Three further programs were selected. Two of these applications – a simple text editing tool and a toolbox software for fast access to individual applications – have been developed using the same graphical interface (Open Look) as the DeAs system. The third program is a drawing program which is already used as example in other scientific publications.

In the following the three main aspects of this book are focused: code-model creation, model analysis and code generation. Each aspect is applied to one of the selected programs. Since the text editor is also based on Open Look, the abstraction of code-models by reusing the existing filter is applied. Due to the code size, the drawing software is analyzed in detail. The original program code is created based on the code-models of the `Toolbar` software.

6.1 `Textedit`

The text editor has been selected because it is an integral part of the Sun Solaris system interface. Its simple structure is illustrated in Figure 6.1. The program code includes 800 lines of C code.

This was at first successfully read by the Elsa parser and thereafter represented as a code-models in jABC. A total of eleven models are created.

Subsequently the original program code is generated from the code-models. The problems, already described in Chapter 5.5.4, emerge again. Due to the age of the application, additional problems appear, which affect

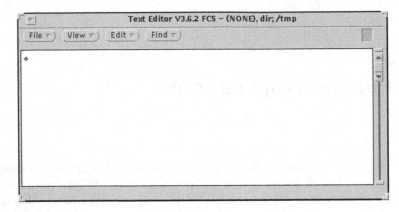

Figure 6.1: Textedit – User interface

the translation of existing program code. In summary the generated code lacks of

- 2 program symbols,
- 12 global variables,
- 14 macro definitions and
- 7 function pointers.

Furthermore, a fault in the developed back-end of the Elsa parser was found. This led to a preprocessor statement that was not removed properly.

Due to the further development of the C/C++ standards, the current compilers examine code much more stringent compared to the development time of the text editor. Because of this, translation errors emerge that are due to missing return values of methods and missing variables from standard libraries. These problems were manually adjusted before processing.

After generating the source code comprises 302 lines. The code increases to 587 lines after adding all global variables and function pointers. The discrepancy of 200 lines of code compared the original program is explained by the frequent use of preprocessor directives for platform independence.

Following the code generation step, the filter described in Chapter 5.6.1 is executed. It abstracts from the code-models and constructs the structure of the graphical interface.

Figure 6.2 illustrates the result. Evident are the window (Text Editor) and the associated panel (textedit:Panel). The four buttons (cf. Figure 6.1) are clustered around. In turn they are linked with the associated code-model.

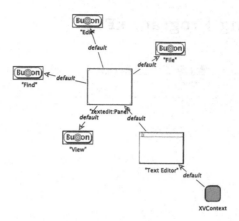

Figure 6.2: Textedit – Structure of the graphical interface

6.2 Toolbar

The Toolbar is implemented in C and is used for quick access of frequently used programs. Thereto the program can be expanded by arbitrary buttons. Each button consists of an icon and a command to start the application.

Figure 6.3: Toolbar – User interface

The original source code consists of 4,104 lines. No problems were encountered during creation of the intermediate format and importing it into the modeling tool. 45 code-models were created. The program code contains 1,564 lines after generation. Compared to the original amount, this gap indicates a larger number of function pointers or global variables.

In conclusion 35 function pointers are missing, which control user actions within the interface. By inserting the functions, the source code doubled to 3,242 lines. The discrepancy to the original size can be explained by the counting of sloccount and by the use of macro directives to enable the code on many platforms. Furthermore, another bug in the developed Elsa parser back-end was found and fixed.

6.3 Drawing Program xFig

Figure 6.4: xFig – User interface

The vector-based drawing program xFig is available on most UNIX/Linux compatible operating systems. The program code is implemented in C. It is open source under the Berkeley Software Distribution (BSD) license. The first version was published in 1985. The program is constantly being refined.

Canfora and Di Penta [CDP07] state that this software has already been used as an example for the analysis by GUPRO [Rie00], Bauhaus [CEK+00], Rigi [MWMW00] as well as Elliot et al. [SHE02]. Their aim was the location of properties and the determination of benchmarks.

Figure 6.4 shows the main window of the software. Altogether, it contains of 72,024 lines of code. These could be successfully transformed into the XML description and imported into jABC. The Elsa parser required 56 s for the conversion of 2,079 models.

Hereinafter the analysis of the xFig program is the focus. The analyzes developed for the DeAs system (Chapter 5.5.2 and Chapter 5.5.3) are applied again. First, the number of methods per XML is calculated. The result is illustrated in Figure 6.5.

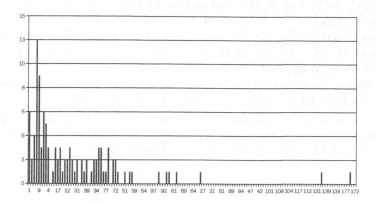

Figure 6.5: Number of methods per XML description

The application consists of 108 transformed files and 2,079 methods. On average each file contains 19.3 functions. Compared to the DeAs system, the density is slightly higher. The apex of the curve is shifted to the right (cf. Figure 5.19, p. 187). Half of the XML descriptions have less than 13, 80 % less than 31 methods.

The first result indicates a slightly higher complexity of xFig compared to DeAs. This assumption can be confirmed by determining the number of programming statements in each method.

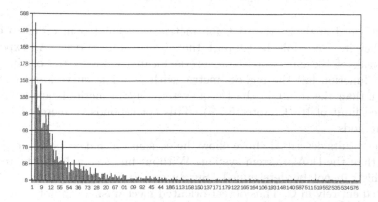

Figure 6.6: Number of nodes per function

Overall, xFig has 70,455 statements. Figure 6.6 shows the number of
nodes for each function (x-axis) on the set of functions that have the same
number (y-axis). The graph is truncated at 250 knots. Hence the results
are easier to compare with DeAs (Figure 5.20, p. 188). The curve for xFig
is much flatter than for the DeAs system. Therefore a method includes a lot
more lines of code (on average 34 lines, DeAs 11 lines). 80 % of the methods
have 38 knots or less (50 % have more than 13 statements).

Furthermore, xFig contains 43 functions with more than 250 statements.
The most extensive method has 2,040 nodes. Overall, these methods involve
about 20,000 lines of code, almost 30 % of the total.

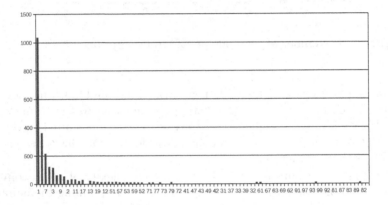

Figure 6.7: Result of the McCabe metric (All values were increased for
better visualization by 10 points.)

The third analysis, the McCabe metric is calculated in order to check
whether it is possible to support the observations above. As expected,
the peak of the curve in Figure 6.7 is located close to the origin. The
main function has the highest metric with 88. The curve is again much
flatter than the result in the DeAs system. 1,943 methods are below the
defined limit of 10 (Chapter 5.5.3). This corresponds to merely 93.5 % of
all methods.

The results described above allow the conclusion that xFig is more complex than the DeAs-System system. Without further analysis, the reasons
for this can not be determined. Surely one cause is that xFig is implemented entirely in C. Thus object-oriented mechanisms can not be applied.
Secondly the life cycle and development of the application certainly play a
central role.

In the last step was the original program code from the existing code-models was restored. After code generation (duration 38 s), the code has an amount of merely 21,929 lines. A more detailed analysis revealed that xFig makes extensive use of function pointers and global variables. The selected parser is not suitable here. A determination of dead code was not performed. Therefore a manual examination of all function pointers inside the source code is required.

6.4 Summary

The reengineering of the three selected applications have shown that the developed procedure and the tool chain are applicable to other programs. Nevertheless, due to their design and programming, there are increasing problems with function pointers and global variables. Again this illustrates clearly the limits of the selected and implemented tool chain.

The C programming language seems less suitable for the developed method. The restriction usually affects the regeneration of the source code. Unaffected by this are the analysis as well as the API-based abstraction. The abstraction naturally is tied to the API of an interface.

7 Conclusions

The following two sections summarize the results of the work and present still open as well as emerging research questions. These include the further development of the project.

7.1 Summary

In the present book the conversion of code-centric software systems towards a *model-driven evolution* is fully demonstrated. A method for *model-driven migration* of software systems was designed for the first time. It was successfully applied to the central application – the DeAs system – and three other applications. Furthermore, it was confirmed that software reengineering and migration are always go with extensive resources and manual effort.

The first results of the model-driven migration justify this effort. The border between *creatio ex nihilo* and *creatio ex aliquo* is removed and the system's evolution is shifted to the model level. The associated code is properly generated from the migrated models. Therefore the developed approach corresponds to the ideal conception illustrated in Figure 3.2.

Moreover, the approach includes the integration of existing code into the model-driven development. The migration of the DeAs system demonstrates the successful integration of original functionality on model level. The definition of a minimum amount of necessary interfaces within the existing system as well as simple and flexible reuse of already migrated functionalities are the essential features.

The work has five key features for the implementation of the project:

- the development of a concrete process model,
- the transformation of program code on model level,
- the analysis of program code,
- the migration and
- the application on a specific in-use software system.

Methodology

The developed methodology is based on the life cycle models presented in
Chapter 2. A continuous, model-driven approach for the evolution of existing systems is derived. The CMDE as a model-driven methodology and
its concrete form – the XMDD method – form the basis. Previously this
method was applied in the development of software systems only. Therefore,
a process model was developed, which is extended by analysis, transformation and integration of existing software.

The overall concept contains of two basic phases: In model-driven reengineering a unique step from a code-centric to a model-driven software evolution is carried out. For this purpose an application is mapped as a control
flow graph on the model level. The graph representation is the basis for the
application understanding and the remodeling. The result of the latter step
describes the behavior of the program as a process model. From the model
the corresponding source code is generated.

The method itself as well as the fragments are described in a formal
notation which has already been applied successfully. The XPDDs cover
conditions and results of an activity within the method. The model-driven
migration consists of several XPDD models. The activities, and their order
play a central role. These are partly automated by different tools.

Transformation of Program Code into the Model Level

Based on the languages C/C++, it could be demonstrated that a transformation to model level is possible. Therefore a C/C++ parser back-end was
developed. It converts the textual representation of the program code into a
machine-readable form. The annotated AST is the fundamental data structure. The structure is translated into a platform-independent description
via the back-end.

The result is enriched with a variety of information about each statement
in the source code. A line in the source file may contain a statement type,
but also more complex data like a fully qualified name or a declaration.

The modeling tool jABC imports this description and translates it into
a code-model. The model consists of nodes that represent the grammar of
C/C++. Each node in the graph is enriched with all available information.
In addition, code-models representing function calls are associated with each
other. Therefore benefits arise both in the inter-procedural analysis of the
program code as well as for the maintenance engineer. The latter can browse
through the source code to improve the application understanding. Since

there is a very large amount of information in the models. However, this must be reduced by targeted analyzes and abstractions.

Analysis of the Source Code

The analysis of the program code enables the participants to improve the knowledge about the existing application and to identify potential problem areas. The analyzes are not described in a programming language. Instead a process model is created using the same modeling tool.

The jABC has been expanded with a range of process modules that can evaluate specific properties of individual nodes in the code-models. Therefore, it is possible to describe the calculation of program lines or the determination of metrics as a process model. Furthermore, it was shown that external tools can also be integrated into this process. A variety of possibilities are available to the maintenance engineer at minimal effort. This book only presented small examples, which by no means exploit the potential of the approach at all.

Migration of a Software System

For the migration of software the generated code-models provide a valuable starting point. However, they contain too much information. The aim of migration is to transfer the functionality expected from the user to a new target system. The developed method can not automate this process yet.

To reduce the amount of information, useful abstraction criteria need to be defined. Thus the *API-based abstraction* is developed and successfully implemented. It is applied and tested with a graphical user interface. The development is based on the following considerations:

- A system consists of a set of process sequences which can be triggered by a user or another mechanism.
- When migrating a system this sequences should be considered and prepared for a new environment.
- GUI systems are advantageous, since all process sequences are usually triggered on the interface.
- For the remodeling, the maintenance engineer is to be supported with regard to examining the process sequences. The actual migration is carried out manually.
- An automated method extracts parts of the sequences and presents them graphically.

The API-based abstraction is again described as a process model. Similar to the analyzes, this enables harnessing the benefits of model-driven development. The result of the abstraction step is a structural model of the graphical interface. It contains all GUI components that are displayed in a tree structure. All elements that can trigger a process sequence are marked separately. Additionally they are linked to the underlying implementation in the form of a code-model. The total quantity of sequences to be transformed is determined automatically for migration.

Next, the maintenance engineer creates a model, which contains the functions to be migrated. By analyzing the code-models the semantics of the process sequence could be evaluated. It has been determined that in general, a search level of two to three layers is sufficient.

Based on this study, the existing system can be remodeled and connected to the model level. For one thing in this approach process graphs are developed that describe the system on an abstract level, for another thing the number of interfaces to the existing system is minimal and limited to merely the necessary ones.

Concrete Application

The concrete application of model-driven software migration could be demonstrated in the present book. The example is a medium-sized legacy system. The examined part of the DeAs system includes nearly 100,000 lines of code and consists of 21 applications based on several libraries.

The overall system has been fully translated into code-models as well as analyzes on the model level. Also external tools for visualizing dependencies have been used. The developed API-based abstraction was successfully applied to all programs. A model of the process sequences was generated for each.

Based on two selected DeAs applications, the manual part of the migration is implemented prototypically. The remodeled process models describe the applications on an abstract level. They illustrate all possible process sequences as well as the components of a DeAs application.

The remodeled process modules are connected via CORBA to the original functionality. Thus it is possible to animate the models in jABC and hence to generate fully executable program code. The validation of existing and remodeled applications is proven by comparing the program output. No differences are observed.

7.2 Future Work

Due to the flexibility and adaptability, the reference implementation of the model-driven migration method can be enhanced continuously. Furthermore new research questions on specific issues are raised. The following section briefly introduces and discusses the key issues. These can be divided into conceptual and tool-specific issues.

Exchange of the Elsa Parser

The application of the Elsa parser has shown that it is not invariably suitable without exception for the necessary processing of the existing program code. Its weaknesses mainly are macros and global variables.

In Chapter 4.1 the Clang parser is discussed as alternative. It was already evaluated at the beginning of the project, but due to its early stage of development it was not selected. In the meantime, it provides a meaningful option: The Clang parser includes, in contrast to the Elsa parser, a preprocessor. Hence, the manual replacement of all macros is redundant. This simplifies the analysis of the original program. Furthermore it includes the analysis of global variables, structures, and functions in order to simplify the code-model generation. Again this reduces the manual rework to a minimum. Its interface is similar to the Elsa parser.

Common Data Exchange Format

The result of the parsing step is a data format, which is composed of various properties of the formats presented in Chapter 4.2. In order to ensure interoperability and comparability with other tools, the transition or conversion of the existing format into GXL is necessary. This results in a plethora of possibilities, e.g. the application and comparison with other reengineering tools like Columbus, GUPRO or Bauhaus.

From a scientific point of view, the comparison of code-centered tools to a tool solely working on the model level is interesting and essential for basic research. Hence the quality of the results, the performance, the flexibility and the resources required for the migration of software systems can be determined and compared.

Extension of the Analysis Processes

So far, the developed analysis processes show only a small subset of the possible potential. Due to the density of the information inside the code-models many code-centric analyzes can be transferred to the model-layer. The calculation of Def/Use-Sets originating from the data flow analysis shall form the basis for subsequent projects.

The aim should be to describe the analysis algorithms at process level and to implement the appropriate process modules. The extension of the SIB library enables rapid and easy development as well as the adaptation of analyzes. The application of XMDD and the modeling tool jABC has opened the opportunity to make the models accessible to other user groups.

In addition, the integration of external tools is possible. Thus, the redeployment of algorithms is avoided and already tested functionality is reused.

Code-Models as Documentation and Test Basis

It has already been indicated that the code-models are not only suitable for program analysis. Other scenarios could be the creation of documentation as well as the generation of test classes. Especially for the primary uses case presented here, such an option is necessary since the system is neither documented nor has a test case.

The creation of classes and method bodies is desirable. Complete testing methods are not possible since information about data types and their semantics are missing. Nevertheless, additional information can be stored. For a path coverage test the mapping of all branches and loops (for example as a comment) of a method will support the testing phase. The result of the procedure consists of the complete set of all methods that are to be tested.

Analysis of Graph Databases

Both the analysis and the migration of the code are based on graphs. These are usually stored in a file as a structured description. Access to files is not efficient, especially regarding search for items on multiple graphs.

A group of databases are designed specifically for graphs. In particular, they can serve as a central collection and access point for the code-models. In this book no detailed consideration is performed in this context. Neo4j[1], HyperGraphDB[2] or VertexDB[3] are example products. It can be assumed that the performance of the method would considerably gain.

A side effect of using a database developed for this purpose are the custom query languages. Hence atomic operations can be defined and mapped

---

[1] http://neo4j.org/
[2] http://www.kobrix.com/hgdb.jsp
[3] http://www.dekorte.com/projects/opensource/vertexdb/

to process nodes. These provide the basis for the description of complex analysis on the model level.

Partial Code Generation

The generation of program code from the code-models leads to the maintenance engineer focusing on the relevant parts of the program, and this helps to significantly reduce complexity.

According to this book, the reduction to the intrinsically indispensable source code supports the code-centric development. Therefore the extension of existing development environments is necessary. These should be able to hide all elements not belonging to the examined application. The procedure is identical to the code-model generation. The whole program code is initially disabled. Thereafter the user selects a method which is analyzed for function calls. The process continues with the associated methods until all parts of the program are examined.

Extension of the transformation language

The previously developed transformation language for API-based abstraction is rudimentary and has few, mostly very complex process nodes. Therefore one of the transformation languages presented in Chapter 4.5 shall be considered. It should be made available as process nodes, in order to model complex transformations.

Here, the distinction between coarse and fine-grained modeling is a relevant research question. It is to be investigated whether and in what contexts atomic or composite operations are useful for modeling. In addition, the comparison of textual and graphical approaches from a research perspective is necessary.

Transformation of the Graphical Interface

The previously developed filter extracts the static aspects of a graphical interface solely. The dynamic aspects, such as disabling windows or buttons for certain actions, are still lacking and need to be implemented manually by the maintenance engineer. The analysis of the models can filter out the dynamic aspects. By examining the xv_set and xv_get methods this information can be reconstructed.

Primarily problems persist in the preparation and the assignment of the elements to the dynamic behavior as well as in the detection of the triggering action. The result can be presented for example as UML diagram or as CEP.

Use of Empirical/Statistical Methods for Interface Detection

The use of empirical methods may support the manual work of the maintenance engineer, e.g. to find components of the process sequences and to ensure the detection of interfaces. These additional filters could classify the program code and can color the individual processing nodes specifically.

The present approach indicates the boundary between empirical research and static analysis. For the use of empirical methods, in Chapter 5.6.6 the first indications for the detection of interfaces in an existing system have been summarized.

Change to the Eclipse Platform

The next version of the jABC modeling tool is developed based on the EMF. With this change a multitude of new possibilities present themselves. These include the description of the model-driven migration at meta-model level as well as the use of integrated EMF tools. Furthermore, there are several software reengineering projects (see Chapter 4.6) that can be incorporated.

- For jABC an own meta-model must be defined in EMF. Based on this, meta-models are derived for control flow graphs and code-models.
- Next, it is possible to describe a general code-model transformation. Different transformation languages are already integrated in EMF.
- Furthermore, Eclipse contains multiple parsers for the supported languages. They can interpret the source code and extract information. Additionally various code generators are available which allow for the original program code to be created from the code-models.
- For each yet to be examined programming language a separate meta-model is defined. It describes the basic elements of a grammar. Therefore, the nodes of the code-models can be generated in advance. A manual implementation is not necessary.

Further description languages for syntax trees (ASTM) and knowledge models (KDM) are discussed in Chapter 4.2. Their reuse stands to reason, especially since existing analyzes based on these meta-models are instantly executable. A disadvantage of the Eclipse solution mainly is the poor documentation of the project. Changes to the tool itself as well as extensions to the modeling environment entail a lot of effort.

Migration from other Platforms

For the further development of the designed method as well as their fragments, it should be used in subsequent projects. Its application to other platforms and programming languages is essential to show that this approach will scale. The existing tools must be adapted or redeveloped.

The XPDDs supports migration by the concrete representation of this process. The required tool chain as well as the associated input and output data are illustrated.

Interpreter for C/C++

The generated code-models represent a control flow graph and have no execution semantics. Thus, in contrast to the process models, these models can not be animated. To facilitate this, an interpreter is required, which can read the code-models. This supports and extends the possibilities of program analysis. Now additional aspects that can only be determined at runtime are examinable (e.g. function pointers). Furthermore, the mixing of code-models and migrated system parts during migration will benefit.

7.3 Result

The predominant code-centric development of software systems and the associated difficulties in software migration make further research in this area essential. As explained in the previous section, a number of open issues arise resulting from this work, which have to be examined subsequently.

The complexity of the subject area is due to the heterogeneity of systems, platforms and development methodologies. Thus, a simple tool chain is not sufficient. This inevitably has to be evolved to a tool box – similar to existing approaches (cf. Chapter 4) so far implemented partially only.

This is the strength of the outlined approach: First, it is described formally using the XPDD notation. Any new approaches, data formats, and analysis tools can be integrated into this process. On the other hand, a continuous modeling approach forms the base. This makes it possible, due to its conception and design flexibility, to adapt the process of migration to specific project requirements as well as to integrate new methods and building blocks. Simultaneously XMDD is the framework for the resulting tool box.

The consistent application of models as representatives for all artifacts plays a central role in the migration of software. It enables a continuous, coordinated and progressive development approach. The representation of program code, the description and evaluation of analysis, the definition of filters, as well as the description of the process to migrate software originate from one source. None other approach and none other tool implement the model-driven approach in such a rigorous manner so far.

Bibliography

[AEK05]   AL-EKRAM, R. ; KONTOGIANNIS, K.:   An XML-Based
           Framework for Language Neutral Program Representation and
           Generic Analysis. In: *Ninth European Conference on Software
           Maintenance and Reengineering (CSMR)*, 2005. – ISSN 1534–
           5351, S. 42 – 51. – DOI 10.1109/CSMR.2005.10 [XV, 121]

[AFMT95]   ANTONIOL, G. ; FIUTEM, R. ; MERLO, E. ; TONELLA, P.: Ap-
           plication and user interface migration from BASIC to Visual
           C++. In: *Proceedings of the International Conference on Soft-
           ware Maintenance*. Washington, DC, USA : IEEE Computer
           Society, 1995 (ICSM '95). – ISBN 0–8186–7141–6, S. 76– [144]

[AK01]   ATKINSON, Colin ; KÜHNE, Thomas: The Essence of Multilevel
           Metamodeling. In: *Proceedings of the 4th International Confer-
           ence on The Unified Modeling Language, Modeling Languages,
           Concepts, and Tools*. London, UK, UK : Springer-Verlag, 2001
           (UML '01). – ISBN 3–540–42667–1, S. 19–33 [47, 51]

[AK02]   ATKINSON, Colin ; KÜHNE, Thomas: Rearchitecting the UML
           infrastructure. In: *ACM Transactions on Modeling and Com-
           puter Simulation* 12 (2002), October, S. 290–321. – ISSN 1049–
           3301. – DOI 10.1145/643120.643123 [47, 52, 55]

[AK03]   ATKINSON, Colin ; KÜHNE, Thomas: Model-Driven Devel-
           opment: A Metamodeling Foundation. In: *IEEE Softw.* 20
           (2003), September, S. 36–41. –   ISSN 0740-7459. –   DOI
           10.1109/MS.2003.1231149 [47, 48, 54, 71]

[ALB11]   AGRAWALA, Maneesh ; LI, Wilmot ; BERTHOUZOZ, Floraine:
           Design principles for visual communication. In: *Communica-
           tions of the ACM* 54 (2011), April, S. 60–69. – ISSN 0001–0782.
           – DOI 10.1145/1924421.1924439 [177]

[APMV03]   ANTONIOL, G. ; PENTA, M. D. ; MASONE, G. ; VILLANO, U.:
           XOgastan: XML-Oriented gcc AST Analysis and Transforma-
           tions. In: *Third IEEE International Workshop on Source Code
           Analysis and Manipulation* 00 (2003), S. 173. ISBN 0–7695–
           2005-7. – DOI 10.1109/SCAM.2003.1238043 [112]

[Arn93] ARNOLD, Robert S.: *Software Reengineering.* Los Alamitos, CA, USA : IEEE Computer Society Press, 1993. – ISBN 0818632712 [34, 85]

[ASAU99] AHO, R.S.A.V. ; SETHI, R. ; AHO, A.V. ; ULLMAN, J.D.: *Compilerbau.* Oldenbourg, 1999 (Compilerbau Teil 1). – ISBN 9783486252941 [86]

[ASRW02] ABRAHAMSSON, Pekka ; SALO, Outi ; RONKAINEN, Jussi ; WARSTA, Juhani: Agile Software Development Methods: Review and Analysis / VTT Publications. 2002 (478). – Forschungsbericht. – ISBN 951–38–6009–4. – "" [14]

[Bad00] BADROS, Greg J.: JavaML: a markup language for Java source code. In: *Computer Networks* 33 (2000), Nr. 1, S. 159–177 [119, 120]

[BBG+93] BODIN, F. ; BECKMAN, P. ; GANNON, D. ; YANG, S. ; KESAVAN, S. ; MALONY, A. ; MOHR, B.: Implementing a Parallel C++ Runtime System for Scalable Parallel Systems. In: *ACM Conference on Object-Oriented Programming Systems, Languages, and Applications (OOPSLA'95).* Portland, Oregon, USA : ACM, Nov. 1993 1993 (Supercomputing Conference), S. 588–597 [111]

[BBG+94] BODIN, F. ; BECKMAN, P. ; GANNON, D. ; GOTWALS, J. ; NARAYANA, S. ; SRINIVAS, S. ; WINNICKA, B.: Sage++: An Object Oriented Toolkit and Class Library for Building Fortran and C++ Restructuring Tools. In: *Proceedings of the Object-Oriented Numerics Conference (Oonski '94), Oregon,* 1994, S. 122–136 [111]

[BBJ07] BEZIVIN, Jean ; BARBERO, Mikael ; JOUAULT, Frederic: On the Applicability Scope of Model Driven Engineering. In: *Proceedings of the Fourth International Workshop on Model-Based Methodologies for Pervasive and Embedded Software.* Washington, DC, USA : IEEE Computer Society, 2007 (MOMPES '07). – ISBN 0–7695–2769–8, S. 3–7. – DOI 10.1109/MOMPES.2007.16 [45, 47, 48, 55, 56, 84, 140]

[BDMG+94] BUSS, E. ; DE MORI, R. ; GENTLEMAN, W. M. ; HENSHAW, J. ; JOHNSON, H. ; KONTOGIANNIS, K. ; MERLO, E. ; MÜLLER, H. A. ; MYLOPOULOS, J. ; PAUL, S. ; PRAKASH, A. ; STANLEY, M. ; TILLEY, S. R. ; TROSTER, J. ; WONG, K.: Investigating reverse engineering technologies for the CAS program understanding project. In: *IBM Systems Journal* 33 (1994), July, Nr. 3, S. 477–500. – ISSN 0018–8670. – DOI 10.1147/sj.333.0477

[23]

[BE08]   BILDHAUER, Daniel ; EBERT, Jürgen: Querying Software Ab-
           straction Graphs. In: *Working Session on Query Technologies
           and Applications for Program Comprehension (QTAPC 2008)*
           (2008) [138]

[BEH+01]   BRANDES, Ulrik ; EIGLSPERGER, Markus ; HERMAN, Ivan ;
           HIMSOLT, Michael ; MARSHALL, M. S.: GraphML Progress Re-
           port (Structural Layer Proposal). In: MUTZEL, Petra (Hrsg.) ;
           JÜNGER, Michael (Hrsg.) ; LEIPERT, Sebastian (Hrsg.): *Graph
           Drawing, Vienna, Austria, September 23-26, 2001*, Springer,
           2001, S. 501–512 [118]

[BEL12]   BRANDES, Ulrik ; EIGLSPERGER, Markus ; LERNER, Jürgen:
           GraphML Primer. http://graphml.graphdrawing.org/
           primer/graphml-primer.html. Version: zuletzt besucht:
           09.01.2012 [118]

[Ben95]   BENNETT, Keith: Legacy Systems: Coping with Success. In:
           IEEE Software 12 (1995), S. 19–23. – ISSN 0740-7459. – DOI
           10.1109/52.363157 [10, 27, 32, 37]

[Ber78]   BERGLAND, Glenn D.: Structured design methodologies. In:
           Proceedings of the 15th conference on Design automation, IEEE
           Press, 1978, S. 475–493 [36, 61]

[Ber05]   BERG, Klaus P.: Softwareevolution und Wartung: Situations-
           analyse und Entwicklungsmöchkeiten. In: *OBJEKTSpektrum* 2
           (2005), S. 54–59 [9, 15, 17, 21, 23, 35, 67]

[BF10]   BEYER, Dirk ; FARAROOY, Ashgan: A Simple and Effective
           Measure for Complex Low-Level Dependencies. In: *Interna-
           tional Conference on Program Comprehension*, IEEE Computer
           Society, 2010. – ISBN 978-0-7695-4113-6, S. 80–83 [195]

[BFG05]   BESZÉDES, Á. ; FERENC, R. ; GYIMÓTHY, T.: Columbus:
           A Reverse Engineering Approach. In: *Proceedings of the 13th
           IEEE Workshop on Software Technology and Engineering Prac-
           tice (STEP 2005)*, IEEE Computer Society, sep 2005, S. 93–96
           [125, 215]

[BG01]   BÉZIVIN, Jean ; GERBÉ, Olivier: Towards a Precise Defini-
           tion of the OMG/MDA Framework. In: *Proceedings of the 16th
           IEEE international conference on Automated software engineer-
           ing*. Washington, DC, USA : IEEE Computer Society, 2001
           (ASE '01), S. 273– [49]

[BJKO00]   BRAND, Mark ; JONG, Hayco A. ; KLINT, Paul ; OLIVIER,
           Pieter A.: Efficient annotated terms. Amsterdam, The Nether-

lands : CWI (Centre for Mathematics and Computer Science), 2000. – Forschungsbericht [137]

[BJM09]   BAKERA, Marco ; JÖRGES, S. ; MARGARIA, T.: Test your Strategy: Graphical Construction of Strategies for Connect-Four. In: *Proc. of the 14th IEEE International Conference on Engineering of Complex Computer Systems, ICECCS 2009*, IEEE Computer Society, June 2009, S. 172–181 [80]

[BJO85]   BERGSTRA, J. ; JONKERS, H. ; OBBINK, J.: ESPRIT'84: Status report of ongoing work. (1985). – ISSN 9780444877406 [60]

[BLP05]   BRANDES, Ulrik ; LERNER, Jürgen ; PICH, Christian: GXL to GraphML and Vice Versa with XSLT. In: *Electronic Notes in Theoretical Computer Science* 127 (2005), Nr. 1, S. 113–125 [119]

[BLWG99a] BISBAL, Jesús ; LAWLESS, Deirdre ; WU, Bing ; GRIMSON, Jane: Legacy Information System Migration: A Brief Review of Problems, Solutions and Research Issues. Dublin, Ireland : Trinity College, Mai 1999 (TCD-CS-1999-38). – Forschungsbericht. – "" [43]

[BLWG99b] BISBAL, Jesús ; LAWLESS, Deirdre ; WU, Bing ; GRIMSON, Jane: Legacy Information Systems: Issues and Directions. In: *IEEE Software* 16 (1999), S. 103–111. – ISSN 0740–7459. – DOI 10.1109/52.795108 [28, 29, 40, 43]

[BM06]   BAJOHR, Markus ; MARGARIA, Tiziana: MaTRICS: A service-based management tool for remote intelligent configuration of systems. In: *ISSE* 2 (2006), Nr. 2, S. 99–111 [80]

[Boe86]   BOEHM, B: A spiral model of software development and enhancement. In: *SIGSOFT Software Engineering Notes* 11 (1986), Nr. 4, S. 14–24. – ISSN 0163–5948. – DOI 10.1145/12944.12948 [9, 12, 13]

[Bri96]   BRINKKEMPER, Sjaak: Method Engineering: Engineering of Information Systems Development Methods and Tools. In: *Information and Software Technology* 38 (1996), April, Nr. 4, S. 275–280 [9, 60, 61]

[BRM99]   BENNETT, Keith H. ; RAMAGE, Magnus ; MUNRO, Malcolm: Decision model for legacy systems. In: *IEEE Proceedings - Software* 146 (1999), Nr. 3, S. 153–159 [27]

[Bro95]   BROOKS, Frederick P.: *The Mythical Man-Month: Essays on Software Engineering, Anniversary Edition (2nd Edition)*. 2. Addison-Wesley Professional, 1995. – ISBN 0201835959 [40]

[Bro04]   BROWN, Alan W.: Model driven architecture: Principles and
           practice. In: *Software and Systems Modeling* 3 (2004), S. 314–
           327. – ISSN 1619–1366. – 10.1007/s10270-004-0061-2 [44, 46, 48,
           70, 82, 100]

[BS95]   BRODIE, Michael L. ; STONEBRAKER, Michael: *Migrating
           Legacy Systems: Gateways, Interfaces, and the Incremental Ap-
           proach*. Morgan Kaufmann, 1995. – ISBN 1–55860–330–1 [27,
           40, 42, 43]

[BSH99]   BRINKKEMPER, Sjaak ; SAEKI, Motoshi ; HARMSEN, Frank:
           Meta-modelling based assembly techniques for situational
           method engineering. In: *Information Systems* 24 (1999), Nr.
           3, S. 209 – 228. – ISSN 0306–4379. – 10th International Con-
           ference on Advanced Information Systems Engineering [60]

[BTD11]   BECK, Martin ; TRÜMPER, Jonas ; DÖLLNER, Jürgen: A Visual
           Analysis and Design Tool for Planning Software Reengineerings.
           In: *Proceedings of the International Workshop on Visualizing
           Software for Understanding and Analysis*, IEEE Computer So-
           ciety, 2011, S. 54–61 [197]

[Byr92]   BYRNE, E.J.: A conceptual foundation for software re-
           engineering. In: *Conference on Software Maintenance*, IEEE
           Computer Society, 1992. – ISSN 0–8186–2980–0, S. 226 – 235.
           – DOI 10.1109/ICSM.1992.242539 [36]

[Bé05]   BÉZIVIN, Jean: On the Unification Power of Models. In: *Soft-
           ware and System Modeling (SoSym)* 4 (2005), Nr. 2, S. 171–188
           [47, 54, 82, 100]

[can00]   CANADA, bell: DATRIX Abstract Semantic Graph Reference
           Manual (Version 1.4) / Bell Canada. 2000. – Forschungsbericht
           [122]

[CC90]   CHIKOFSKY, Elliot J. ; CROSS, James H.: Reverse Engineer-
           ing and Design Recovery: A Taxonomy. In: *IEEE Software* 7
           (1990), Nr. 1, S. 13–17 [30, 31, 35, 88]

[CC00]   CANFORA, Gerardo ; CIMITILE, Aniello: Software Maintenance.
           Benevento Palazzo Bosco Lucarelli, Piazza Roma 82100 : Uni-
           verstity of Sannio, November 2000 (""). – Forschungsbericht. –
           "" [1, 24, 26, 29, 32, 83, 102]

[CDP07]   CANFORA, Gerardo ; DI PENTA, Massimiliano: New Fron-
           tiers of Reverse Engineering. In: *2007 Future of Software En-
           gineering*. Washington, DC, USA : IEEE Computer Society,
           2007 (FOSE '07). – ISBN 0–7695–2829–5, S. 326–341. – DOI
           10.1109/FOSE.2007.15 [31, 244]

[CEK+00] CZERANSKI, Jörg ; EISENBARTH, Thomas ; KIENLE, Holger ; KOSCHKE, Rainer ; SIMON, Daniel: Analyzing xfig Using the Bauhaus Tool. In: *Proceedings of the Seventh Working Conference on Reverse Engineering (WCRE'00)*. Washington, DC, USA : IEEE Computer Society, 2000 (WCRE '00). – ISBN 0–7695–0881–2, S. 197– [126, 244]

[CH80] CASHMAN, Paul M. ; HOLT, Anatol W.: A communication-oriented approach to structuring the software maintenance environment. In: *SIGSOFT Software Engengineering Notes* 5 (1980), Nr. 1, S. 4–17. – ISSN 0163–5948. – DOI 10.1145/1010782.1010783 [16]

[Chi95] CHIBA, S.: A Metaobject Protocol for C++. In: *ACM Conference on Object-Oriented Programming Systems, Languages, and Applications (OOPSLA'95)*. Austin, Texas, USA : ACM, Oktober 1995 (SIGPLAN Notices 30(10)), S. 285–299 [111]

[CHN06] CHANG, Bor-Yuh E. ; HARREN, Matthew T. ; NECULA, George: Analysis of Low-Level Code Using Cooperating Decompilers / EECS Department, University of California, Berkeley. 2006 (UCB/EECS-2006-86). – Forschungsbericht. – "" [113]

[CLC04] COHEN, David ; LINDVALL, Mikael ; COSTA, Patricia: An introduction to agile methods. In: *Advances in Computers* 62 (2004), S. 2–67 [14]

[CLM03] CHAN, Keith ; LIANG, Zhi Cong L. ; MICHAIL, Amir: Design recovery of interactive graphical applications. In: *Proceedings of the 25th International Conference on Software Engineering*. Washington, DC, USA : IEEE Computer Society, 2003 (ICSE '03). – ISBN 0–7695–1877–X, S. 114–124 [143]

[CM08] CEPA, Vasian ; MEZINI, Mira: Language support for model-driven software development. In: *Science of Computer Programming* 73 (2008), September, Nr. 1, S. 13–25. – ISSN 0167–6423. – DOI 10.1016/j.scico.2008.05.003 [124]

[CON12] CONNECT - EMERGENT CONNECTORS FOR ETERNAL SOFTWARE INTENSIVE NETWORKED SYSTEMS: *http://www.connect-forever.eu.* zuletzt besucht: 09.03.2012 [9, 63]

[Cor06a] CORDY, James R.: Source transformation, analysis and generation in TXL. In: *Proceedings of the 2006 ACM SIGPLAN symposium on Partial evaluation and semantics-based program manipulation*. New York, NY, USA : ACM, 2006 (PEPM '06). – ISBN 1–59593–196–1, S. 1–11. – DOI 10.1145/1111542.1111544 [138]

[Cor06b] CORDY, James R.: The TXL source transformation language. In: *Sci. Comput. Program.* 61 (2006), August, Nr. 3, S. 190–210. – ISSN 0167–6423. – DOI 10.1016/j.scico.2006.04.002 [137]

[CS06] CLAUS, Volker ; SCHWILL, Andreas ; MEYERS LEXIKONREDAKTION (Hrsg.): *Duden Informatik A–Z. Fachlexikon für Studium und Praxis.* 4., überarb. u. aktualis. Aufl. Mannheim, Leipzig, Wien, Zürich : Bibliographisches Institut, 2006. – ISBN 3–411–05234–1 [21, 35]

[DDN09] DEMEYER, S. ; DUCASSE, S. ; NIERSTRASZ, O.M.: *Object-oriented reengineering patterns.* 2009-09-28. Square Bracket Associates, October 7, 2009. – 360 S. – ISBN 978–3–9523341–2–6 [25, 40, 41, 42, 68, 92]

[DGGD06] DOYLE, Duncan ; GEERS, Hans ; GRAAF, Bas ; DEURSEN, Arie van: Migrating a Domain-Specific Modeling Language to MDA Technology. In: FAVRE, Jean M. (Hrsg.) ; GASEVIC, Dragan (Hrsg.) ; LAMMEL, Ralf (Hrsg.) ; WINTER, Andreas (Hrsg.): *Proceedings of the 3rd International Workshop on Metamodels, Schemas, Grammars, and Ontologies for Reverse Engineering (ateM 2006)*, Johannes Gutenberg-Universitat Mainz, 2006. – ISBN ISSN 0931–9972, S. 47–54. – Informatik Bericht [128]

[Die02] DIETZSCH, Andreas: Adapting the UML to Business Modelling's Needs - Experiences in Situational Method Engineering. In: *Proceedings of the 5th International Conference on The Unified Modeling Language.* London, UK : Springer-Verlag, 2002 (UML '02). – ISBN 3–540–44254–5, S. 73–83 [61, 62]

[DMH01] DEAN, Thomas R. ; MALTON, Andrew J. ; HOLT, Ric: Union Schemas as a Basis for a C++ Extractor. In: *Proceedings of the Eighth Working Conference on Reverse Engineering (WCRE'01).* Washington, DC, USA : IEEE Computer Society, 2001 (WCRE '01). – ISBN 0–7695–1303–4, S. 59– [112]

[DMT10] DETTEN, M. von ; MEYER, M. ; TRAVKIN, D.: Reverse Engineering with the Reclipse Tool Suite. In: *Proceedings of the 32nd ACM/IEEE International Conference on Software Engineering (ICSE 2010), Cape Town, South Africa, May 2-8, 2010,* 2010 [135]

[DR95] DEBAUD, J.-M. ; RUGABER, S.: A software re-engineering method using domain models. In: *Proceedings of the International Conference on Software Maintenance.* Washington, DC, USA : IEEE Computer Society, 1995 (ICSM '95). – ISBN 0–8186–7141–6, S. 204–213 [98, 101]

[DRN78]   DE ROZE, B. C. ; NYMAN, T. H.:   The Software Life Cy-
            cle A Management and Technological Challenge in the Depart-
            ment of Defense. In: *IEEE Transactions on Software Engineer-
            ing* 4 (1978), Nr. 4, S. 309–318. – ISSN 0098–5589. – DOI
            10.1109/TSE.1978.231517 [16]

[DVW07]   DEURSEN, Arie van ; VISSER, Eelco ; WARMER, Jos: Model-
            Driven Software Evolution: A Research Agenda. In: TAMZALIT,
            D. (Hrsg.): *CSMR Workshop on Model-Driven Software Evolu-
            tion (MoDSE 2007)*. Amsterdam, The Netherlands : "", March
            2007, S. 41–49 [45, 52, 57, 59, 82, 84, 100, 103]

[EKRW02]   EBERT, Jürgen ; KULLBACH, Bernt ; RIEDIGER, Volker ; WIN-
            TER, Andreas: GUPRO - Generic Understanding of Programs
            An Overview. In: *Electronic Notes in Theoretical Computer
            Science* 72 (2002), Nr. 2, S. 47 – 56. – ISSN 1571–0661. – Gra-
            BaTs 2002, Graph-Based Tools (First International Conference
            on Graph Transformation) [125]

[EKW99]   EBERT, Jürgen ; KULLBACH, Bernt ; WINTER, Andreas: GraX
            - An Interchange Format for Reengineering Tools. In: *Proceed-
            ings of the Sixth Working Conference on Reverse Engineering
            (WCRE)*. Washington, DC, USA : IEEE Computer Society,
            1999. – ISBN 0–7695–0303–9, S. 89– [117, 125]

[EKW00]   EBERT, Jürgen ; KULLBACH, Bernt ; WINTER, Andreas: GraX:
            Graph Exchange Format. In: *Proceedings ICSE 2000 Workshop
            on Standard Exchange Format (WoSEF)*, 2000 [117]

[Erl00]   ERLIKH, Len: Leveraging Legacy System Dollars for E-Business.
            In: *IT Professional* 2 (2000), May, S. 17–23. – ISSN 1520–9202.
            – DOI 10.1109/6294.846201 [16]

[EWD+96]   EBERT, Jürgen ; WINTER, Andreas ; DAHM, Peter ; FRANZKE,
            Angelika ; SÜTTENBACH, Roger: Graph Based Modeling and
            Implementation with EER / GRAL. In: *Proceedings of the 15th
            International Conference on Conceptual Modeling*. London, UK
            : Springer-Verlag, 1996 (ER '96). – ISBN 3–540–61784–1, S.
            163–178 [125]

[Fav04a]   FAVRE, Jean-Marie: Foundations of Model (driven) (Reverse)
            Engineering - Episode I: Story of the Fidus Papyrus and the
            Solarus. (2004) [9, 47, 50, 51, 53, 57, 59, 60, 70, 79]

[Fav04b]   FAVRE, Jean-Marie: Towards a Basic Theory to Model Model
            Driven Engineering. (2004), October [47, 57]

[Fav05]   FAVRE, Jean-Marie: Foundations of meta-pyramids: Languages
            vs. metamodels Episode II: Story of thotus the baboon. In:

Language Engineering for Model-Driven Software Development 4101 (2005) [47, 54, 55]

[FB02]   FERENC, Rudolf ; BESZEDES, Arpad: Data Exchange with the Columbus Schema for C++. In: *Proceedings of the Sixth European Conference on Software Maintenance and Reengineering.* Washington, DC, USA : IEEE Computer Society, 2002 (CSMR '02), S. 59– [125]

[FBB+99] FOWLER, Martin ; BECK, Kent ; BRANT, John ; OPDYKE, William ; ROBERTS, Don: *Refactoring: Improving the Design of Existing Code.* Boston, MA, USA : Addison-Wesley Longman Publishing Co., Inc., 1999. – ISBN 0–201–48567–2 [23, 29]

[FBTG02] FERENC, Rudolf ; BESZÉDES, Árpád ; TARKIAINEN, Mikko ; GYIMÓTHY, Tibor: Columbus - Reverse Engineering Tool and Schema for C++. In: *ICSM*, IEEE Computer Society, 2002. – ISBN 0–7695–1819–2, S. 172–181 [124, 125]

[FED+01] FAVRE, Jean-Marie ; ESTUBLIER, Jacky ; DUCLOS, Frédéric ; SANLAVILLE, Remy ; AUFFRET, Jean-Jacques: Reverse Engineering a Large Component-Based Software Product. In: *Proceedings of the Fifth European Conference on Software Maintenance and Reengineering.* Washington, DC, USA : IEEE Computer Society, 2001 (CSMR '01). – ISBN 0–7695–1028–0, S. 95– [85]

[FGH06]   FEILER, Peter H. ; GLUCH, David P. ; HUDAK, John J.: The architecture analysis & design language (AADL): An introduction. Pittsburgh, PA 15213 : Software Engineering Institut Carnegie Mellon University, February 2006 (CMU/SEI-2006-TN-011). – Forschungsbericht. – "" [62]

[FH79]   FJELDSTAD, R. K. ; HAMLEN, W. T.: Application Program maintenance study: report to our respondents. In: *Proceedings of GUIDE 48.* Philedalphia : The Guide Corporation, 1979 [24]

[FHW10]   FUHR, Andreas ; HORN, Tassilo ; WINTER, Andreas: Model-Driven Software Migration. In: ENGELS, Gregor (Hrsg.) ; LUCKEY, Markus (Hrsg.) ; SCHÄFER, Wilhelm (Hrsg.): *Software Engineering* Bd. 159, GI, 2010 (LNI). – ISBN 978–3–88579–253–6, S. 69–80 [98, 123, 138, 141]

[FLM95]   FRICK, Arne ; LUDWIG, Andreas ; MEHLDAU, Heiko: A Fast Adaptive Layout Algorithm for Undirected Graphs. In: *Proceedings of the DIMACS International Workshop on Graph Drawing.* London, UK : Springer-Verlag, 1995 (GD '94). – ISBN 3–540–58950–3, S. 388–403 [180]

[FR91]   FRUCHTERMAN, Thomas M. J. ; REINGOLD, Edward M.: Graph drawing by force-directed placement. In: *Software: Practice and Experience* 21 (1991), November, Nr. 11, S. 1129–1164. – ISSN 0038–0644. – DOI 10.1002/spe.4380211102 [180]

[GC87]   GRADY, Robert B. ; CASWELL, Deborah L.: *Software metrics: establishing a company-wide program.* Upper Saddle River, NJ, USA : Prentice-Hall, Inc., 1987. – ISBN 0–13–821844–7 [16, 24]

[GDD06]   GAŠEVIĆ, D. ; DJURIĆ, D. ; DEVEDŽIĆ, V.: *Model driven architecture and ontology development.* Springer-Verlag, 2006. – ISBN 9783540321804 [54]

[GHJV09]   GAMMA, Erich ; HELM, Richard ; JOHNSON, Ralph ; VLISSIDES, John: *Entwurfsmuster.* Addison Wesley Verlag, 2009. – ISBN 978–3–8273–2824–3 [114, 168, 170, 227]

[GHK95]   GEISEN, H. ; HARMENING, M. ; KOSEL, W.: DeAs 1.0 Designbeschreibung / Deutsche Forschungsanstalt für Luft- und Raumfahrt e.V. 1.0. 1995. – Forschungsbericht [148]

[GHK00]   GEISEN, H. ; HARMENING, M. ; KOSEL, W.: DeAs 2.4 Designbeschreibung / Deutsche Forschungsanstalt für Luft- und Raumfahrt e.V. 2.4. 2000. – Forschungsbericht [148]

[GLZ06]   GRAY, Jeff ; LIN, Yuehua ; ZHANG, Jing: Automating Change Evolution in Model-Driven Engineering. In: *IEEE Computer* 39 (2006), S. 51–58. – ISSN 0018–9162. – DOI 10.1109/MC.2006.45 [57, 59]

[Gor98]   GORDON, Rob: *Essential JNI: Java Native Interface.* Upper Saddle River, NJ, USA : Prentice-Hall, Inc., 1998. – ISBN 0–13–679895–0 [102, 161]

[Gou05]   GOUGH, Brian: *An Introduction to GCC for the GNU Compilers gcc and g++.* Network Theory Limited, 2005. – ISBN 0–954–16179–3 [110]

[GPHS06]   GONZALEZ-PEREZ, Cesar ; HENDERSON-SELLERS, Brian: A powertype-based metamodelling framework. In: *Software and Systems Modeling* 5 (2006), S. 72–90. – ISSN 1619–1366. – DOI 10.1007/s10270-005-0099-9 [47]

[Gra12]   *Graphviz - Graph Visualization Software.* http://www.graphviz.org/, zuletzt besucht: 28.03.2012 [92]

[HBLR04]   HEARNDEN, David ; BAILES, Paul A. ; LAWLEY, Michael ; RAYMOND, Kerry: Automating Software Evolution. In: *IWPSE*, IEEE Computer Society, 2004. – ISBN 0–7695–2211–4, S. 95–100 [73]

[HBO94] HARMSEN, Frank ; BRINKKEMPER, Sjaak ; OEI, J. L. H.: Situational method engineering for informational system project approaches. In: *Proceedings of the IFIP WG8.1 Working Conference on Methods and Associated Tools for the Information Systems Life Cycle*. New York, NY, USA : Elsevier Science Inc., 1994. – ISBN 0–444–82074–4, S. 169–194 [60, 62]

[HDD+03] HATCLIFF, John ; DENG, Xinghua ; DWYER, Matthew B. ; JUNG, Georg ; RANGANATH, Venkatesh P.: Cadena: an integrated development, analysis, and verification environment for component-based systems. In: *Proceedings of the 25th International Conference on Software Engineering*. Washington, DC, USA : IEEE Computer Society, 2003 (ICSE '03). – ISBN 0–7695–1877–X, S. 160–173 [135, 136]

[HE11] HORN, Tassilo ; EBERT, Jürgen: The GReTL transformation language. In: *Proceedings of the 4th international conference on Theory and practice of model transformations*. Berlin, Heidelberg : Springer-Verlag, 2011 (ICMT'11). – ISBN 978–3–642–21731–9, S. 183–197 [138]

[HHKR89] HEERING, J. ; HENDRIKS, P. R. H. ; KLINT, P. ; REKERS, J.: The syntax definition formalism SDF – reference manual. In: *SIGPLAN Not.* 24 (1989), November, Nr. 11, S. 43–75. – ISSN 0362–1340. – DOI 10.1145/71605.71607 [137]

[Hid97] HIDDING, Gezinus J.: Reinventing methodology: who reads it and why? In: *Communications of the ACM* 40 (1997), November, Nr. 11, S. 102–109. – DOI 10.1145/265684.265697 [62]

[HJM+10] HOWAR, Falk ; JONSSON, Bengt ; MERTEN, Maik ; STEFFEN, Bernhard ; CASSEL, Sofia: On Handling Data in Automata Learning - Considerations from the CONNECT Perspective. In: MARGARIA, Tiziana (Hrsg.) ; STEFFEN, Bernhard (Hrsg.): *ISoLA (2)* Bd. 6416, Springer, 2010 (Lecture Notes in Computer Science). – ISBN 978–3–642–16560–3, S. 221–235 [63]

[HM01] HERMAN, Ivan ; MARSHALL, M. S.: GraphXML - An XML-Based Graph Description Format. In: *Proceedings of the 8th International Symposium on Graph Drawing*. London, UK : Springer-Verlag, 2001 (GD '00). – ISBN 3–540–41554–8, S. 52–62 [119]

[HM08] HESSE, Wolfgang ; MAYR, Heinrich C.: Modellierung in der Softwaretechnik: eine Bestandsaufnahme. In: *Informatik Spektrum* 31 (2008), Nr. 5, S. 377–393. – DOI 10.1007/s00287-008-0276-7 [51]

[HMM⁺08] HÖRMANN, Martina ; MARGARIA, Tiziana ; MENDER, Thomas ; NAGEL, Ralf ; STEFFEN, Bernhard ; TRINH, Hong: The jABC Approach to Rigorous Collaborative Development of SCM Applications. In: *ISoLA*, 2008, S. 724–737 [80]

[Hol02] HOLT, Ric: *TA: The Tuple Attribute Language*. Juli 2002 [112, 117, 122]

[Hol06] HOLTEN, Danny: Hierarchical Edge Bundles: Visualization of Adjacency Relations in Hierarchical Data. In: *IEEE Transactions on Visualization and Computer Graphics* 12 (2006), S. 741–748. – ISSN 1077–2626. – DOI 10.1109/TVCG.2006.147 [197]

[HSM10] HOWAR, Falk ; STEFFEN, Bernhard ; MERTEN, Maik: From ZULU to RERS - Lessons Learned in the ZULU Challenge. In: MARGARIA, Tiziana (Hrsg.) ; STEFFEN, Bernhard (Hrsg.): *ISoLA (1)* Bd. 6415, Springer, 2010 (Lecture Notes in Computer Science). – ISBN 978–3–642–16557–3, S. 687–704. – DOI 10.1007/978-3-642-16558-0 [9]

[HSSW12a] HOLT, Richard C. ; SCHÜRR, Andy ; SIM, Susan E. ; WINTER, Andreas: *GXL - Graph eXchange Language.* http://www.gupro.de/GXL/, zuletzt besucht: 10.01.2012 [117]

[HSSW12b] HOLT, Richard C. ; SCHÜRR, Andy ; SIM, Susan E. ; WINTER, Andreas: *GXL - Graph eXchange Language.* http://www.gupro.de/GXL/Introduction/intro.html, zuletzt besucht: 13.03.2012 [117]

[HT02] HUNT, Andy ; THOMAS, Dave: Software Archaeology. In: *IEEE Software* 19 (2002), S. 20–22. – ISSN 0740–7459. – DOI 10.1109/52.991327 [67]

[Hum88] HUMPHREY, Watts S.: Characterizing the Software Process: A Maturity Framework. In: *IEEE Software* 5 (1988), March, S. 73–79. – ISSN 0740–7459. – DOI 10.1109/52.2014 [61]

[HV99] HENNING, M. ; VINOSKI, S.: *Advanced CORBA programming with C++*. Addison-Wesley, 1999 (Addison-Wesley professional computing series). – ISBN 9780201379273 [224, 225]

[HWS00] HOLT, Richard C. ; WINTER, Andreas ; SCHÜRR, Andy: GXL: Towards a Standard Exchange Format. Rheinau 1, D-56075 Koblenz : Universität Koblenz-Landau, Institut für Informatik, 2000 (1–2000). – Forschungsbericht. – "" [112]

[IEE90] IEEE STD. 610.12: Standard Glossary of Software Engineering Terminology. Los Alamitos, CA, USA : Computer Society Press, 1990 (""). – Forschungsbericht. – "" [22]

[IEE99]   IEEE STD. 1219-1998: IEEE Standard for Software Main-
            tenance, IEEE Std 1219-1998.   IEEE Press, 1999 (""). –
            Forschungsbericht. – "" [23, 32, 35]

[III81]   III, John R.: Maintenance is a management problem and a pro-
            grammer's opportunity. In: AFIPS National Computer Confer-
            ence Bd. 50, AFIPS Press, 1981 (AFIPS Conference Proceed-
            ings), S. 343–347 [9, 16, 23, 24]

[ISJ⁺09]   ISSARNY, Valérie ; STEFFEN, Bernhard ; JONSSON, Bengt ;
            BLAIR, Gordon S. ; GRACE, Paul ; KWIATKOWSKA, Marta Z.
            ; CALINESCU, Radu ; INVERARDI, Paola ; TIVOLI, Massimo ;
            BERTOLINO, Antonia ; SABETTA, Antonino: CONNECT Chal-
            lenges: Towards Emergent Connectors for Eternal Networked
            Systems. In: ICECCS, IEEE Computer Society, June 2009, S.
            154–161 [9]

[ISO99]   ISO/IEC 14764: Information technology - Software Mainte-
            nance. Joint Technical Commitee International Standards Orga-
            nization/International Electrotechnique Commission, 1999 ("").
            – Forschungsbericht. – "" [23]

[ISO02]   ISO: Information technology – Z formal specification notation
            – Syntax, type system and semantics / International Organiza-
            tion for Standardization. 2002 (ISO/IEC 13568). – Forschungs-
            bericht [53]

[JKPM07]   JÖRGES, Sven ; KUBCZAK, Christian ; PAGEAU, Fèlix ; MAR-
            GARIA, Tiziana: Model Driven Design of Reliable Robot Control
            Programs Using the jABC. In: Proc. of 4th IEEE International
            Workshop on Engineering of Autonomic and Autonomous Sys-
            tems (EASe 2007), 2007, S. 137–148 [80]

[JMPWI93]   JOHANSON, Henry J. ; MCHUGH, Patrick ; PENDLEBURY, A. J.
            ; WHEELER II, William A.:   Business process reengineering :
            breakpoint strategies for market dominance. Chichester, England
            : John Whiley & Sons Ltd, 1993. ISSN 0–471–93883–1 [39]

[JMS06]   JÖRGES, Sven ; MARGARIA, Tiziana ; STEFFEN, Bernhard: For-
            mulaBuilder: A Tool for Graph-Based Modelling and Genera-
            tion of Formulae. In: Proceedings of the 28th international con-
            ference on Software engineering, ACM, 2006 (ICSE '06). – ISBN
            1–59593–375–1, S. 815–818 [80]

[JMS08]   JÖRGES, S. ; MARGARIA, T. ; STEFFEN, B.: Genesys: Service-
            Oriented Construction of Property Conform Code Generators.
            In: Innovations in Systems and Software Engineering 4 (2008),
            Nr. 4, S. 361–384 [78]

[Jon90]   JONES, Cliff B.: *Systematic software development using VDM (2nd ed.)*. Upper Saddle River, NJ, USA : Prentice-Hall, Inc., 1990. – ISBN 0–13–880733–7 [53]

[Jör11]   JÖRGES, Sven: *Genesys: A Model-Driven and Service-Oriented Approach to the Construction and Evolution of Code Generators*, TU Dortmund, Chair of Programming Systems, PhD Thesis, 2011. – to appear [77, 81, 131, 133, 135, 202]

[Jun07]   JUNG, Georg: *Structured interrelations of component architectures*. Manhattan, KS, USA, Diss., 2007 [136]

[JVV01]   JONGE, Merijn de ; VISSER, Eelco ; VISSER, Joost: XT: a bundle of program transformation tools. In: *Electronic Notes in Theoretical Computer Science* 44 (2001), Nr. 2, S. 79–86 [137]

[JWMB10] JUNG, Georg ; WAGNER, Christian ; MARGARIA, Tiziana ; BAKERA, Marco: Formalizing a Methodology for Design- and Runtime Self-Healing. In: *Proceedings of the 2010 Seventh IEEE International Conference and Workshops on Engineering of Autonomic and Autonomous Systems*. Washington, DC, USA : IEEE Computer Society, 2010 (EASE '10). – ISBN 978–0–7695–4004–7, S. 106–115. – DOI 10.1109/EASe.2010.21 [63, 82]

[KA04]   KARLSSON, Fredrik ; ÅGERFALK, Pär J.: Method configuration: adapting to situational characteristics while creating reusable assets. In: *Information and Software Technology* 46 (2004), Nr. 9, S. 619 – 633. – ISSN 0950–5849. – DOI 10.1016/j.infsof.2003.12.004 [60, 61, 62]

[Kel04]   KELLY, Steven: Comparison of Eclipse EMF/GEF and MetaEdit+ for DSM. In: *OOPSLA*, 2004 [134]

[Ken81]   *Kapitel* A Survey of Data Flow Analysis Techniques. In: KENNEDY, Ken: *Program Flow Analysis: Theory and Applications*. Englewood Cliffs, New York : Prentice-Hall, 1981. – ISBN 0–137–29681–9, S. 5–54 [23]

[KJMS09] KUBCZAK, Christian ; JÖRGES, Sven ; MARGARIA, Tiziana ; STEFFEN, Bernhard: eXtreme Model-Driven Design with jABC. In: *Proc. of the Tools and Consultancy Track of the 5th European Conference on Model-Driven Architecture Foundations and Applications (ECMDA-FA)*, CTIT, 2009 (Volume WP09-12 of CTIT proceedings), S. 78–99 [73, 77, 78]

[KK01]   KAMP, M. ; KULLBACH, B.: GReQL - Eine Anfragesprache für das GUPRO–Repository, Sprachbeschreibung / Universität Koblenz-Landau, Institut für Softwaretechnik. 2001 (Projektbericht 8/2001). – Forschungsbericht [126]

[KK02]   KARAGIANNIS, Dimitris ; KÜHN, Harald: Metamodelling Plat-
           forms. In: *Proceedings of the Third International Conference
           on E-Commerce and Web Technologies*. London, UK : Springer-
           Verlag, 2002 (EC-WEB '02). – ISBN 3–540–44137–9, S. 182–
           [51, 80, 84, 101, 140]

[KLR96]   KELLY, Steven ; LYYTINEN, Kalle ; ROSSI, Matti: MetaEdit+ A
           fully configurable multi-user and multi-tool CASE and CAME
           environment. In: CONSTANTOPOULOS, Panos (Hrsg.) ; MY-
           LOPOULOS, John (Hrsg.) ; VASSILIOU, Yannis (Hrsg.): *Advanced
           Information Systems Engineering* Bd. 1080. Springer Berlin /
           Heidelberg, 1996. – ISBN 978–3–540–61292–6, S. 1–21 [134]

[KM06]   KARUSSEIT, Martin ; MARGARIA, Tiziana: Feature-based Mod-
           elling of a Complex, Online-Reconfigurable Decision Support
           Service. In: *Electronic Notes in Theoretical Computer Science*
           157 (2006), Nr. 2, S. 101–118 [80]

[KM10]   KIENLE, Holger M. ; MÜLLER, Hausi A.: Rigi-An environment
           for software reverse engineering, exploration, visualization, and
           redocumentation. In: *Science of Computer Programming* 75
           (2010), April, Nr. 4, S. 247–263. – ISSN 0167–6423. – DOI
           10.1016/j.scico.2009.10.007 [126, 127]

[KMSN09]   KUBCZAK, Christian ; MARGARIA, Tiziana ; STEFFEN, Bern-
           hard ; NAGEL, Ralf: Service-oriented Mediation with jABC/-
           jETI. In: *Semantic Web Services Challenge* Bd. 8. Springer,
           2009. – ISBN 978–0–387–72495–9, S. 71–99 [81]

[KN02]   KOUTSOFIOS, Eleftherios ; NORTH, Stephen C.: *Drawing graphs
           with dot*. Murray Hill, NJ, February 4, 2002 [92]

[KP09]   KELLY, Steven ; POHJONEN, Risto: Worst Practices for
           Domain-Specific Modeling. In: *IEEE Software* 26 (2009), S.
           22–29. – ISSN 0740–7459. – DOI 10.1109/MS.2009.109 [52]

[KR90]   KERNIGHAN, B.W. ; RITCHIE: *Programmieren in C: mit dem
           C-Reference-Manual*. Carl Hanser Verlag und Prentice-Hall In-
           ternational, 1990. – ISBN 3–446–15497–3 [166]

[Kru95]   KRUCHTEN, Philippe: The 4+1 View Model of Architecture.
           In: *IEEE Software* 12 (1995), S. 42–50. – ISSN 0740–7459. –
           DOI 10.1109/52.469759 [45]

[Kru03]   KRUCHTEN, Philippe: *The Rational Unified Process: An In-
           troduction*. Boston, MA, USA : Addison-Wesley Longman Pub-
           lishing Co., Inc., 2003. – ISBN 0321197704 [11]

[KW92]   *Kapitel* Methodology Engineering: a proposal for situation-
           specific methodology construction. In: KUMAR, K. ; WELKE,

R.J: *Challenges and strategies for research in systems development.* New York : John Wiley & Sons, 1992 (Information Systems), S. 257–269 [61]

[KWC98] KAZMAN, Rick ; WOODS, Steven G. ; CARRIÈRE, S. J.: Requirements for Integrating Software Architecture and Reengineering Models: CORUM II. In: *Proceedings of the Working Conference on Reverse Engineering (WCRE'98)* 0 (1998), S. 154–. ISBN 0–8186–8967–6. – DOI 10.1109/WCRE.1998.723185 [36, 37]

[Kü06] KÜHNE, Thomas: Matters of (Meta-) Modeling. In: *Software and Systems Modeling* 5 (2006), S. 369–385. – ISSN 1619–1366. – 10.1007/s10270-006-0017-9 [9, 45, 50, 51, 54, 57, 88, 98]

[Lan96] LANO, Kevin: *The B Language and Method: A Guide to Practical Formal Development.* 1st. Secaucus, NJ, USA : Springer-Verlag New York, Inc., 1996. – ISBN 3540760334 [53]

[LB85] LEHMAN, M. M. (Hrsg.) ; BELADY, L. A. (Hrsg.): *Program evolution: processes of software change.* San Diego, CA, USA : Academic Press Professional, Inc., 1985. – ISBN 0–12–442440–6 [15, 22]

[Lie10] LIEBHART, Daniel: Die 10 Regeln der Modernisierung. In: *Java Magazin* 1 (2010), S. 90–95. – ISSN 1619–7951 [41, 101, 102]

[LLL01] LAPIERRE, Sébastien ; LAGUË, Bruno ; LEDUC, Charles: Datrix source code model and its interchange format: lessons learned and considerations for future work. In: *SIGSOFT Software Engineering Notes* 26 (2001), January, S. 53–56. – ISSN 0163–5948 [122]

[LMS08] LAMPRECHT, Anna-Lena ; MARGARIA, Tiziana ; STEFFEN, Bernhard: Seven Variations of an Alignment Workflow - An Illustration of Agile Process Design and Management in BiojETI. In: *Bioinformatics Research and Applications* Bd. 4983. Springer, 2008, S. 445–456 [80]

[LS80] LIENTZ, Bennett P. ; SWANSON, E. B.: *Software Maintenance Management.* Boston, MA, USA : Addison-Wesley Longman Publishing Co., Inc., 1980. – ISBN 0201042053 [16, 23, 24]

[LS81] LIENTZ, Bennet P. ; SWANSON, E. B.: Problems in application software maintenance. In: *Communications of the ACM* 24 (1981), November, S. 763–769. – ISSN 0001–0782. – DOI 10.1145/358790.358796 [23]

[Lud03] LUDEWIG, Jochen: Models in software engineering – an introduction. In: *Software and Systems Modeling* 2 (2003), S. 5–14. – ISSN 1619–1366. – 10.1007/s10270-003-0020-3 [44, 51, 57]

[Lyo81]   LYONS, Michael J.: Salvaging your software asset: (tools based maintenance). In: *Proceedings of the National Computer Conference.* New York, NY, USA : ACM, 1981 (AFIPS '81), S. 337–341. – DOI 10.1145/1500412.1500459 [21]

[Lyy87]   LYYTINEN, Kalle: Different perspectives on information systems: problems and solutions. In: *ACM Computing Surveys* 19 (1987), March, S. 5–46. – ISSN 0360–0300. – DOI 10.1145/28865.28867 [61]

[MBE⁺00] MANN, Stefan ; BORUSAN, Er ; EHRIG, Hartmut ; GROSSE-RHODE, Martin ; GROSSE-RHODE, Martin ; MACKENTHUN, Rainer ; MACKENTHUN, Rainer ; SÜNBÜL, Asuman ; SÜNBÜL, Asuman ; WEBER, Herbert ; WEBER, Herbert: Towards a Component Concept for Continuous Software Engineering / Fraunhofer ISST. 2000 (55/00). – Forschungsbericht. – "" [18]

[McC76]   MCCABE, Thomas J.: A complexity measure. In: *Proceedings of the 2nd international conference on Software engineering.* Los Alamitos, CA, USA : IEEE Computer Society Press, 1976 (ICSE '76), S. 407– [193]

[McC92]   MCCLURE, Carma: *The three Rs of software automation: reengineering, repository, reusability.* Upper Saddle River, NJ, USA : Prentice-Hall, Inc., 1992. – ISBN 0–13–915240–7 [34]

[MCF03]   MELLOR, Stephen J. ; CLARK, Anthony N. ; FUTAGAMI, Takao: Guest Editors' Introduction: Model-Driven Development. In: *IEEE Software* 20 (2003), S. 14–18. – ISSN 0740–7459. – DOI 10.1109/MS.2003.1231145 [45, 51, 53, 57, 71, 75, 76, 78]

[McK84]   MCKEE, James R.: Maintenance as a function of design. In: *AFIPS '84: Proceedings of the July 9-12, 1984, national computer conference and exposition* Bd. 53. New York, NY, USA : ACM, 1984 (AFIPS Conference Proceedings). – ISBN 0–88283–043–0, S. 187–193. – DOI 10.1145/1499310.1499334 [16]

[McP12]   MCPEAK, Scott: *cc.ast: The Abstract Syntax Tree description* . http://scottmcpeak.com/elkhound/sources/elsa/doc/cc.ast.html, zuletzt besucht: 17.01.2012 [168]

[MD08]   MENS, Tom (Hrsg.) ; DEMEYER, Serge (Hrsg.): *Software Evolution.* Springer, 2008. – ISBN 978–3–540–76439–7 [27]

[MGK⁺93a] MERLO, Ettore ; GIRARD, Jean-Francois ; KONTOGIANNIS, Kostas ; PANANGADEN, Prakash ; MORI, Renato de: Reverse Engineering of User Interfaces. In: *WCRE'93*, 1993, S. 171–179 [97, 143]

[MGK+93b] MERLO, Ettore ; GIRARD, Jean-Francois ; KONTOGIANNIS, Kostas ; PANANGADEN, Prakash ; MORI, Renato de: Reverse Engineering of User Interfaces. In: *Proc. Working Conference on Reverse Engineering*, IEEE CS Press, 1993, S. 171–179 [143]

[Mic02] MICHAIL, Amir: Browsing and searching source code of applications written using a GUI framework. In: *Proceedings of the 24th International Conference on Software Engineering*. New York, NY, USA : ACM, 2002 (ICSE '02). – ISBN 1–58113–472–X, S. 327–337. – DOI 10.1145/581339.581381 [142]

[Mil76] MILLS, Harlan D.: Software Development. In: *IEEE Transactions on Software Engineering* 2 (1976), Nr. 4, S. 265–273 [13, 15, 16]

[Mil98] MILLER, Howard W.: *Reengineering legacy software systems*. Newton, MA, USA : Digital Press, 1998. – ISBN 1–55558–195–1 [13]

[Mil02] MILICEV, Dragan: Domain Mapping Using Extended UML Object Diagrams. In: *IEEE Softw.* 19 (2002), March, Nr. 2, S. 90–97. – ISSN 0740–7459. – DOI 10.1109/52.991369 [139]

[Mis11] MISRA: *The Motor Industry Software Reliability Association*. http://www.misra.org.uk/, zuletzt besucht: 07/2011 [73]

[MJ82] MCCRACKEN, Daniel D. ; JACKSON, Michael A.: Life cycle concept considered harmful. In: *SIGSOFT Softw. Eng. Notes* 7 (1982), April, S. 29–32. – ISSN 0163–5948. – DOI 10.1145/1005937.1005943 [13]

[MK00] MAMAS, E. ; KONTOGIANNIS, K.: Towards Portable Source Code Representations Using XML. In: *Proceedings of the Seventh Working Conference on Reverse Engineering (WCRE)*. Washington, DC, USA : IEEE Computer Society, 2000. – ISBN 0–7695–0881–2, S. 172– [120]

[MKM97] MENAPACE, Julia ; KINGDON, Jim ; MACKENZIE, David: The stabs Debug Format / Cygnus Support. 1997 (""). – Forschungsbericht. – "" [109]

[MKS08] MARGARIA, Tiziana ; KUBCZAK, Christian ; STEFFEN, Bernhard: Bio-jETI: a service integration, design, and provisioning platform for orchestrated bioinformatics processes. In: *BMC Bioinformatics* 9 (2008), Nr. S-4 [80]

[MM83] MARTIN, James ; MCCLURE, Carma L.: *Software Maintenance: The Problems and Its Solutions*. Prentice Hall Professional Technical Reference, 1983. – ISBN 0138223610 [24]

[MM03] MILLER, J. ; MUKERJI, J.: MDA Guide / Object Management Group (OMG). 2003 (omg/2003-06-01). – Forschungsbericht. – Version 1.0.1 [46]

[MMN02] MCARTHUR, G. ; MYLOPOULOS, J. ; NG, Siu Kee K.: An extensible tool for source code representation using XML. In: *Proceedings of the Ninth Working Conference on Reverse Engineering (WCRE)*, 2002. – ISSN 1095–1350, S. 199–208. – DOI 10.1109/WCRE.2002.1173078 [122]

[MN04] MCPEAK, Scott ; NECULA, George C.: Elkhound: A Fast, Practical GLR Parser Generator. In: *Proceedings of Conference on Compiler Constructor (CC04)*, 2004, S. 73–88 [113]

[MNS95] MURPHY, Gail C. ; NOTKIN, David ; SULLIVAN, Kevin: Software reflexion models: bridging the gap between source and high-level models. In: *SIGSOFT Software Engineering Notes* 20 (1995), Oktober, Nr. 4, S. 18–28. – ISSN 0163–5948. – DOI 10.1145/222132.222136 [128]

[Moa90] MOAD, J.: Maintaining the competitive edge. In: *Datamation* 36 (1990), Februar, Nr. 4, S. 61–62, 64, 66. – ISSN 0011–6963 [16, 19]

[Moo09] MOODY, Daniel L.: The "'Physics'" of Notations: Toward a Scientific Basis for Constructing Visual Notations in Software Engineering. In: *IEEE Transactions on Software Engineering* 35 (2009), S. 756–779. – ISSN 0098–5589. – DOI 10.1109/TSE.2009.67 [58, 79, 177]

[Mos09] MOSLER, Christof: *Graphbasiertes Reengineering von Telekommunikationssystemen*, Fakultät für Mathematik, Informatik und Naturwissenschaften der RWTH Aachen, Diss., November 2009 [35, 141]

[MOSS99] MÜLLER-OLM, Markus ; SCHMIDT, David A. ; STEFFEN, Bernhard: Model-Checking: A Tutorial Introduction. In: CORTESI, Agostino (Hrsg.) ; FILÉ, Gilberto (Hrsg.): *SAS* Bd. 1694, Springer, 1999 (Lecture Notes in Computer Science). – ISBN 3–540–66459–9, S. 330–354 [78]

[MS04] MARGARIA, Tiziana ; STEFFEN, Bernhard: Lightweight coarse-grained coordination: a scalable system-level approach. In: *STTT* 5 (2004), Nr. 2-3, S. 107–123 [74, 76, 77, 79, 80, 130, 131, 132]

[MS08] MARGARIA, Tiziana ; STEFFEN, Bernhard: Agile IT: Thinking in User-Centric Models. In: MARGARIA, Tiziana (Hrsg.) ; STEFFEN, Bernhard (Hrsg.): *ISoLA* Bd. 17, Springer, 2008 (Communications in Computer and Information Science). – ISBN 978–3–540–88478–1, S. 490–502 [79]

[MS09a] MARGARIA, Tiziana ; STEFFEN, Bernhard: Continuous Model-Driven Engineering. In: *Computer* 42 (2009), S. 106–109. – ISSN 0018–9162. – DOI 10.1109/MC.2009.315 [18, 73, 74, 76, 79]

[MS09b] *Kapitel* Business Process Modeling in the jABC: The One-Thing Approach. In: MARGARIA, Tiziana ; STEFFEN, Bernhard: *Handbook of Research on Business Process Modeling*. Information Science Reference, 2009 ISSN 9781605662886, S. 1–26. – DOI 10.4018/978-1-60566-288-6.ch001 [73, 74, 75, 77, 78, 79, 129, 133]

[MWMW00] MARTIN, Johannes ; WINTER, Bruce ; MÜLLER, Hausi ; WONG, Kenny: Analyzing xfig Using the Rigi Tool Suite. In: *Proceedings of the Seventh Working Conference on Reverse Engineering (WCRE)*. Washington, DC, USA : IEEE Computer Society, 2000. – ISBN 0–7695–0881–2, S. 207– [244]

[Mü86] MÜLLER, Hans A.: *Rigi: a model for software system construction, integration, and evolution based on module interface specifications*. Houston, TX, USA, Diss., 1986. – AAI8718755 [127]

[Mü97] MÜLLER, Bernd: *Reengineering: Eine Einführung*. Stuttgart : B.G. Teubner, 1997. – ISBN 3–519–02942–1 [16, 17, 19, 23, 24, 25, 32, 38, 40, 41]

[NNH99] NIELSON, F. ; NIELSON, Riis H. ; HANKIN, C. L.: *Principles of Program Analysis*. Second printing, 2005. Springer, 1999 [91]

[NNWZ00] NICKEL, U. A. ; NIERE, J. ; WADSACK, J. P. ; ZÜNDORF, A.: Roundtrip Engineering with FUJABA. In: *Proc of 2nd Workshop on Software-Reengineering (WSR), Bad Honnef, Germany*, 2000 [135]

[NP90] NOSEK, J. T. ; PALVIA, P.: Software maintenance management: changes in the last decade. In: *Journal of Software Maintenance* 2 (1990), September, S. 157–174. – ISSN 1040–550X. – DOI 10.1002/smr.4360020303 [16, 24]

[NZ99] NIERE, J. ; ZÜNDORF, A.: Tool Demonstration: Testing and Simulating Production Control Systems Using the Fujaba Environment. In: *Proc. of International Workshop and Symposium on Applications Of Graph Transformations With Industrial Relevance (AGTIVE), Kerkrade, The Netherlands*, 1999 [135]

[Obj07] OBJECT MANAGEMENT GROUP: MOF 2.0/XMI Mapping / Object Management Group. Version: December 2007. http://

www.omg.org/spec/XMI/2.1.1/PDF/. 2007 (formal/2007-12-01). – Forschungsbericht. – Version 2.1 [54]

[Obj10]   OBJECT MANAGEMENT GROUP: *OMG Unified Modeling Language (OMG UML),Superstructure.* http://www.omg.org/spec/UML/2.3/Superstructure. Version: May 2010. – Version 2.3 [54]

[Obj11a]   OBJECT MANAGEMENT GROUP: *Architecture-driven Modernization: Abstract Syntax Tree Metamodel (ASTM).* http://www.omg.org/spec/ASTM/1.0/PDF. Version: January 2011. – Version 1.0 [123]

[Obj11b]   OBJECT MANAGEMENT GROUP: *Architecture-Driven Modernization (ADM): Knowledge Discovery Meta-Model (KDM).* http://www.omg.org/spec/KDM/1.3/PDF/. Version: August 2011. – Version 1.3 [123]

[Obj11c]   OBJECT MANAGEMENT GROUP: *Meta Object Facility (MOF) 2.0 Query/View/Transformation Specification.* http://www.omg.org/spec/QVT/1.1/PDF/. Version: January 2011. – Version 1.1 [58, 138]

[OMG12a]   *Architecture-Driven Modernization.* http://adm.omg.org/, zuletzt besucht: 28.03.2012 [60]

[OMG12b]   *MDA Model Driven Architecture.* http://www.omg.org/mda, zuletzt besucht: 28.03.2012 [46]

[OMG12c]   *UML Unified Modeling Language.* http://www.omg.org/spec/UML/2.3/, zuletzt besucht: 28.03.2012 [45]

[OMG12d]   *Object Management Group.* http://www.omg.org/, zuletzt besucht: 28.03.2012 [44]

[OR23]   OGDEN, C. K. ; RICHARDS, C. K.: *The Meaning of Meaning: A Study of the Influence of Language Upon Thought and of the Science of Symbolism.* Reissue (June 1989). Harcourt, 1923 [52]

[Par94]   PARNAS, David L.: Software aging. In: *Proceedings of the 16th international conference on Software engineering.* Los Alamitos, CA, USA : IEEE Computer Society Press, 1994 (ICSE '94). – ISBN 0–8186–5855–X, S. 279–287 [17, 19]

[Pet62]   PETRI, Carl A.: *Kommunikation mit Automaten.*, Bonn: Institut für Instrumentelle Mathematik, Schriften des IIM Nr. 2, Diss., 1962. – Second Edition:, New York: Griffiss Air Force Base, Technical Report RADC-TR-65–377, Vol.1, 1966, Pages: Suppl. 1, English translation [45]

[Pig96]   PIGOSKI, Thomas M.: *Practical Software Maintenance: Best Practices for Managing Your Software Investment*. New York, NY, USA : John Wiley & Sons, Inc., 1996. – ISBN 0471170011 [22]

[Pre86]   PRESSMAN, Roger S.: *Software engineering: a practitioner's approach (2nd ed.)*. 2nd. New York, NY, USA : McGraw-Hill, Inc., 1986. – ISBN 0–070–50783–X [35, 38]

[Rad00]   RADA, Roy: *Reengineering Software: How to Reuse Programming to Build New, State-of-the-Art Software*. Glenlake Publishing Company, Limited, The, 2000. – ISBN 188899861X [27]

[RDR03]   RALYTÉ, Jolita ; DENECKÈRE, Rébecca ; ROLLAND, Colette: Towards a generic model for situational method engineering. In: *Proceedings of the 15th international conference on Advanced information systems engineering*. Berlin, Heidelberg : Springer-Verlag, 2003 (CAiSE'03). – ISBN 3–540–40442–2, S. 95–110 [62]

[RGD06]   REUS, T. ; GEERS, H. ; DEURSEN, A. van: Harvesting Software Systems for MDA-Based Reengineering. In: RENSINK, Arend (Hrsg.) ; WARMER, Jos (Hrsg.): *European Conference on Model Driven Architectures: Foundations and Applications* Bd. 4066, Springer-Verlag, 2006 (Lecture Notes in Computer Science). – ISBN 0302–9743, S. 213–225 [32, 81, 124, 128]

[Rie00]   RIEDIGER, Volker: Analyzing XFIG with GUPRO. In: *Proceedings of the Seventh Working Conference on Reverse Engineering (WCRE)*. Washington, DC, USA : IEEE Computer Society, 2000. – ISBN 0–7695–0881–2, S. 194– [244]

[Rol97]   ROLAND, Colette: A Primer For Method Engineering. Toulouse, France : Proceedings of the conferance INFormatique des ORganisations et Systèmes d'Information et de Décision (INFORSID), June 1997 (97-06). – Forschungsbericht [60, 61]

[Roy70]   ROYCE, W. W.: Managing the Development of Large Software Systems. In: *Technical Papers of Western Electronic Show and Convention (IEEE WesCon)*, TRW, August 1970, S. 1–9. – Reprinted in Proc. Int'l Conf. Software Engineering (ICSE) 1989, ACM Press, pp. 328-338 [10, 11]

[RP96]   ROLLAND, Colette ; PRAKASH, Naveen: A proposal for context-specific method engineering. In: *Proceedings of the IFIP TC8, WG8.1/8.2 working conference on method engineering on Method engineering : principles of method construction and tool support*. London, UK : Chapman & Hall, Ltd., 1996. – ISBN

0–412–79750–X, S. 191–208 [62]

[RPTU84] RAMAMOORTHY, C. V. ; PRAKASH, Atul ; TSAI, Wei-Tek ; USUDA, Yutaka: Software Engineering: Problems and Perspectives. In: *IEEE Computer* 17 (1984), Nr. 10, S. 191–209 [14, 16, 19, 24, 38]

[RS04] RUGABER, Spencer ; STIREWALT, Kurt: Model-Driven Reverse Engineering. In: *IEEE Software* 21 (2004), July, S. 45–53. – ISSN 0740–7459. – DOI 10.1109/MS.2004.23 [59, 82, 92, 127, 128, 201, 239]

[RTR⁺00] ROSSI, Matti ; TOLVANEN, Juha-Pekka ; RAMESH, Balasubmaraniam ; LYYTINEN, Kalle ; KAIPALA, Janne: Method Rationale in Method Engineering. In: *Hawaii International Conference on System Sciences* 2 (2000), S. 2036. – ISSN 1530–1605. – DOI 10.1109/HICSS.2000.926680 [62]

[RVP06] RAZA, Aoun ; VOGEL, Gunther ; PLÖDEREDER, Erhard: Bauhaus: a tool suite for program analysis and reverse engineering. In: *Proceedings of the 11th Ada-Europe international conference on Reliable Software Technologies*. Berlin, Heidelberg : Springer-Verlag, 2006 (Ada-Europe'06). – ISBN 3–540–34663–5, 978–3–540–34663–0, S. 71–82. – DOI 10.1007/11767077_6 [126]

[Sac97] SACHS, W.: DeAs 2.1 Schnittstelle: DeAs - Geräte / Deutsche Forschungsanstalt für Luft- und Raumfahrt e.V. 2.1.0. 1997. – Forschungsbericht [148]

[Sae03] SAEKI, Motoshi: Embedding Metrics into Information Systems Development Methods: An Application of Method Engineering Technique. In: EDER, Johann (Hrsg.) ; MISSIKOFF, Michele (Hrsg.): *CAiSE* Bd. 2681, Springer, 2003 (Lecture Notes in Computer Science). – ISBN 3–540–40442–2, S. 374–389 [63]

[SB89] SWANSON, E. B. ; BEATH, Cynthia M.: *Maintaining information systems in organizations*. New York, NY, USA : John Wiley & Sons, Inc., 1989. – ISBN 0–471–91969–1 [22]

[SB10] SOHR, Karsten ; BERGER, Bernhard J.: Idea: Towards Architecture-Centric Security Analysis of Software. In: MASSACCI, Fabio (Hrsg.) ; WALLACH, Dan S. (Hrsg.) ; ZANNONE, Nicola (Hrsg.): *ESSoS* Bd. 5965, Springer, 2010 (Lecture Notes in Computer Science). – ISBN 978–3–642–11746–6, S. 70–78 [126]

[SCDP07] STUERMER, Ingo ; CONRAD, Mirko ; DOERR, Heiko ; PEPPER, Peter: Systematic Testing of Model-Based Code Generators. In: *IEEE Transactions on Software Engineering* 33 (2007), September, S. 622–634. – ISSN 0098–5589. – DOI 10.1109/TSE.2007.70708 [201]

[Sch06]   SCHMIDT, Douglas C.: Model-Driven Engineering. In: *IEEE Computer* 39 (2006), February, Nr. 2, S. 25–31 [46, 52, 53, 54, 59]

[Sei03]   SEIDEWITZ, Ed: What Models Mean. In: *IEEE Software* 20 (2003), September, S. 26–32. – ISSN 0740–7459. – DOI 10.1109/MS.2003.1231147 [45, 47, 48, 50, 51, 53, 55, 62]

[Sel03]   SELIC, Bran: The Pragmatics of Model-Driven Development. In: *IEEE Software* 20 (2003), S. 19–25. – ISSN 0740–7459. – DOI 10.1109/MS.2003.1231146 [53, 56, 59, 71, 73, 75]

[SERIS03] STROULIA, E. ; EL-RAMLY, M. ; IGLINSKI, P. ; SORENSON, P.: User Interface Reverse Engineering in Support of Interface Migration to the Web. In: *Automated Software Engg.* 10 (2003), July, Nr. 3, S. 271–301. – ISSN 0928–8910. – DOI 10.1023/A:1024460315173 [143]

[SFZ10]   SCALISE, Eugenio P. ; FAVRE, Jean-Marie ; ZAMBRANO, Nancy: Model-Driven Reverse Engineering and Program Comprehension: an Example. In: *Ingeniare. Revista chilena de ingeniería* 18 (2010), Nr. 1, S. 76–83. – ISSN 0718–3305. – DOI 10.4067/S0718-33052010000100009 [26, 59, 82, 128, 139]

[SH96]   SLOOTEN, Kees van ; HODES, B.: Characterizing IS development projects. In: *Proceedings of the IFIP TC8, WG8.1/8.2 working conference on method engineering on Method engineering : principles of method construction and tool support*. London, UK : Chapman & Hall, Ltd., 1996. – ISBN 0–412–79750–X, S. 29–44 [60]

[SH05]   SINGH, Munindar P. ; HUHNS, Michael N.: Service-Oriented Computing: Key Concepts and Principles. In: *IEEE Internet Computing* 9 (2005), January, S. 75–81. – ISSN 1089–7801. – DOI 10.1109/MIC.2005.21 [28]

[SH09]   STOBER, Thomas ; HANSMANN, Uwe: WebSphere Portal 6.1: an agile development success story. In: *Informatik-Spektrum* 32 (2009), S. 378–392. – ISSN 0170–6012. – 10.1007/s00287-009-0358-1 [11]

[SHA08]   SHADOWS EU IST FP6 PROJECT: Methodology for the Development of Self-Healing Systems / SHADOWS. 2008 (D6.5). – Deliverable. – 83 S. – "" [9, 63]

[SHA12]   *SHADOWS. A Self-healing Approach to Designing Complex Software Systems.* https://sysrun.haifa.ibm.com/

shadows/, zuletzt besucht: 27.03.2012 [9, 63]

[SHE02] SIM, Susan E. ; HOLT, Richard C. ; EASTERBROOK, Steve: On Using a Benchmark to Evaluate C++ Extractors. In: *Proceedings of the 10th International Workshop on Program Comprehension*. Washington, DC, USA : IEEE Computer Society, 2002 (IWPC '02). – ISBN 0–7695–1495–2, S. 114– [244]

[She08] SHEHORY, O.: SHADOWS: Self-healing complex software systems. In: *23rd IEEE/ACM Int. Conf. on Automated Software Engineering - Workshops (ASE)*, IEEE, 2008. – ISBN 978–1–4244–2776–5, S. 71–76 [9, 63]

[Sim92] SIMON, A.R.: *Systems migration: a complete reference*. Van Nostrand Reinhold, 1992 ([VNR computer library]). – ISBN 9780442308537 [42, 95]

[SJWM09] STEFFEN, Bernhard ; JÖRGES, Sven ; WAGNER, Christian ; MARGARIA, Tiziana: Maintenance, or the 3rd dimension of eXtreme model-driven design. In: *Software Maintenance, IEEE International Conference on* 0 (2009), S. 483–486. ISBN 978–1–4244–4897–5. – DOI 10.1109/ICSM.2009.5306281 [57]

[SK03] SENDALL, Shane ; KOZACZYNSKI, Wojtek: Model Transformation: The Heart and Soul of Model-Driven Software Development. In: *IEEE Software* 20 (2003), S. 42–45. – ISSN 0740–7459. – DOI 10.1109/MS.2003.1231150 [58, 71, 99]

[SLT00] STÉPHANE DUCASSE ; LANZA, Michele ; TICHELAAR, Sander: Moose: an Extensible Language-Independent Environment for Reengineering Object-Oriented Systems. In: *Proc. Int'l Symp. Constructing Software Engineering Tools (CoSET)*, 2000 [128]

[SM99] STEFFEN, Bernhard ; MARGARIA, Tiziana: METAFrame in Practice: Design of Intelligent Network Services. In: *Correct System Design*, 1999, S. 390–415 [80, 129]

[SMC⁺96] STEFFEN, Bernhard ; MARGARIA, Tiziana ; CLASSEN, Andreas ; BRAUN, Volker ; NISIUS, Rita ; REITENSPIESS, Manfred: A Constraint-Oriented Service Creation Environment. In: *Proceedings of the Second International Workshop on Tools and Algorithms for Construction and Analysis of Systems*. London, UK : Springer-Verlag, 1996. – ISBN 3–540–61042–1, S. 418–421 [80]

[SMN⁺07] STEFFEN, Bernhard ; MARGARIA, Tiziana ; NAGEL, Ralf ; JÖRGES, Sven ; KUBCZAK, Christian: Model-driven development with the jABC. In: *Proceedings of the 2nd international Haifa verification conference on Hardware and software, verifi-*

cation and testing. Berlin, Heidelberg : Springer-Verlag, 2007 (HVC'06). – ISBN 978–3–540–70888–9, S. 92–108 [XV, 76, 131, 133]

[Sne84] SNEED, H.M.: Software Renewal: A case Study. In: *IEEE Software* 1 (1984), S. 56–63. – ISSN 0740–7459. – DOI 10.1109/MS.1984.234710 [26, 67]

[SO06] SOLEY, Richard ; OARA, Mike: Extracting UML from legacy applications. In: *SOA Web Services Journal* (2006), October [123]

[Som06] SOMMERVILLE, Ian: *Software Engineering: (Update) (8th Edition)*. 8. Addison Wesley, 2006. – ISBN 0321313798 [10, 21, 29, 35, 67]

[SPL03] SEACORD, Robert C. ; PLAKOSH, Daniel ; LEWIS, Grace A.: *Modernizing Legacy Systems: Software Technologies, Engineering Process and Business Practices*. Boston, MA, USA : Addison-Wesley Longman Publishing Co., Inc., 2003. – ISBN 0321118847 [16, 17, 20, 27, 28, 29, 30, 33, 40, 41, 43, 94]

[SR98] STIREWALT, Kurt ; RUGABER, Spencer: Automating UI Generation by Model Composition. In: *ASE*, 1998, S. 177– [142, 216]

[Sta73] STACHOWIAK, H.: *Allgemeine Modelltheorie*. Springer-Verlag, Wien New York, 1973. – ISBN 9783211811061 [44]

[Sta07a] STAIGER, Stefan: Reverse Engineering of Graphical User Interfaces Using Static Analyses. In: *Proceedings of the 14th Working Conference on Reverse Engineering*. Washington, DC, USA : IEEE Computer Society, 2007 (WCRE '07). – ISBN 0–7695–3034–6, S. 189–198. – DOI 10.1109/WCRE.2007.44 [142]

[Sta07b] STAIGER, Stefan: Statische Analyse von Graphischen Oberflächen. In: KOSCHKE, Rainer (Hrsg.) ; HERZOG, Otthein (Hrsg.) ; RÖDIGER, Karl-Heinz (Hrsg.) ; RONTHALER, Marc (Hrsg.): *GI Jahrestagung (2)* Bd. 110, GI, 2007 (LNI). – ISBN 978–3–88579–204–8, S. 247–253 [142]

[Str98] STROUSTRUP, B.: *Die C++-Programmiersprache*. Addison-Wesley, 1998 (Professionelle Programmierung). – ISBN 9783827312969 [169, 177]

[STT81] SUGIYAMA, Kozo ; TAGAWA, Shojiro ; TODA, Mitsuhiko: Methods for Visual Understanding of Hierarchical System Structures. In: *IEEE Transactions on Systems, Man, and Cybernetics* 11 (1981), Nr. 2, S. 109–125. – ISSN 0018–9472. – DOI 10.1109/TSMC.1981.4308636 [180]

[Sun01]   SUN MICROSYSTEMS: Introduction to Sun WorkShop / Sun Microsystems, Inc. July 2001 (806-7980-10). – Forschungsbericht. – Revision A [109]

[SVEH07]   STAHL, Thomas ; VÖLTER, Markus ; EFFTINGE, Sven ; HAASE, Arno: *Modellgetriebene Softwareentwicklung - Techniken, Engineering, Management*. dpunkt.verlag, 2007. – I–XV, 1–441 S. – ISBN 978–3–89864–310–8 [53, 54]

[SW98]   SCHÜRR, Andy ; WINTER, Andreas J.: UML Packages for PROgrammed Graph REwriting Systems. In: EHRIG, Hartmut (Hrsg.) ; ENGELS, Gregor (Hrsg.) ; KREOWSKI, Hans-Jörg (Hrsg.) ; ROZENBERG, Grzegorz (Hrsg.): *TAGT* Bd. 1764, Springer, 1998 (Lecture Notes in Computer Science). – ISBN 3–540–67203–6, S. 396–409 [117]

[Swa76]   SWANSON, E. B.: The dimensions of maintenance. In: *ICSE '76: Proceedings of the 2nd international conference on Software engineering*. Los Alamitos, CA, USA : IEEE Computer Society Press, 1976, S. 492–497 [1, 22]

[SWM10]   *Kapitel* Round-Trip Engineering vs. One-Thing Approach. In: STEFFEN, Bernhard ; WAGNER, Christian ; MARGARIA, Tiziana: *Encyclopedia of software engineering*. Auerbach Publications, 2010 ISSN 978–1–4200597–7–9 [56, 72, 123]

[TMD09]   TAYLOR, R. N. ; MEDVIDOVIC, N. ; DASHOFY, E. M.: *Software Architecture: Foundations, Theory, and Practice*. Wiley Publishing, 2009. – ISBN 0470167742, 9780470167748 [131]

[TPK07]   TOLVANEN, Juha P. ; POHJONEN, Risto ; KELLY, Steven: Advanced Tooling for Domain-Specific Modeling: MetaEdit+. In: *Object-Oriented programming systems, languages, and applications (OOPSLA)*. Portland, Oregon, USA, 2007 [134]

[TS95]   TILLEY, S. R. ; SMITH, D. B.: Perspectives on Legacy System Reengineering / Software Engineering Institute, Carnegie Mellon University. 1995 (""). – Forschungsbericht. – "" [24, 34, 38]

[TS99]   TUCKER, K. ; STIREWALT, R. E. K.: Model Based User-Interface Reengineering. In: *Proceedings of the Sixth Working Conference on Reverse Engineering*. Washington, DC, USA : IEEE Computer Society, 1999 (WCRE '99). – ISBN 0–7695–0303–9, S. 56– [142]

[Val00]   VALIENTE, Gabriel: *A Simple XML Exchange Format for Graph Transformation*. http://www2.cs.uni-paderborn.de/cs/ag-engels/Conferences/APPLIGRAPH_XML/

`Valiente.html`. Version: 2000. – APPLIGRAPH Subgroup Meeting on Exchange Formats for Graph Transformation, Paderborn University, Germany, September 5-6 [116]

[Van93]   VANRAALTE, T.:   *XView reference manual.*   O'Reilly, 1993 (Definitive guides to the X window system). – ISBN 9780937175897 [217]

[Vas08]   VASSEV, E.: *Towards a Framework for Specification and Code Generation of Autonomic Systems*, Department of Computer Science and Software Engineering, Concordia University, Montreal, Canada, Diss., 2008 [62]

[Vis04]   VISSER, Eelco: Program Transformation with Stratego/XT: Rules, Strategies, Tools, and Systems in StrategoXT-0.9. In: LENGAUER, C. (Hrsg.) u. a.: *Domain-Specific Program Generation* Bd. 3016. Spinger-Verlag, June 2004, S. 216–238 [137]

[Vli08]   VLIET, Hans v.: *Software Engineering: Principles and Practice.* 3rd. Wiley Publishing, 2008. – ISBN 9780470031469 [10, 16, 24, 25]

[W3C01]   *XML Linking Language (XLink)*. `http://www.omg.org/`, Juni 2001. – Version 1.0, zuletzt besucht: 28.03.2012 [119]

[War99]   WARREN, Ian: *The Renaissance of Legacy Systems: Method Support for Software-System Evolution.* 1st.   Springer-Verlag London, 1999. – ISBN 1852330600 [28, 30, 32, 33, 96, 140]

[WBST97]   WEIDERMAN, Nelson W. ; BERGEY, John K. ; SMITH, Dennis B. ; TILLEY, Scott R.: Approaches to Legacy System Evolution. Pittsburgh, PA 15213 : Software Engineering Institut Carnegie Mellon University, Dezember 1997 (CMU/SEI-97-TR-014). – Forschungsbericht. – "" [19, 38, 87]

[WBSV06]   WEERD, Inge van d. ; BRINKKEMPER, Sjaak ; SOUER, Jurriaan ; VERSENDAAL, Johan: A situational implementation method for web-based content management system-applications: method engineering and validation in practice. In: *Software Process: Improvement and Practice* 11 (2006), July, Nr. 5, S. 521–538. – DOI 10.1002/spip.293 [9, 61, 63]

[WBV07]   *Kapitel* Concepts for Incremental Method Evolution: Empirical Exploration and Validation in Requirements Management. In: WEERD, Inge van d. ; BRINKKEMPER, Sjaak ; VERSENDAAL, Johan: *Lecture Notes in Computer Science.* Bd. 4495/2007: *Advanced Information Systems Engineering.* Springer, 2007, S. 469–484. – DOI 10.1007/978-3-540-72988-4_33 [9, 63, 64, 65]

[Web99]   WEBER, Herbert: Continuous Engineering of Information and
          Communication Infrastructures (Extended Abstract). In: *Pro-
          ceedings of the Second Internationsl Conference on Fundamental
          Approaches to Software Engineering*. London, UK : Springer-
          Verlag, 1999. – ISBN 3–540–65718–5, S. 22–29 [17, 18]

[Wei84]   WEISER, Mark: Program Slicing. In: *IEEE Transactions on
          Software Engineering* 10 (1984), Nr. 4, S. 352–357 [38]

[Wes09]   WEST, Dave: Best Practices: Software Development Processes.
          Forrester Research In., April 2009 (47913). – Forschungsbericht.
          – " " [11]

[WH04]   WALL, Kurt ; HAGEN, Willian von: *The definitive guide to
          GCC*. Apress, 2004. – ISBN 1–59059–109–7 [110]

[WK06]   WIMMER, Manuel ; KRAMLER, Gerhard: Bridging grammar-
          ware and modelware. In: *Proceedings of the 2005 international
          conference on Satellite Events at the MoDELS*. Berlin, Heidel-
          berg : Springer-Verlag, 2006 (MoDELS'05). – ISBN 3–540–
          31780–5, S. 159–168. – DOI 10.1007/11663430_17 [123]

[WKR02]   WINTER, Andreas ; KULLBACH, Bernt ; RIEDIGER, Volker: An
          Overview of the GXL Graph Exchange Language. In: *Revised
          Lectures on Software Visualization, International Seminar*. Lon-
          don, UK : Springer-Verlag, 2002. – ISBN 3–540–43323–6, S.
          324–336 [XV, 117]

[WLB⁺97] WU, Bing ; LAWLESS, Deirdre ; BISBAL, Jesus ; RICHARDSON,
          Ray ; GRIMSON, Jane ; WADE, Vincent ; O'SULLIVAN, Donie:
          The Butterfly Methodology: A Gateway-free Approach for Mi-
          grating Legacy Information Systems. In: *Proceedings of the
          Third IEEE International Conference on Engineering of Com-
          plex Computer Systems*. Washington, DC, USA : IEEE Com-
          puter Society, 1997. – ISBN 0–8186–8126–8, S. 200– [27, 43]

[WMP06]   WAGNER, Christian ; MARGARIA, Tiziana ; PAGENDARM, Hans-
          Georg: Comparative Analysis of Tools for Automated Soft-
          ware Re-engineering Purposes. (2006), S. 433–440. – DOI
          10.1109/ISoLA.2006.67 [108]

[WMP09]   WAGNER, Christian ; MARGARIA, Tiziana ; PAGENDARM, Hans-
          Georg: Analysis and Code Model Extraction for C/C++
          Source Code. In: *Proceedings of the 2009 14th IEEE Inter-
          national Conference on Engineering of Complex Computer Sys-
          tems*. Washington, DC, USA : IEEE Computer Society, 2009
          (ICECCS '09). – ISBN 978–0–7695–3702–3, S. 110–119. – DOI
          10.1109/ICECCS.2009.46 [XIX, 115]

[WNS⁺97] WEIDERMAN, Nelson ; NORTHROP, Linda ; SMITH, Dennis ;
TILLEY, Scott ; WALLNAU, Kurt: Implications of Distributed
Object Technology for Reengineering. Pittsburgh, PA 15213
: Software Engineering Institut Carnegie Mellon University,
Dezember 1997 (CMU/SEI-97-TR-005). – Forschungsbericht.
– "" [33, 41, 94, 102]

[WOL⁺98] WOODS, S. ; O'BRIEN, L. ; LIN, T. ; GALLAGHER, K. ; QUILICI,
A.: An Architecture for Interoperable Program Understanding
Tools. In: *Proceedings of the 6th International Workshop on
Program Comprehension.* Washington, DC, USA : IEEE Com-
puter Society, 1998 (IWPC '98). – ISBN 0–8186–8560–3, S. 54–
[36, 116, 165]

[Wor05] WORKGROUP, Dwarf: *Dwarf Debugging Information Format
Version 3.* http://dwarf.freestandards.org/Dwarf3.pdf, Dezember 20, 2005 [109]

[WUG03] WEIS, Torben ; ULBRICH, Andreas ; GEIHS, Kurt: Model Meta-
morphosis. In: *IEEE Software* 20 (2003), September, S. 46–51.
– ISSN 0740–7459. – DOI 10.1109/MS.2003.1231151 [57, 58, 99,
138]

[Zel04] ZELLER, Thomas: Software-Visualisierung / Virtuelles
Software Engineering Kompetenzzentrum (ViSEK). 2004
(ViSEK/045/D). – Forschungsbericht. – "" [39]

[ZLK⁺04] ZOU, Ying ; LAU, Terence C. ; KONTOGIANNIS, Kostas ; TONG,
Tack ; MCKEGNEY, Ross: Model-Driven Business Process Recovery. In: *Proceedings of the 11th Working Conference on Reverse Engineering.* Washington, DC, USA : IEEE Computer
Society, 2004 (WCRE '04). – ISBN 0–7695–2243–2, S. 224–233
[141]

[ZS95] ZILAHI-SZABÓ, M.G.: *Kleines Lexikon der Informatik
und Wirtschaftsinformatik.* Oldenbourg, 1995. – ISBN
9783486229073 [16, 24, 35]

[ZSG79] ZELKOWITZ, Marvin V. ; SHAW, Alan C. ; GANNON, John D.:
Principles of Software Engineering and Design. Prentice Hall
Professional Technical Reference, 1979. – ISBN 013710202X [16]

[ZWH⁺11] ZILLMANN, C. ; WINTER, Andreas ; HERGET, A. ; TEPPE, W.
; THEURER, M. ; FUHR, Andreas ; HORN, Tassilo ; RIEDIGER,
Volker ; ERDMENGER, Uwe ; KAISER, Uwe ; UHLIG, Denis ;
ZIMMERMANN, Y.: The SOAMIG Process Model in Industrial
Applications. In: MENS, Tom (Hrsg.) ; KANELLOPOULOS, Yian-
nis (Hrsg.) ; WINTER, Andreas (Hrsg.): *15th European Confer-*

ence on Software Maintenance and Reengineering, CSMR 2011, 1-4 March 2011, Oldenburg, Germany, IEEE Computer Society, 2011. – ISBN 978–0–7695–4343–7, S. 339–342. – DOI 10.1109/CSMR.2011.48 [141]

A DTD of XML description

Listing A.1: DTD

```
1  <!ELEMENT graphxml (graph* ,
       map*)>
2
3  <!ELEMENT graph (graph_attr*
       , node*)>
4  <!ATTLIST graph id CDATA #
       REQUIRED>
5
6  <!ELEMENT graph_attr ANY>
7  <!ATTLIST graph_attr
8     type CDATA #IMPLIED
9     loc CDATA #IMPLIED
10    suc CDATA #IMPLIED
11    line CDATA #IMPLIED
12    column CDATA #IMPLIED
13    fnname CDATA #IMPLIED
14    qualifiedname CDATA #
          IMPLIED>
15
16 <!ELEMENT params ANY>
17 <!ATTLIST params>
18
19 <!ELEMENT return ANY>
20 <!ATTLIST return>
21
22 <!ELEMENT node (node_attr* ,
       node*)>
23 <!ATTLIST node id CDATA #
       IMPLIED >
24
25 <!ELEMENT node_attr ANY>
26 <!ATTLIST node_attr
27    id CDATA #IMPLIED
28    type CDATA #IMPLIED
29    loc CDATA #IMPLIED
30    suc CDATA #IMPLIED
31    line CDATA #IMPLIED
32    column CDATA #IMPLIED
33    codeline CDATA #IMPLIED
34    stmtcount CDATA #IMPLIED
35    init CDATA #IMPLIED
36    body CDATA #IMPLIED
37    trycount CDATA #IMPLIED
38    statement CDATA #IMPLIED
39    labelvalue CDATA #IMPLIED
40    statementloc CDATA #IMPLIED
41    branches CDATA #IMPLIED
42    else CDATA #IMPLIED
43    then CDATA #IMPLIED
44    memberlist CDATA #IMPLIED>
45
46 <!ELEMENT declaration ANY>
47 <!ATTLIST declaration
48        declcount CDATA #
              IMPLIED
49        visitDeclaration
              CDATA #IMPLIED>
50
51 <!ELEMENT expression ANY>
52 <!ATTLIST expression>
53
54 <!ELEMENT expr_kind (#PCDATA)
       >
55 <!ATTLIST expr_kind
56    kind CDATA #REQUIRED
57    type CDATA #IMPLIED
58    value CDATA #IMPLIED
59    argscount CDATA #IMPLIED
60    var CDATA #IMPLIED
61    refersto CDATA #IMPLIED
62    operator CDATA #IMPLIED
63    name CDATA #IMPLIED
64    qualifiedname CDATA #
          IMPLIED
65    globalvar CDATA #IMPLIED
66    func CDATA #IMPLIED
```

```
67    address CDATA #IMPLIED
68    ctorvar CDATA #IMPLIED
69  >
70
71  <!ELEMENT condition ANY>
72  <!ATTLIST condition>
73
74  <!ELEMENT e1 ANY>
75  <!ATTLIST e1>
76
77  <!ELEMENT e2 ANY>
78  <!ATTLIST e2>
79
80  <!ELEMENT op (#PCDATA)>
81  <!ATTLIST op
82    operator CDATA #IMPLIED
83
84  <!ELEMENT declarator (#PCDATA
      )>
85  <!ATTLIST declarator
86    context CDATA #IMPLIED
87    var CDATA #IMPLIED
88    loc CDATA #IMPLIED
89    type CDATA #IMPLIED>
90
91  <!ELEMENT ideclarator (#
      PCDATA)>
92  <!ATTLIST ideclarator
93        loc CDATA #IMPLIED
94      paramscount CDATA #
          IMPLIED>
95
96  <!ELEMENT pqname (#PCDATA)>
97  <!ATTLIST pqname
98      pqname CDATA #IMPLIED
99    loc CDATA #IMPLIED
100   name CDATA #IMPLIED
101   refersto CDATA #IMPLIED
102   qualifier CDATA #IMPLIED
103   enumscount CDATA #IMPLIED
104   enumcount CDATA #IMPLIED
105   fakename CDATA #IMPLIED
106   var CDATA #IMPLIED>
107
108 <!ELEMENT initializer (#
      PCDATA)>
```

```
109 <!ATTLIST initializer
110   loc CDATA #IMPLIED
111   refersto CDATA #IMPLIED
112   var CDATA #IMPLIED>
113
114 <!ELEMENT typespecifier (#
      PCDATA)>
115 <!ATTLIST typespecifier
116    id CDATA #IMPLIED
117   loc  CDATA #IMPLIED
118   refersto CDATA #IMPLIED
119   var CDATA #IMPLIED
120   type CDATA #IMPLIED>
121
122 <!ELEMENT init ANY>
123 <!ATTLIST init>
124
125 <!ELEMENT after ANY>
126 <!ATTLIST after>
127
128 <!ELEMENT handlers ANY>
129 <!ATTLIST handlers>
130
131 <!ELEMENT handler ANY>
132 <!ATTLIST handler
133    refersto CDATA #IMPLIED
134    globalvar CDATA #IMPLIED>
135
136 <!ELEMENT exceptionspec ANY>
137 <!ATTLIST exceptionspec
138    typescount CDATA #IMPLIED>
139
140 <!ELEMENT operatorname ANY>
141 <!ATTLIST operatorname
142    operator CDATA #IMPLIED>
143
144 <!ELEMENT map (edge*)>
145 <!ATTLIST map id CDATA #
          IMPLIED>
146
147 <!ELEMENT edge (#PCDATA)>
148 <!ATTLIST edge
149   id CDATA #REQUIRED
150   source CDATA #REQUIRED
151   target CDATA #REQUIRED
152   cyclic CDATA #IMPLIED>
```

B Evaluation of the DeAs system

Table B.1: DeAs – Evaluation of preprocessor

Evaluation of preprocessor				
Program/ Library	LOC	C–Code [Byte]	Prepro. [Byte]	Time [ms]
An_an	1.013	43.635	8.876.480	725
An_be	4.142	157.608	22.333.810	1.813
An_ko	3.673	120.198	17.866.942	1.421
Ap_an	1.249	42.040	8.877.913	879
Ap_au	7.205	242.059	19.543.253	1.753
Ap_be	4.546	149.817	11.980.398	1.101
Aw_be	7.294	277.205	30.035.038	2.646
DeAsManager	818	21.777	2.973.866	235
GPM	860	31.313	1.781.801	289
In_an	1.534	51.449	8.892.230	725
In_be	246	10.872	2.954.242	411
Me_ko	1.054	76.219	11.876.293	959
Mg_be	5.344	163.184	17.896.988	1.966
Mg_se	3.065	93.456	11.907.176	1.081
Mg_wa	4.692	140.704	17.924.084	1.419
Mo_an	1.310	41.722	8.877.007	896
Mo_be	4.656	157.662	22.346.576	2.566
Mo_ko	3.668	117.923	17.871.707	1.608
Mv_an	1.857	58.441	8.899.689	1.086
Pr_as	2.508	87.835	14.849.442	1.321
Pr_aw	760	24.071	5.912.620	468
Vg_be	2.157	67.068	11.865.011	1.144
	96.717	**4.014.027**	**517.419.937**	**47.371**
		3,83 MB	**493,45 MB**	**47,37 s**

Table B.2: DeAs – Evaluation of Elsa-Parsers

Elsa-Parser				
Program/ Library	**ccparse [Byte]**	**Pre/ ccparse**	**Back-end time [ms]**	**Overall time [ms]**
An_an	1.340.669	15,10%	20.356	26.084
An_be	5.510.647	24,67%	51.075	65.464
An_ko	3.921.037	21,95%	40.765	52.265
Ap_an	1.302.976	14,68%	20.269	26.057
Ap_au	8.215.076	42,04%	44.976	57.671
Ap_be	5.349.220	44,65%	28.430	36.248
Aw_be8	10.244.403	34,11%	72.533	92.717
DeAsManager	772.024	25,96%	6.855	8.767
GPM	1.197.262	67,19%	1.800	2.377
In_an	1.716.326	19,30%	20.412	26.151
In_be	291.103	9,85%	6.811	8.714
Me_ko	2.435.324	20,51%	27.310	34.974
Mg_be	6.020.917	33,64%	42.162	53.785
Mg_se	3.418.547	28,71%	27.810	35.603
Mg_wa	4.896.206	27,32%	41.617	53.168
Mo_an	1.371.298	15,45%	21.260	27.151
Mo_be	5.528.025	24,74%	53.669	68.487
Mo_ko	3.918.208	21,92%	41.141	52.637
Mv_an	2.062.661	23,18%	22.379	28.505
Pr_as	2.975.832	20,04%	35.544	45.365
Pr_aw	810.702	13,71%	13.578	17.384
Vg_be	2.242.373	18,90%	27.366	35.019
libDeAs	8.504.084	19,99%	99.589	129.552
libDeAsFenster	12.999.501	25,12%	125.442	160.183
libDeAsKlassen	27.042.512	24,49%	246.361	320.133
libGI	949.902	76,42%	943	1.221
libKorrektur	4.102.916	21,79%	44.685	58.047
libSPS	401.488	28,95%	1.101	1.550
libVGI	1.120.082	22,54%	11.909	15.387
	130.661.321	**29,14%**	**1.198.148**	**1.540.666**
	124,61 MB		**20,0 min**	**25,7 min**

Table B.3: DeAs − Evaluation of jABC-Import

jABC-Import				
Program/ Library	SLG [Byte]	Method	Nodes	Time [ms]
An_an	7.231.084	70	626	4.316
An_be	29.625.117	168	2.171	5.303
An_ko	20.701.473	167	1.653	4.684
Ap_an	6.956.004	60	608	2.578
Ap_au	44.052.313	320	3.620	13.442
Ap_be	28.915.656	216	2.421	9.921
Aw_be	56.635.769	356	4.584	29.991
DeAsManager	4.196.629	48	309	3.322
GPM	7.030.381	39	612	3.350
In_an	9.142.837	69	753	5.768
In_be	1.439.812	2	114	386
Me_ko	12.726.223	100	1.036	8.340
Mg_be	31.787.742	237	2.686	23.801
Mg_se	18.136.544	141	1.489	12.152
Mg_wa	26.235.960	215	2.265	18.968
Mo_an	7.343.819	62	647	11.049
Mo_be	29.902.710	168	2.135	21.110
Mo_ko	20.733.658	167	1.625	19.467
Mv_an	11.068.904	75	872	9.929
Pr_as	15.942.407	106	1.240	18.275
Pr_aw	4.406.717	38	348	4.984
Vg_be	11.900.916	108	1.022	13.659
libDeAs	46.899.683	434	4.805	88.888
libDeAsFenster	69.938.297	509	5.590	72.909
libDeAsKlassen	147.651.057	1.638	16.705	299.712
libGI	5.338.069	30	671	5.520
libKorrektur	22.692.645	48	1.565	19.514
libSPS	1.516.712	8	187	1.280
libVGI	6.188.201	59	692	11.893
	706.337.339	**5.658**	**63.051**	**744.511**
	673,62 MB			**12,4 min**

Table B.4: DeAs – Evaluation of the relation of the code-models

Link Analysis			
Program/ Library	SLG [Byte]	Function-calls	Time [ms]
An_an	7.317.459	114	30.479
An_be	30.002.327	585	90.827
An_ko	20.993.703	383	75.383
Ap_an	7.047.730	121	26.762
Ap_au	44.690.459	918	158.657
Ap_be	29.355.684	590	105.027
Aw_be	57.869.816	1.318	199.259
DeAsManager	4.219.880	36	19.534
GPM	7.125.879	75	16.101
In_an	9.262.423	160	31.535
In_be	1.462.028	36	5.791
Me_ko	12.922.625	252	48.507
Mg_be	32.214.909	696	121.152
Mg_se	18.338.342	353	67.443
Mg_wa	26.609.716	545	103.158
Mo_an	7.419.547	118	27.134
Mo_be	30.233.981	578	89.471
Mo_ko	20.970.720	381	77.126
Mv_an	11.190.396	156	34.775
Pr_as	16.218.188	346	58.102
Pr_aw	4.451.659	71	17.071
Vg_be	12.075.798	255	64.293
libDeAs	47.922.729	740	186.010
libDeAsFenster	71.078.290	1.386	256.940
libDeAsKlassen	152.068.724	7.412	912.606
libGI	5.434.179	91	15.809
libKorrektur	23.137.800	350	51.990
libSPS	1.545.432	28	5.858
libVGI	5.996.599	76	24.926
	719.177.022	**18.170**	**2.921.726**
	685,86 MB		**48,7 min**

Index